# MAKE SPIELBERG GREAT AGAIN

## The Steven Spielberg Chronicles

BOOKS BY ARMOND WHITE PUBLISHED
BY RESISTANCE WORKS, WDC

- *Keep Moving: The Michael Jackson Chronicles*
- *New Position: The Prince Chronicles*
- *Make Spielberg Great Again: The Steven Spielberg Chronicles*

OTHER BOOKS PUBLISHED BY
RESISTANCE WORKS, WDC

- *The Community of Desire: Selected Critical Writings (John Demetry)*
- *Serpents and Doves (John Demetry)*
- *Watch the Throne (John Demetry)*

# MAKE
# SPIELBERG
# GREAT AGAIN

The Steven Spielberg Chronicles

## ARMOND WHITE

*Resistance Works, WDC*

ISBN: 978-0-9842159-1-1

Book Design/Typesetting by Iskon Book Design
Book Cover Design/Layout by Iskon Book Design
Book Cover Artwork Source *First of the Month*
Copy Editing by John Demetry

## ACKNOWLEDGEMENTS

These ideas grew from what connoisseurs Gregory Solman, Keith Gardner, Pauline Kael, Teofilo Colon and John Demetry helped me to know.

These writings were encouraged by Gene Cunningham, Cheryl Head, Robin Little, Utrice Leid, Andrew Cooper, Harlan Jacobson, Benj DeMott, John Strausbaugh, Richard T. Jameson, Jonathan Reider, Jeff Koyen, Albert Mobilio, Daniel McNeil and Kate Walsh.

Armond White is the esteemed, controversial, and brilliantly independent film critic and three-times chair of the New York Film Critics Circle. He won the 2014 American Book Award for Anti-Censorship.

White is a film and cultural critic for *National Review*. Notably, *Out* magazine simultaneously featured his column "Our Bud at the Movies" for many years. Before these posts, he was Editor for *CityArts* and Arts Editor for *The City Sun*. In between which, he was lead film critic for *New York Press* (as selectively catalogued in the book *The Press Gang: Writings on Cinema from New York Press, 1991-2011*). That's a 40-year career as "The Last Honest Film Critic in America," to quote the title of an entire chapter devoted to White from the textbook *Film Criticism in the Digital Age*.

White, himself, wrote four books essential for anyone who loves pop culture: *The Resistance: Ten Years of Pop Culture That Shook the World*, *Rebel for the Hell of It: The Life of Tupac Shakur*, *Keep Moving: The Michael Jackson Chronicles*, and *New Position: The Prince Chronicles*. Now, *Make Spielberg Great Again: The Steven Spielberg Chronicles* joins the ranks of these auspicious tomes.

These books affirm that White practically invented the art of music video criticism, which he demonstrated for over a decade in an annual presentation of music video art at Lincoln Center. It was always the cultural highlight of the year.

# DEDICATION

*Dedicated to Melvin Van Peebles.*
*Profound thanks to Richard Hecht and*
*John Demetry.*

# PREFACE

---

## *The Wailing Wall*

*J*AWS, *CLOSE ENCOUNTERS of the Third Kind*, *Raiders of the Lost Ark, E.T. the Extra-Terrestrial, The Color Purple* weren't just popular movies. Each one changed the world in which they appeared: inflecting spoken language, influencing social concepts and increasing visual appreciation at the movies. They also imprinted a name on the culture: Steven Spielberg.

Name recognition such as Spielberg's means more than just popularity. As for only a few cultural impresarios—Charlie Chaplin, Alfred Hitchcock, Walt Disney—it also indicates broad affection, familiarity and trust. Spielberg is the only filmmaker to win that legendary regard in the second half of the 20ᵗʰ Century—certainly he is the one director of his baby boomer generation whose sensibility is fully conveyed by name alone. This phenomenon came apparent with a surprise—that during one swift decade his sensibility also seemed to be shared by viewers of all ages and around the world.

Spielberg's fame represented the apex of that moment when American filmmakers, inspired by the post-Second World War international art film boom and the French New Wave, reinterpreted their own experiences and art ambitions through the heritage of the movies. The cultural development that defined Hollywood's '70s American Renaissance was personified in the singular figure of Spielberg. Such towering peers as Robert Altman and Francis Ford Coppola made formally radical hits *M\*A\*S\*H* (1970) and *The Godfather* (1972) that demonstrated an instinct for truly popular pop spectacle but Spielberg was able to convey that new, complex motivation uncannily—with the simple, direct, powerful effect and purity of D.W. Griffith's silents. As inheritor of Griffith's vision, Spielberg and each one of his early hits seemed to bring almost all of film history up to date.

During that first stage of Spielberg's renown listed above, moviegoers and the public at large discovered an image for their fear of marine carnivores (*Jaws*); discerned symbols for unearthly delight (*Close Encounters of the Third Kind*); found a source of their traditional moviegoing affection (*Raiders of the Lost Ark*); then—as if to prove the peak of popular response— went further to realize a fresh, rejuvenated expression of their need to communicate (*E. T. the Extra-Terrestrial*) and through communication located a deeper understanding of their common humanity (*The Color Purple*).

While many filmmakers achieved fame with a particular kind of story and storytelling, Spielberg proved to be one of cinema's uniquely adept young masters, much like Jean Vigo, Orson Welles and Jean-Luc Godard and as promptly as *The Sugarland Express* and *Jaws*. But *Close Encounters* importantly suggested that Spielberg had a God-given talent to influence mainstream narrative and viewership. His imprimatur was the only counterweight to the growing cynicism during the Eighties decade of Hollywood corporate procedures and its high-concept filmmaking practices that trashed Nouvelle Vague connoisseurship and was crassly based on imported British advertising methods.

Spielberg's interest in genre purity—like the "romance with the Word" he professed at the 1987 Oscar ceremony when accepting the Irving G. Thalberg Award—was bolstered by his craftsman's aesthetic ingenuity and wit. He avoided the sheer, impersonal calculation of industry peers and imitators who chased his success but lacked his unique personal expressiveness; a movie love that could uniquely blend contradictory emotions—humor and fear, tragedy and hope—into unabashed profundity: spiritual revelation, agape. Yet, after nearly a century of classical innovation and modernist revitalization, in an age of hyper-sophistication, Spielberg's signature technique was often mistaken for mere technique.

The first unexpectedly precise insight about Spielberg described his sensibility as "ecumenical," and the next phase of Spielberg's career confirmed a devotion to spiritual and cinematic practice through more than secular expressivity. The appearance of the uncanny and the supernatural in his films evokes common custom, ritual and tradition—the Ark of the Covenant, the Rainbow Sign, the Holy Grail, even *Jurassic Park*'s admonition of "what ought not to be." These concepts repeat and rehearse traditions that enrich the cultural experience of movies—the screen before one's eyes like a Wailing Wall that receives our genuflection and devotion. As a mass media entertainer and showman, Spielberg spread his awareness of audience expectation, personal feeling and public obligation into the world-citizen expressions of *Always, The Last Crusade, Jurassic Park, Schindler's List, The Lost World, Amistad, Saving Private Ryan*.

Peripatetic creativity characterized his first films of the new millennium—*A.I., Minority Report, Catch Me If You Can*. Then 9/11 hit and the most profoundly American film artist since D.W. Griffith changed. *The Terminal* wasn't called "The Terminal" for nothing. *War of the Worlds* and *Munich* are simultaneous climaxes of both purgation and new beginnings. His artistry sharpened. He changed games with *The Adventures of Tintin* and *War Horse* (his first animation, his first theatrical adaptation). Game-changers or End-gamers?

Then, with the 2008 election, the ecumenicism soured. Can Spielberg be made great again? Can political revolution be transformed back into revelation? Can the once miraculous gift for mass excitement, enchantment and education be offered with his original virtue and guiltlessness? Obama turned him onto guilt, Tony Kushner brought him corrupt sophistication. Griffith's advancement turned into a retreat from what was both moral and aesthetic.

As this narrative resolves itself, one's early great enthrallment becomes great disappointment and now stands as a hope that greatness will return. His best films will line up with the word of God—they pursue truth without sophistry.

# INTRODUCTION

---

## *MSGA*

*Oriana Fallaci: I don't believe in objectivity. A journalist is a historian who writes history in the moment history happens and it is the damn best way to write history.*

S PIELBERG'S EXCEPTIONALISM PARALLELS American exceptionalism. His trajectory from the most popular filmmaker in the world to his current marginal status that no longer guarantees a box-office hit—nor popularity—parallels the trajectory of the nation that produced him. Spielberg once excited the imaginations of America's young cultural consumers, but consumers of the current generation ignore his recent entreaties. The embarrassment felt by Spielberg's hipster detractors, who protested his films as corny and middle-brow, is ingrained and turned into American shame. Not even the odd politicization of Spielberg's latest films can satisfy that unease, which is a personal disdain—the opposite of the common, all-American, "suburban" idealization of family and spirit that is at the heart of even his internationally-set films. American shame is the product of progressive politics that seeks to deny or transform America's history and its soul which Spielberg uniquely expressed like no other filmmaker since D.W. Griffith.

Anyone fortunate enough to go to the movies during the peak moment of Spielberg's exceptionalism—from *Jaws* to *Close Encounters* to *Raiders of the Lost Ark* to *E.T. the Extra-Terrestrial* and *The Color Purple*—knew how special it was for an American pop artist to delight and edify a global audience. That delight was not jingoism but spiritual harmony—unity. Those movies showed the unassumingly sophisticated art form of the cinema going broad and deep into viewers' kinetic and emotional needs. To wonder how Spielberg can be made great again parallels one's hope that America—and its cinema— be rescued from its current crisis, the manic contempt for creativity, originality and ecumenical humanism.

Spielberg's avowed fealty to liberal politics has not only hobbled his miraculous "touch," but prevented him from openly embracing the values implicit in President Donald Trump's optimistic campaign slogan "Make America Great Again." Those values seem hidden from view in Spielberg's recent films, just like the personal treasures hoarded in the *Citizen Kane* (1941) storehouse at the end of *Raiders of the Lost Ark*. Spielberg's best chance at renewed popularity is to retrieve his unifying vision and Millennial moviegoers (perhaps future moviegoers) wanting that unity.

Besides sharing a middle name with Steven Allen Spielberg, his filmmaking career parallels my own practice of professional film criticism starting at the peak of the American Renaissance (1967-1983) and through that halcyon period of the culture when I wrote for Wayne State University's *The South End* newspaper and my national launch at New York's *The City Sun*, *New York Press* and *National Review*. This collection of reviews and essays chronicles the warm, radiant, eye-widening light that Spielberg brought to the cinema. For me, each piece reads like a diaristic memory of how I thought at the time that they were written, taking note of Spielberg's astonishing, developing art and its effect on the world.

There are humble regrets here (every critic has them), but also in-the-moment ideals. Oriana Fallaci was right to reject objectivity—most especially when it comes to the critical branch of journalism. Criticism is never objective but it should be informed and honest and inquiring—and that's the aim of these chronicles. Here's a history of Spielberg's multifarious art, a history of my impressions and a history of American greatness.

# CONTENTS

**Preface**

*The Wailing Wall*.......................................................................*xi*

**Introduction**

*MSGA* ........................................................................... *xv*


# PART ONE: AMERICA AND THE WORLD ...................................25

### The Sugarland Express (1974)

*The Sugarland Express*.............................................. *27*

*The Sugarland Express and Duel on DVD* ............................ *31*

### Jaws (1975)

*The Fanged Failure*................................................... *33*

*A Jawful Black Christmas*........................................ *37*

*Jaws Redux* ................................................................ *40*

### Close Encounters of the Third Kind (1977)

*Close Encounters of the Third Kind* ........................... *41*

### 1941 (1979)

*1941* .......................................................................... *49*

### Raiders of the Lost Ark (1981)

*Flashback: The Mountain and the Gun* ................................. *55*

### Poltergeist (1982)

*Poltergeist* .................................................................. *61*

### E.T. the Extra-Terrestrial (1982)

*E.T. vs Resident Evil*................................................. *67*

### Twilight Zone: The Movie (1983)

*A Boomer-rang Remake*........................................ *73*

### Indiana Jones and the Temple of Doom (1984)

*Temple of Gremlins* ............................................... *77*

**The Color Purple (1985)**

*Rethinking Hollywood Archetypes* ........................................... 85

*National Board of Review: Best Film, Best Director* ............... 92

*The Black Image A.C.P.* .......................................................... 95

*Fiction into Film: Best Adaptations* ..................................... 100

*Hollywood's Greatest Gay Film* ............................................ 102

# PART TWO: A.C.P. .............................................................. 107

**Empire of the Sun (1987)**

*Spielberg Strikes Again* ......................................................... 109

**Indiana Jones and the Last Crusade (1989)**

*Indiana Jones Makes History and Progress* ............................ 113

*Keeping Up with the Joneses* .................................................. 116

**Always (1989)**

*The Spectacle of Always Recalled* ........................................... 123

**Hook (1991)**

*Hook Gives Serious Happiness Its Due* ................................... 129

**Jurassic Park (1993)**

*In Jurassic Park, Spielberg Satirizes Capitalism* ..................... 137

**Schindler's List (1993)**

*Toward a Theory of Spielberg History* ................................... 143

*My Schindler's List Problem—And Yours* .............................. 158

**The Lost World: Jurassic Park (1997)**

*Dino and Might* .................................................................... 167

**Amistad (1997)**

*Titanic: Sinking* .................................................................... 173

*Bitter?* ................................................................................... 179

*Emancipating Movie History* ................................................ 186

*Against the Hollywood Grain* ................................................ 195

*Playing the Favorite Atrocity Game* ...................................... 216

**Saving Private Ryan (1998)**

*Saving Private Ryan*........................................................ 223

*Disturbing Behavior*........................................................ 231

# PART THREE: 9/11 ....................................................................239

**A.I. Artificial Intelligence (2001)**

*A.I. Artificial Intelligence*.................................................. 241

*Intelligence Quotient*........................................................ 248

**Minority Report (2002)**

*Spielberg Goes to Alphaville*............................................... 255

**Catch Me If You Can (2002)**

*Catch Spielberg If You Can*................................................ 261

**The Terminal (2004)**

*Now Playing: The Terminal*................................................ 267

**War of the Worlds (2005)**

*La Guerra de Todos Mundos*............................................... 271

*Refugees and Searchers to the Movies*................................... 272

**Munich (2005)**

*Spielberg Climbs Another Mountain*.................................... 281

**Indiana Jones and the Kingdom of the Crystal Skull (2008)**

*Another Indy Classic*........................................................ 289

*The Whip and the Fedora*.................................................. 297

**DreamWorks SKG**

*The Big Picture: The Men Who Would Be King*.................... 301

**The Adventures of Tintin (2011) AND War Horse (2011)**

*Game Changers*.............................................................. 307

# PART FOUR: OBAMA ............................................................. 317

### Lincoln (2012)
*On the Immediate Future of the Arts* ................................... 319
*The Pageantry of Rhetoric* ..................................................... 322
*After the Debate: Fact-Checking Hollywood's Propaganda* .... 328

### Steven Spielberg's Obama (2013)
*Spielberg's Obama* ................................................................. 329

### Bridge of Spies (2015)
*The Dark Days of Spielberg* .................................................... 335

### The BFG (2016)
*The Notorious BFG* ................................................................ 339

### The Post (2017)
*Spielberg Rides Politics' Slippery Slope* .................................. 345

### Ready Player One (2018)
*Spielberg's Crowd-Pleasing Escapism* ..................................... 351

### Spielberg Meets the Zeitgeist
*Spielberg in the Whorehouse of Cannes* .................................. 357
*Better-Than* ........................................................................... 360
*Spielberg Recovers His Political Courage* ............................... 363
*Spielberg Meets the Zeitgeist* ................................................. 366

## Index .................................................................................. 371

PART ONE

# AMERICA AND THE WORLD

# THE SUGARLAND EXPRESS (1974)

## *The Sugarland Express*

C ARS AND MOVIES are probably the two most identifiably American phenomena of the century. They both provide different sorts of unprecedented transport and have had an incalculable influence on contemporary American life, by making us travelers and dreamers of a daring, romantic sort. They have the unusual ability to, at a single-time, hold many people and involve them in a shared experience.

*The Sugarland Express* is a film that glories in the existence, the use and the beauty of automobiles, and it does something unique in that it expresses human nature through automobiles, through the way people act in and with them. This isn't as weird as it may sound, for is there any aspect of $20^{th}$ century life that cannot and has not happened on wheels?

There is a central scene in *The Sugarland Express* in which the lead characters—fugitives flouting the law—spend the night in a trailer watching a drive-in movie. In this scene, they illustrate the inextricable faults and good points of their nature (their awareness and their naiveté). The scene indicates what it is that gives the film its unusual energy and meaning: The intrinsic value of cars and movies in modern American life. Take them away and we lose our color—they are our color; part of our own peculiar style and quality of living.

Cars and motor vehicles of all sorts are more than just a motif throughout this film they also become characters that are keys to the exclusively American spirit of the movie's energy and humor. The director, Steven Spielberg (who makes a stunning debut with this film) shows an inordinate and exhilarating love for cars; so much love that he sees them as toys—things he can manipulate to show what he knows and feels about modern American life.

The film uses the phenomena of our culture to express a profound knowledge of it. It does this playfully, but the glee it imparts doesn't lessen the movie's impact; it's a hilariously wry vision of modern behavior, and is at all times, very effective. Even when there are toys on screen, they are formidable portents also invested with character. One of the saddest and most memorable images in the movie is the sight of car tires crushing and overturning a Teddy Bear on a dusty road. That's the kind of movie this is—crazily sweet and charming with a touch of pathos.

The Teddy Bear belongs to Lou Jean and Clovis Poplin (Goldie Hawn and William Atherton) an escaped convict and his wife, who kidnap a Texas policeman (Michael Sacks) and drive his patrol car to Sugarland, the town where their baby (put under court custody when Lou Jean herself served a jail sentence), has been put up for adoption in the home of foster parents. In their headstrong endeavor, the Poplins go across Texas dragging behind them in frenetic pursuit what looks like the entire state police force.

The film is based on a true story that happened in 1969, but it has the pleasure of an extraordinary fable. It's like a great, profound joyride in a car with its motor started before one realizes it. In no time at all after the opening, you discover, engrossed and laughing, that the film built up a good head of steam.

It's as invigorating as anyone could want a movie to be, yet when the film takes a dramatic turn and then ends, one may feel there's a fault in its not having the definitive power of the endings of *Bonnie and Clyde* (1967) and *McCabe & Mrs. Miller* (1971). This joyride of a movie doesn't come to a psychologically or emotionally jolting end. It isn't like a pretentious touch of cynicism, or a try for a classic dramatic close; the ending is right. There's a limit to the knowingness of the picture—its theme is expounded early and brilliantly, but it doesn't deepen. Yet, it does an emotional about-face with great surety and persuasiveness. The ending leaves us with our feelings for the characters and for their story's meaning. We mull it over and are profoundly, almost inexplicably touched.

Lou Jean and Clovis Poplin are impetuous daredevils, prowled by Justice figure Captain Tanner (Ben Johnson). They befriend their hostage and all of them are put under stress. The movie is effective in showing the import of their behaviors, but what elevates it are the automobiles. They're alternately giddy, affectionate figures, then pathetic ones, ruthlessly destroyed, or even a medium upon which a person vents his rage. Innumerable police cars with their lights flashing pursue Lou Jean, Clovis and Slide and that, along with the vivid neon of roadside establishments and the parades and congregations of rural folk who sympathize with the Poplins and cheer them on, makes the film like a great dazzling circus that displays and incarnates wondrous human folly.

At the beginning of her career, Hawn had a bright, shrill daffiness that was often cute, but not much to brag about or build a career on. I had come to accept it, thinking it was the best and probably all she could do. It hardly shows in his movie and I didn't miss it. Here she has a human glow and energy—gumption instead of kookiness. She uses that glow and energy to beguile the three men, and to entice wary Clovis out of prison, even out of his senses and onto his fate. Atherton (who sings "What'll I Do" in *The Great Gatsby* (1974)) portrays Clovis equally well, and Michael Sacks redeems himself after his showing his limitations in *Slaughterhouse-Five* (1972).

It's said that people buy cars to fit their personalities. Spielberg takes off from that axiom using cars to express and embody the soul of his characters, his story, and American life. There's more spirit to his direction that there was to Peckinpah's mechanical marvels in *The Getaway* (1972), and it's quite a feat. It's a bit shallow but like the careening, hopping, sashaying automobiles, it's funny and touching.

Spielberg may not be an artist of deep ideas, but he's able to transmute affection and give a story fullness without depth—that's what a lot of the best movie entertainments have had, and an audience can respond deeply to that.

*The Sugarland Express* is an effervescent, clear-cut movie. It takes one through a gamut of emotions, and is marvelously entertaining. There hasn't been a comedy nearly this good since *M\*A\*S\*H* and I'm almost sure this is going to be a big hit—it really deserves to be.

*The South End*
March 1974

# The Sugarland Express and Duel on DVD

**S**OME PEOPLE LIKED Steven Spielberg better when they felt like they didn't have to take him seriously. For a long while, these contrarians preferred *Duel* (1971) to the large scale and large ambitions of such theatrical productions as *Close Encounters* and *The Color Purple*. Even after *Schindler's List*, one mainstream New York reviewer argued with me that *Raiders of the Lost Ark* was Spielberg's best movie. (Was he pulling my leg or just shortening his intelligence?)

This dilemma is refreshed with the new restoration of *Duel*, a made-for-tv movie that Spielberg just barely transcends. The square frame and spare plot (motorist Dennis Weaver is menaced by an 18-wheeler along the California highways) don't lend themselves to grand themes, but Spielberg makes the most he can out of camera velocity and surprise edits. It's a textbook example of how virtuosity can lift a B-movie into a new level.

*Duel* offers mystery and threat. It is the most plainly manipulative of all Spielberg films, but you have to be attuned to the potency of movie grammar to see anything more in it than the kind of portentous graphics that buffs love in Kubrick. By releasing *Duel* along with the first DVD version of *The Sugarland Express*, Universal has helped clarify the difference between a B-movie with potential and a full-scale movie vision. *Sugarland* belongs to the same lovers-on-the-lam genre as *Bonnie and Clyde*, *Thieves Like Us* (1974) and *Badlands* (1973), but it is the most dynamic of the bunch. The feel for the pop-culture landscape (endless ribbons of police cars stretched along the highways in pursuit of Goldie Hawn and William Atherton) is made almost tactile by Vilmos Zsigmond. But this 1974 movie still astonishes through its combination of folk and pop humor and visual panache.

The difference from *Duel* is like that between an idea and an experience. The outlaw couple of *Sugarland* trying to reclaim their baby from foster parents is not mysterious. It can be appreciated as a parable (based on a real-life incident) of the younger generation testing its allegiance to the values that the older generation thinks are solely theirs. (Ben Johnson plays the first of Spielberg's ambivalent authority figures.) A key moment is Atherton realizing the gravity of his heartfelt folly when pantomiming a Road Runner cartoon. The meta-movie complexity is way beyond *Duel*—way beyond Guy Maddin. You'd have to be blind not to take this kind of talent seriously.

*New York Press*
September 2004

# JAWS (1975)

―――

## *The Fanged Failure*

**W**HAT DO PEOPLE expect to get out of a movie like *Jaws*? I can't even call it a passable entertainment because I wasn't entertained one wit, and the reason is not that I'm no longer a child who responds to imaginative fantasy; the reason is that there is no imagination in *Jaws* to respond to.

*Time* magazine said it right in its cover story-cum-press release: "In *Jaws*, the only thing to fear is fear itself." What audiences scream at in the movie is the processed fear they bring with them—the shark-phobia Universal has fomented during the past year while promoting Peter Benchley's book.

I don't think anyone on land has an abiding fear of sharks—we just know enough not to swim with them—but for months now Universal's high-pressure promotion has been telling us, "Be afraid of sharks! Be afraid of sharks!" and audiences at this film react accordingly. The movie hasn't touched them, the media sludge has.

*Jaws* is the most solidly manufactured pre-sold product since *Love Story* (1970). Its publicity machine is so powerful everyone jumps on the *Jaws* bandwagon because it makes them seem "With it." These results should convince some slick politician to hire Universal's press department to manage his presidential campaign.

As the corny, cattle-prodding music pounds on the soundtrack, one thinks this facile horror story will be a cinch for the director Steven Spielberg, who showed such an exhilarating display of movie craft last year in *The Sugarland Express*. I had thought of Spielberg as a genial William Friedkin, but now that he's entered Friedkin's shock-thriller territory, he's marred his own reputation.

Spielberg's gifts don't compare with Friedkin's. *Jaws* isn't a work of skill like *The French Connection* (1971) or the despicable *The Exorcist* (1973) were; it is just clever, yet not clever enough.

All Spielberg can do is spring surprises, there isn't enough human feeling for tension or apprehensiveness. There's no long wait for violence, we are fed it constantly like a Roman circus audience, but the many displays of it are so cold that they are dull anyway.

As a contrast to Spielberg, Friedkin really knows how to put the screws on, and he can squeeze the fear out of you even though you're aware of his tactics—which isn't a talent I admire but I acknowledge it as phenomenal. Compared to *The French Connection*, *Jaws* is kindergarten stuff. There's no real excitement, which goes along with the lack of emotion. The characters all have silicone running through their veins except for Roy Scheider's police chief, one of the few "common man" movie characters who isn't a pain (though Robert Shaw as a macho fisherman and Richard Dreyfuss as a smart aleck make up for that).

We all know why there's no emotion in *Jaws*—because it's working on the same audience-as-zombie principles as Universal's disaster epics. The story, about a shark that terrorizes a beach resort, is based on Benchley's pseudo-novel and from it, Spielberg has made a synthetic movie.

Spielberg could make a crushed teddy bear an image of pathos in *Sugarland* but the shark in *Jaws*, which we don't see enough of, has no character. It's just rubber and metal, which also marks the difference between *Jaws* and movies like *The Creature from the Black Lagoon* (1954), which entertained me as a child and still do (as camp). Such a monster, the product of a make-up man's imagination, was something to project onto, but a shark is a very mundane antagonist, as dull a figure as Jonathan Livingston Seagull. Its attacks are mundane, too—not bizarrely out of character like Hitchcock's birds.

The one example of skill (when two fishermen fall off a pier and frantically scramble back on) isn't much for a movie that comes on as a big-deal ultimate thriller and it is virtually buried among the film's other junk by the haphazard plotting and fussy, self-conscious editing which tries to outdo both Eisenstein and Bob Fosse.

Nothing dazzles you in *Jaws* the way the incredible assassination attempts mixed with gymnasium practice did in *S\*P\*Y\*S* (1974) or almost any single moment in the slower-paced thrillers *The Conversation* (1974) and *The Parallax View* (1974). There was visceral excitement even in *The Towering Inferno* (1974) but there's really nothing to see in *Jaws*. You can imagine it better than it actually is, even the crappy book is better.

Spielberg seems to have deteriorated with this film. Its sensibility is inhumane, and technically it is very scrappy, with lighting that doesn't match from shot to shot, action that isn't fast but jumbled up, and outdoor scenes that look for all the world like soundstage reproductions.

*The Sugarland Express* was a commercial flop but it had zest and feeling to it, while this commercial blockbuster hasn't any. It's a very thin experience. Spielberg graduates to the

Hollywood big time with *Jaws*; it's an eight-million-dollar hack job and that is real failure.

*The South End*
May 1975

# A Jawful Black Christmas

THERE'S TOO MUCH talent in a picture like *Jaws* for it to be anything other than dispiriting. The material isn't just unworthy of Steven Spielberg's talent, but Spielberg's handling of it is sloppy compared to what one knows he is capable of (*The Sugarland Express*).

For all the talent at work, *Jaws* should be better than what it is. As it is, the film only proves that the adage "Build a better mousetrap…" is wrong. It's "Build a better cattle-prod…"

But a certain amount of schlockiness can be liberating to an audience. *Black Christmas* (1975), the Canadian thriller filmed under the title *Silent Night, Evil Night*, is no better than *Jaws*. And though I suspect that the director Bob Clark is less talented than Steven Spielberg, *Black Christmas* is just as effective. In fact, I found it more enjoyable.

Crudeness slicked over with Hollywood flash is still crudeness, and I appreciated *Black Christmas'* honesty about it. There are never any static moments, as in *Jaws*; it goes about its business efficiently.

This film, about a mysterious murderer who preys on a sorority house during the holiday season, has no originality and the plotting is often inconsistent. However, the fact that it is minimally effective proves that the tricks people fawn over in *Jaws* are no big deal. When Clark's subjective camera roams the landings and staircases of a sorority house with the ghastly, apprehensive music increasing its volume (and it's less campy than the bass-strumming *Jaws* music) you can't help but gulp.

It is part of the mechanism. Clark and Spielberg have mastered the same schlock technique.

Both films are designed to scare the hell out of you, but *Black Christmas* succeeds at surrounding that crass aim with a story. It's not much (and when Keir Dullea as the boyfriend of one of the sorority members gets angry and busts up a piano, the film gets absolutely silly) but the story —which is like a sex-obsessed horror version of *Stage Door* (1937)—is watchable.

There's always something going on, the emotions don't seem left out as in *Jaws* and the girls are attractive—the best the men in *Jaws* could do was cross legs with each other like a hairy white octopus.

Olivia Hussey (Zeffirelli's Juliet) plays the girl whose neurotic musician boyfriend (Dullea) is the chief suspect in the murders. Hussey is a perfect victim for horror films, she has a fragility you can't help feeling protective about, like Bambi. The movies have never had an ingénue quite like her. Her fresh beauty, like Merle Oberon's, doesn't conform to the Hollywood images of glamour and her acting talent is considerable.

So is Margot Kidder's, whose appeal is entirely different. Non-innocent, non-ethereal, she's a snarling, sexy babe. She updates the old Joan Blondell-Ginger Rogers heroine until she seems the girl of tomorrow—liberated beyond any sexual mores. And so she's a match for the obscene phone caller who keeps the sorority house phone line jumping (the calls are porno-camp).

But movies are overdoing Kidder's sting. In this film she often verges on parodying curtness the way she did all through her older woman role in *The Reincarnation of Peter Proud*

(1975). But together she and Hussey give *Black Christmas* a sense of life. I didn't care about the shark's tooth in Robert Shaw's stomach or Richard Dreyfuss going into the ocean in that steel cage (and have people not noticed how Dreyfuss' inane hiding from the shark destroys the entire logic of *Jaws*!!). But I feared for Kidder and Hussey.

Lively, hysterical women are part of the pleasure of horror movies. In *Jaws*, Roy Scheider's wife was as responsive as a piece of bait, but Hussey screams wonderfully.

The movie ends with a daring conceit—John Saxon, playing the policeman who investigates the murder, is unable to solve the case. I first thought this was very trite but a few nights after seeing the film the lights were out when I arrived home, reminding me of the movie, and I laughed at the trepidation I felt.

Though at first it looked like the writer of *Black Christmas* ran out of ideas at the end, it might be that he came up with a genuinely effective one. By leaving the mystery in a suspense story, the movie builds up some real suspense that gets a delayed reaction.

None of this is to say that *Black Christmas* is a great film. I don't even think it is a very good one, but I make a point of it because while watching it I recognized how easy scare techniques are in the movies and that the less pretentious it is, the more fun it can be.

*The South End*
November 1975

# *Jaws Redux*

**T**HIS IS YOUR last chance to go teasing movie sharks before the summer is over. Steven Spielberg's classic scary movie is a combination action-thriller and action-comedy. It's not the death-by-big-mechanical-teeth that's thrilling and funny but Spielberg's out-in-the-open toying with audience expectation and still surprising them through crack timing and awesome, looming imagery. This is the movie that made his name. *Jaws* begins with bloody subtlety; swims into character depth (Roy Scheider, Richard Dreyfuss and Robert Shaw in a macho competition); and with John Williams' unforgettable score raising anxiety, it all climaxes with exhilaration. Summer may be ending but *Jaws* will entertain forever.

*Black Book*
September 2016

# CLOSE ENCOUNTERS OF THE THIRD KIND (1977)

## *Close Encounters of the Third Kind*

S TEVEN SPIELBERG, THE writer-director of *Close Encounters of the Third Kind*, is a true child of the century. He's fascinated by electronic technology and finds the way that technology and mechanics have become a "natural" part of our way of life (through TV, cars, washing machines, electric trains, gadgets and, especially, movies)—altogether crazy, baffling and amusing. Spielberg can show us a circuit light bulb or a machine and make us feel the wonder of the whole modern world.

Movies are, of course, Spielberg's art form, and not just because of their mechanical principles but primarily because this technological medium can, miraculously, express, enrich and (in a sense) preserve our lives. The wit and technical proficiency of Spielberg's movies—the new and improved use of old formula as in *The Sugarland Express* and *Jaws*—seems to almost reciprocate the pleasure he has gotten from other films and their presentations of life. And though he is not yet a particularly "sensitive" artist, it's clear that Steven Spielberg loves both the art and the mechanics of movies, and *Close Encounters* is a strange, wondrous, incandescent salute to both.

This movie has a space-age heart but instead of being set in the future where machines take over like typical science fiction, it's set in the present in which machines, even when they act up on us, still have a wittiness about them. They don't overwhelm us. They're toys, they have a wondrousness like gifts from heaven and so the plot centers on the most heavenly gift a space-age kid could think: A flying saucer.

The UFO genre of the 1950s doesn't need updating, it's still a modern subject, but what gives this film substance (what makes it less frivolous than *Jaws*) is that Spielberg makes UFOs seem possible by highlighting the flash and dazzle of present-day technology (thing that were undreamed of 20, 50 years ago) so that alien technology doesn't seem so remote or far-fetched. In this film the "common man" character, Roy (Richard Dreyfuss) works for the Indian Power Company so he isn't altogether "simple" and another hero, Barry (Cary Guffey), a young toddler, has his whole world filled with a bevy of mechanical, motorized toys. And in one of the most complexly affecting scenes in movie history, his toys come to life as the UFOs approach Earth. When Barry sees the spaceships coming through the clouds, he says, "Toys! Toys! Toys!" and Spielberg fills the whole movie with that sense of expectant joy.

Throughout the film, various UFO sightings and encounters are being traced by a French scientist, Lacombe (Francois Truffaut). The first close-up in the film is of Truffaut as he questions a man who says he has seen UFOs, and the understanding and love that one senses in Truffaut's own movies is right there in Lacombe's face. It's a look of innocence and trust—faith—and that's the motivation he shares with Roy, Barry and Barry's mother Jillian (Melinda Dillon) who all, once Barry has been kidnapped by the UFOs, converge on a mountain in Wyoming where a personal encounter with the aliens—the climax of the film—has been set.

*Close Encounters* is more than its story. Its highpoint, in which the aliens and earthlings converse through music and light, is an almost abstract demonstration of the sheer dazzlement of movies—it's a marvelous, transcendent demonstration that goes beyond technology into magic or poetry, take your pick.

It must be admitted that the plot itself tends to fall apart in the second half, but it is never infantile or laughable like *Star Wars* (1977). We stay with *Close Encounters* emotionally and are carried away by it because it has what *Star Wars* doesn't: it has visual beauty and grandeur which, for a technological director like Spielberg, is the manifestation of his feeling for the subject. Vilmos Zsigmond was the director of photography (aided by such notables as William A. Fraker, László Kovács, John A. Alonzo, Douglas Slocombe and Frank Stanley), and the film is nothing less than the best-looking American movie of the year. Plus, it's only glorious good sense that a science fiction movie should have a visionary power. Through the magically clear sky- and landscapes, and special effects artist Douglas Trumbull's luminous designs of the crafts that race at night on our turnpikes and highways like drag-racing Ferris wheels, this picture is full of scenes you won't forget. The special effects have a surreality that sparks one's imagination. This is the rare movie in which the modern world is depicted so imaginatively that it looks enchanted. You'll never be able to look at a toy, a set of headlights, a produce truck, an appliance or a helicopter the same way again.

Despite the advertising hype for the film, *Close Encounters* is not a tract on extraterrestrial life. It's not scary and it's not serious. It's a funny, genial film. A fantasy about the delight that superior technology can bring, and in the final sequence it becomes a celebration of the kinds of delight movies alone can bring us: Aurally the conversation John Williams has composed between Earthlings and aliens is a buoyant, witty music exchange. Listen: [Music from the five-note theme is played].

It's marvelous. And, visually, the thousands of flashing, codified lights that accompany the music are marvelous, too. But Spielberg also has faith in *movies* as communication, and in a daring stroke for a mass-appeal filmmaker, he epitomizes this by having the alien that comes out of the spaceship look remarkably like Jean Renoir and greet Truffaut (who is the direct inheritor of Renoir's humanistic filmmaking approach). It is a priceless moment, a sublime movie joke and a further reminder that the pleasures of movies are not sterile or inhuman despite all the mechanics. It is artistry, a special human faith and endeavor that makes it more than mechanics, that transforms technology into something very like a life force—and what a surprising, prodigious message for Spielberg of all people to espouse.

The giant flying saucer that lands in the film's climax is a bountiful symbol of technology. It's lit-up like a city at night, like the dream of every big city skyline that manifests mankind's soaring ambition and aspiration, like the diamond-studded blanket one sees out of an airplane window at night. Coming from the heavens, it's a Promethean spaceship—majestic and invigorating. And when we see it in full, with the city on top, it's like Spielberg is saying "Here is the ultimate marvel of technology and look—the whole developed world is based on it!"

Spielberg's poetic message isn't articulated literally but is delineated through his plot and dialogue but we feel that special, heightened sense of wonder for ourselves, and not only personally but when little Barry's toys take on their own life and go berserk, when the mailboxes on a road shake as if animated by some inner E.T.A. Hoffmann enchantment, when Jillian's appliances dance, when a character watching a TV set is inspired beyond the news and commercialism, and when the lights go out on a whole town, even its most flamboyant hamburger and gasoline drive-ins.

On the simplest level, *Close Encounters* is a supreme entertainment, a witty, ingenious, pretty treatment of a pop subject. But what relates it to great art are its resonances—about movies and about ingenuity. After Roy and Jillian sight UFOs they become obsessed with the image of a mountain where the great rendezvous eventually takes place. They don't know why, but they feel compelled to build or to draw the shape of the mountain. It's a baffling, intriguing idea (linking the creation of art and technology with muses) and we don't know why it's here in a sci-fi movie, especially in the long scene where the obsessed Roy ransacks his home and neighborhood sick with a creative urge. But the scene has an equivalent when the big spaceship lands: The scientists awaiting it are so dumbfounded they start talking their jargon all at once; it's gibberish but we know it's their attempt to describe the unbelievable thing they're seeing and have been seeking toward. I think Edison and da Vinci would have understood this moment perfectly. And I don't think it's farfetched to say that in these scenes, Spielberg comes as close as any filmmaker to uncovering the indefinable, if romantic, reason for creativity; i.e., man's attempt to comprehend the ineffable.

Spielberg may be treating his own creative crisis, his fascination with movies and his wonder why he loves them even though he doesn't make them like Renoir or Truffaut. To get at this, there are countless movie references in the film—even a take-off on the interview scene in Truffaut's *The 400 Blows* (1959) which Truffaut, himself, here takes part in.

But why Spielberg or any of us love and appreciate the technological miracle of the movies is best encapsulated in the very plot contrivance that gets the story started: in the opening scene, a squadron of planes missing in WWII show up in a Mexican desert, good as new. And in the climax, when the spaceship lands, unloading little Barry, it also unloads inhabitants of other places and eras, including the pilots of those planes. They come out of the spaceship walking toward us like a diverse group of extras on a Hollywood backlot. Surprisingly, they come out preserved, the same age and in the same dress as when they were "captured." It's an ecstatic, super-photographic, nearly metaphysical occasion recalling the sense of awe we get at a period film that also brings the past to us good-as-new—a visual and literal resurrection.

For me this homecoming scene put *Close Encounters* right over the top. I felt exultantly happy. Emotionally and sensually, it is overwhelming and this happens surprisingly often: in scenes like Roy and Jillian finding each other in a crowd. It's what is meant by "movie magic."

Scientists, but not many artists, have perceived the marvel of this redemptive, life-capturing potential in $20^{th}$ century technology; Renoir and Truffaut have and in his own way, Spielberg does, too.

Spielberg takes on a child's infatuation with technology contrary to the generally-accepted anti-industrialist, pro-proletariat view of technology in films like *Modern Times* (1936), *Metropolis* (1927), *Playtime* (1967) and even such a whimsy as *À nous la liberté* (1931), and by doing so he alerts us to the beauty of it.

The most valuable artists show us things about life that we may have missed or overlooked and what makes Spielberg's uniquely American, pro-machine stance acceptable and charming is that it is not also anti-human. He suggests to us the lofty human dreams that technology represents. The spaceship that holds the scientists in thrall is the very thing that they (like Roy, Jillian and Barry) have been dreaming of and reaching toward. And, obliquely, Spielberg presents a distinction between technology being used for good or evil. So this film doesn't just have heart, it has soul; it is Spielberg's electronic poem—his masterpiece.

Scenes like Barry summoning a UFO envoy by tinkering on a musical toy have a sublime innocence and thrill. If the story is not completely coherent (which the UFO genre can never be) a scene like that—a magnificent piece of visual poetry—makes all the difference.

*Close Encounters*—that title comes from the terminology used in UFO research. An Encounter of the First kind is a UFO sighting; of the Second kind, it's a trace of physical evidence; and of the Third kind, it's contact. But in the correct context of the film Spielberg has made the title *Close Encounters* also stand as a finer synonym for the effect movies have on us—a synonym for what people usually call "vicarious experience."

The experience of *Close Encounters of the Third Kind* is not just the greatest movie vision of 1977, but a fitting milestone for the 50th anniversary of talking pictures.

"The Movie Report," *Community Concerns*, WDET
January 1978

# 1941 (1979)

---

## *1941*

A PATTERN SEEMS TO be developing in Steven Spielberg's career: he makes one absolutely entertaining and honestly felt film like his debut *The Sugarland Express* and then follows it with a big, horribly manipulative piece of trash like *Jaws*. He has now followed the incandescent, wonderful *Close Encounters* with *1941*. Spielberg himself had differentiated this movie by calling *Sugarland* and *Close Encounters* his: films that originate from his own interest, that contain his expressive ideas while the others are simply jobs, work to which he brings only his craftsmanship. As craftsmanship, at least, *1941* can hardly be faulted, but Spielberg of all directors has no need to function as a hack and even on a project he did not originate it is utterly dispiriting to see him work with so little feeling, such crass imagination. *1941* is the most joyless movie experience from a major director since Altman's *A Perfect Couple* (1979).

What happens here is not unlike what happens in *Apocalypse Now* (1979): the director conducts an epic tale, pulling off many impressive, technically and physically awesome scenes without ever bringing depth to the story. At least for Coppola this is not a failure of effort (and it's the straining for depth that makes *Apocalypse Now* respectable, admirable, even heroic) but in *1941* Spielberg doesn't even try. The screenplay by Robert Zemeckis and Bob Gale (from an idea hatched with John Milius) is a collection of broad, obvious gags (spoken and visual) that for a director can only be a diagram of stunts. Spielberg's essential failure is in not activating the gags and or stunts with humanity or a sense of life. He doesn't treat his huge cast as people but sub-humanly, as if they were clowns— or gag props like Stanley Kramer's handling of his *It's a Mad, Mad, Mad, Mad World* (1963) cast though with far less reason than Kramer had. Spielberg attempts no understanding of the frantic behavior of West Coast Americans who (as the story has it) in the days following the bombing of Pearl Harbor were so panicky with fear of a mainland invasion from Japan that the mere sighting of an unidentified airplane would cause havoc. The film hypes the havoc into what one of the characters calls "Pure pandemonium." The exaggeration is beyond even that depicted in the recent TV dramatization of Orson Welles' *War of the Worlds* (1938) hoax (*The Night America Panicked* (1975)). And this exaggeration is *forced*, the picture's tone is *silly*, or determined silliness. Spielberg gets nowhere near the more drastic and serious incidents of U.S. war panic like the martialing and encampment of Oriental-American citizens, and he jokes about '40s segregation and racism. (He's a liberal though; whenever we're affronted with a large-faced clownish Black, we also catch sight of his white counterpart. Pure Hollywood fairness.)

The subject here ran the risk of chafing the American public, caught as we are now in the fervid near-panic of incipient war due to the hostage crisis in Iran which many view as an insult to American dignity, thereby reason enough to fight. I can't say that by neglecting to examine this attitude in its early '40s incarnation Spielberg has become a shameless, late-'70s war-monger, but the intentional, bland innocuousness of this movie does encourage the public's ignorance and disregard for history, when a regard for it is needed now more than ever.

Spielberg may aspire to Entertainment pure and simple, but his talent goes beyond that and so one has a right to expect more from him. Perhaps not a solemn discourse on mob psychology or psychopathology in America during World War II, but some semblance of real life, some vision or insight into the Tom Swift impetuosity Spielberg has sensed in American life during moments of his past work. In *Close Encounters*, toy-obsessed little Cary Guffey was Spielberg's stand-in epitomizing man's fascination with machines and technology. In *1941*, Spielberg and his insensitive characters lay waste to a lavishly constructed Los Angeles with cold dumbness. The sets and special effects are justly lovely (and Michael Kahn's editing nearly defines "quick") but this kind of destruction, as done here, has a moronic, childish aspect like Burt Reynolds car chases. And it's not done as well as in James Bond films: Ken Adams designs so wittily that the disassembling of his sets fulfills our interest in their assembly (like the billiard room in *Goldfinger* (1964) that was made to come apart).

*1941* opens with a mock restaging of the beginning of *Jaws*. Not only is it too early in his career for Spielberg to indulge in self-parody but the joke itself is poor. The film starts off on the wrong foot and throughout his *missteps*, based on other movies, just get bigger: We see John Belushi as a mad pilot stuffing food in his flight jacket as if he were still doing *Animal House* (1978) and the gratuitous destruction orgy takes its cue from the dullest moments in *The Great Race* (1965) (a tank running through a paint warehouse is reminiscent of the pie fight in that film). And there's much, much more involving

Slim Pickens, Ned Beatty and Lorraine Gary, Toshiro Mifune, Christopher Lee, Murray Hamilton, Robert Stack as General Stilwell, Warren Oates, Lucille Benson that is too idiotic to mention. A lot of this comes from the screenwriters Zemeckis and Gale who have synthetic/film-school memories; the closest they get to characterization is the imitation of Preston Sturges' maniacal Americans in a mixed-up love quartet enacted by Bobby Di Cicco, Dianne Kay, Treat Williams and Wendie Jo Sperber. But Spielberg merely works within his writers' limits, the characters and situations remain stock.

Last year, Spielberg was the producer on *I Wanna Hold Your Hand* (1978) which Zemeckis directed from another gag-ridden script by he and Gale. However, it was a sweet-tempered, innocent picture. It didn't merely view American hysteria through Sturges and Kramer, but it had a genuine (and ingenious) concept: Beatlemania as slapstick. It was a beautiful little movie—the best rock film yet because the filmmakers, though playful, respected and felt their subject. The cast was marvelous, convincingly young and exuberant—I couldn't wait to see them all again, but the way Spielberg uses some of them—Di Cicco, Sperber, Nancy Allen and Eddie Deezen—is without feeling or respect and the performers seem callow and stupid. Nancy Allen gave a classic enactment of rock fetishism in *I Wanna Hold Your Hand* that out-did Ann-Margret all the way from *Bye Bye Birdie* (1963) to *Tommy* (1975), but here Spielberg merely substitutes airplane fetishism in a dumb, smarmy running gag featuring Tim Matheson who blandly redoes his playboy role in *Animal House*.

Even so, Di Cicco and Sperber give the movie its best moments and the picture reaches its peak during a USO dance contest at the Crystal Ballroom. Feverishly choreographed, spectacularly shot (by William A. Fraker who did *American Hot Wax* (1978)) and with the liveliest bit of music scoring John Williams musters in the whole picture, this jangly, eye-popping sequence is like something by a modern, high-tech Gene Kelly. I began to hope Spielberg would turn the whole thing into a musical because following the rhythms of this dance sequence evinced the only conviction he showed during the whole picture. Spielberg is an unrivalled technician, but the extra—and the surprise—of his films is the moods he's capable of creating: in *Sugarland*, pathos; in *Jaws*, bursts of kinetic humor; in *Close Encounters*, sheer wondrous fantasy; and for a brief time in *1941*, music and dance. The rest of the picture is a fiasco.

"The Movie Report," *Community Concerns*, WDET
December 1979

# RAIDERS OF THE LOST ARK (1981)

## Flashback: The Mountain and the Gun

**R**AIDERS OF THE *Lost Ark* was released in 1981, the same year as *Take It Off*, the disco band Chic's most perfect album. Both artifacts exemplify pop culture infectiousness. That Spielberg's film, the first in what would become an ongoing series, had audiences lining up for admission needed no explanation (I attended a preview screening-plus-regular feature-attraction—an economic boon for me and my eager film school friends highly anticipating the newest Spielberg opus), but Chic provided the rationale in the *Take It Off* track "Flashback:" "The reason for the teasin' was the pleasin'."

Although *Raiders of the Lost Ark* has come to be known as Reagan-era escapism, expressing America-first imperialist might and arrogance, it doesn't really play that way. It works like Chic said: as pop satisfaction. This film epitomized the summit of Movie Brat, American Renaissance sophistication. Spielberg's collaboration with George Lucas (and screenwriter Lawrence Kasdan) showed how Boomer boys understood and related to Hollywood's entertainment tradition, both high and low, from tacky serials made on shoe-string budgets to lavish extravaganzas that offered James Bond-style stunts, action spectacle and panache. No wonder the film opens with the most erudite trope of any postmodern Hollywood production:

The Paramount Studio logo of a snow-capped mountaintop morphs into what semiotic students recognize as a synecdoche. That famous mountain (known from playful Hope-Crosby road movies as well as George Stevens' prestigious *A Place in the Sun* (1951)) symbolizes the Hollywood promise of ambitious entertainment, a fulfillment of what all movie brats trusted and loved—which would become the essence of the Indiana Jones serial.

The teasin', pleasin' audacity of that opening was proof of post-'70s style, complexity and knowingness. Indy's exploits felt fresh without feeling new. What was new was the acknowledgement of audience familiarity with the Everest peak of showbiz amusement. More than Spielberg and Lucas' wink of the eye, that mountaintop represented the crest of popular expectation and satisfaction.

From there, *Raiders of the Lost Ark* could communicate with viewers as nostalgia-plus—a refinement of Buck Rogers, William S. Hart, Tarzan, Hopalong Cassidy, Terry and the Pirates and James Bond adventure. (Flash Gordon's interstellar exploits were left to *Star Wars*; Spielberg would put his own imprimatur on this epic.)

Starting with the appropriation of Han Solo—Harrison Ford—as the intrepid professor/adventurer, Spielberg finds a figure who personifies his cross-cultural ambivalent identity: A boyish he-man embodying American ingenuity whose worldly sophistication combined respect for ancient rituals, religious reverence and the need for speed. (This was five years before Paramount's *Top Gun* (1986).) Appreciation of Indy's manly virtues were teased in the classroom scene where romantic co-eds stared breathlessly, one with "I Love You" written on her eyelids, revealed when she closed them to dream, and a furtive male student expressed his own crush by leaving a polished apple on Professor Jones' desk before hastily retreating off screen.

Starting with *Raiders*, Indy goes through the series as a bildungsroman, a worldly coming-of-age for the American political sensibility. This entertainment features a larky foreign policy. No more serious than James Bond foiling the maniacal intentions of various arch nemeses, Indy struts through the Middle East as if the world was his own museum. He's purposeful, not casual, but part of his erudition comes from the experience gained by awareness of his singularity, his distinction as Western interloper.

Just over a year into Reagan's first term, we film students understood that this excursion wasn't just American intervention but had a more innocent origin: *Raiders* was the latest response to what historian and Middle East scholar Edward Said called Orientalism. But instead of an unconscious expression of Western cultural dominance, Spielberg and Lucas had been made conscious of difference through the exoticism of fantasy-adventure movies. For Spielberg, the 1940 *The Thief of Bagdad* is essential. It overcomes the timely tensions of the U.S.-Iran hostage crisis—not suppressing that anxiety but overwhelming it with remarkable wish fulfillment, an allegiance to humane movie imagination. Indy's coming-of-age starts there in Alexander Korda's technicolor extravaganza and, specifically, the appeal to childhood wonder and purpose.

At the sentimental heart of *The Thief of Bagdad*, after child actor Sabu has gone through a transformation as a dog and back to loyal, faithful, impetuous but good-hearted and adventurous youth, he approaches a Persian priest whose advice describes a prophecy Spielberg will fulfill:

For you we have been waiting twice 2000 years. This is the land of legend where everything is possible when seen through the eyes of youth. We are the remnants of the Golden Age. Golden because gold was nothing; no more than the sand beneath your feet or the stone that we became. We were petrified with horror for the evil done among men when they cease to be children and to believe in the beauty of the impossible. Whenever the heart of a child returns to us and comes in to us we live again. And so, as that child, you are to be my successor.

Much of the wonderment of *Raiders of the Lost Ark*, that made its 1981 appearance seem fresh, owes to the childlike spirit that re-imagined the adventure serial as well as the fantasy action film so that those genres—from Buck Rogers to *The Crimson Pirate* (1952)—felt renewed. Spielberg's signature gift for editing, pace and humor comes from both an instinct and a learned skill that paid homage to those genres so that even a striking visual stylist like Robert Siodmak's all-out jamboree of bravado, jokes, fighting, explosions and romance were now updated. It's not a demonstration of new technology, it answered modern adolescent thrill and attention spans. Ironically, Spielberg's action filmmaking didn't become more streamlined (*Raiders of the Lost Ark* is actually longer than *The Crimson Pirate*) or minimalist (like the work of Luc Besson and his acolytes) but shows-off more elaborate narration and modernist wit.

Essential to Spielberg's artistry is the ambassadorial idea of film, cinema, movies as a bridge of communication—

between cultures, nations, people. His sense of humor prevents him from being pious about it too often—the piety usually comes through best as visual slapstick or satire. In that sense, it also comes across as practicality, and *Raiders* demonstrates that best in the frequently mentioned moment when Indy is faced with a threat through a black-robed swordsman. The Oriental's whooshing, dazzling display of a scimitar and its implicitly obscure skills calls up foreign prowess and enigmatic tradition. Caught facing the terrifying menace of Third World proficiency, Indy responds pragmatically: he pulls out a revolver and shoots the Oriental: Modern Western technology vs antiquity. Oriental fantasy instantly changed into Cowboy-Gangster movie. That joke is not about racist aggression as symbolized by Indy's gun but the gun itself is a joke—not a venal weapon but a mechanism of cognitive, *American*, speed. Like movies.

The Ark itself, emblem of Jewish heritage and Biblical mysticism, appears good naturedly as part of a story gimmick that also epitomizes Spielberg's ecumenical discourse. The Symbol's power is unleashed during the film's climax, interestingly a hybrid of Spielberg's Orthodox teaching and his film-buff savvy: the special effects pay homage to George Pal and Ray Harryhausen but especially to Cecil B. DeMille's *The Ten Commandments* just like the roiling clouds that part to reveal the earth-bound arrival of heaven-sent flying saucers in *Close Encounters of the Third Kind*. It's all a cultural flashback—to the Torah and to the Hollywood repository of Western imagination. Spielberg raids the stockpile of cinematic narrative, eventually concealing the Ark amidst the flashback to Charles Foster Kane's bounty.

# POLTERGEIST (1982)

*Poltergeist*

T OBE HOOPER'S *THE Texas Chainsaw Massacre* has a
unique brilliance different from *Poltergeist* which is why you
know Spielberg directed the latter. Hooper caught Spielberg's
attention because *The Texas Chainsaw Massacre* initiated a new
genre of horror film when it was first released in 1974. The
renegade tale of a remorseless, predatory psychopath, hidden
in the American Southwest backroads as also hidden in the
American psyche, had undeniable B-movie virtues. It was so
coarse as to be more potent than suspense films made at a higher
grade. Hooper's sophistication, coming from a background in
the production of advertising commercials, drew viewers into
the terror-run-amuck storyline so that their appreciation grew
unsuspectingly—out of surprise but also in line with exact and
efficient presentation of character types and tense situations
that were already familiar from generic narratives but would,
as a result, become conventional. Hooper's technique created
a new genre that influenced all the horror films made after it.

Spielberg belonged to the new generation of mainstream
Hollywood filmmakers who appreciated B-movies along with
prestige classics. And although *Jaws* conquered the world, it
did so partly due to the new sense of fright that Hooper had
simultaneously articulated. Hooper's energy and wit—the

brazen remorselessness of a daytime horror story—offered unexpected delight. And that's what producer Spielberg sought for *Poltergeist*: a similar prestidigitation but magic tricks that came from his own hands, bearing his own fingerprints.

Ten years before *Poltergeist*'s release, Spielberg did his apprenticeship on the Universal Studios made-for-TV film *Something Evil* (1972).

It was a 73-minute occult horror story devised to take advantage of the popular best-selling book *The Exorcist*. Spielberg got a jump on the child-torture elements of William Friedkin's 1973 film through *Something Evil*'s simplified story of a boy (Johnny Whitaker) possessed by a malign presence when his advertising executive father (Darren McGavin) and artist mother (Sandy Dennis) buy a new house in exurban New York. Made on low-budget TV terms, *Something Evil* is a mere programmer. Unexceptional except for a few film-school-trite experiments: a man falling through a window in slo-mo (a gimmick seldom used by Spielberg, soon worked out of his system), a traveling shot from the p.o.v. of a hand-held flashlight and a jump-cut montage of Dennis threading a series of clay disc talismans.

*Something Evil*, with its mostly routine and undistinguished gimmicks, is only notable for motifs that will be refined in future Spielberg endeavors: Scenes of household objects flying in a vortex as in *Close Encounters* and *Poltergeist*. Another towhead female toddler as in *Poltergeist*. There's also a frightening moment when a possessed child is suspended in air, alarming his concerned parent, that would reappear in Brian De Palma's *The Fury* (1978). And a mother's courageous, dedicated life-or-death struggle over the fate of her child when Dennis grasped the flailing Whitaker in the midst of that vortex shouting a powerful declaration: "Stevie, I love you! I won't let them have you!"

Fear and benevolence—the basic elements of *Poltergeist*—are already bows in Spielberg's quiver. His supervision of the film's production, however shrouded in mystery, discretion and denial is aesthetically apparent but it can definitively be felt in its temperament and tone. *Poltergeist*'s ghost story works as a satire on haunted house movies, the joke pinning the supernatural and the super annoying on the medium of TV (Spielberg's cheeky appreciation that he has graduated to the big time).

Steve and Diane Freeling (Craig T. Nelson, JoBeth Williams) live in Cuesta Verde, a suburban planned community, with their three children aging from pre-school to adolescence. Their suburban domestic harmony is interrupted by ghosts who contact the youngest child (towhead Carol Anne) through an off-broadcast TV set.

A thematic reading of *Poltergeist* won't yield much of interest; best to observe the film through that perennial film pundit term "a thrill ride." Here's where resemblances to *Something Evil* matter. Years later, post-William Friedkin's film of *The Exorcist*, Spielberg teases childhood fright as well as his own past as a television wunderkind. It is the movie that most consistently and profitably indulges Spielberg's taste for juvenile anarchy.

This film's genre simplicity lets Spielberg exercise his extraordinary craft without care for niceties of theme and plotting because saying "Boo!" is the point. Just like the slapstick routines that turned *1941* into *Hellzapoppin'* (1941), that later would barge into such serious films as *The Color Purple* (that infelicitous roof-crash) and *Minority Report* (the gross-out refrigerated food and truly witty jet-pack chase scene in an alley between Tom Cruise and his Precrime cop colleagues).

*Poltergeist* is a testament to Spielberg's fanboy jokiness that often erupts in chase scenes. It is both a distraction from solemnity and an aesthetic weakness. (Spielberg's cameo appearance in John Landis' *The Blues Brothers* (1980) is no accident; it is the *raison d'etre* of the overwrought car-crash folderol in that clamorous joke fest.) The only excuse is that *Poltergeist* is a series of media jests (from cinema and television) that, as in *Raiders of the Lost Ark*, succeed by reminding viewers of their cinematic memories and the erudition (of genre and technique) that accounted for their response to Hooper's *Texas Chainsaw Massacre*, a less ferocious experience than Friedkin's *The Exorcist*. Hooper's film was not obscene but a film geek extravaganza, from the stroboscopic scenes, where the ghost-world's portals which mirrors the fluttering effects of Hooper's *The Funhouse* (1981), to the mother-love sequence of Joanne's determination to save her children, filmed as a Hitchcockian reverse pullback in *Poltergeist* of JoBeth Williams running down the hallway. This is the culmination of *Something Evil's* "Stevie, I love you!" scene, but by this point, Spielberg has found his footing as a director. The wittily storyboarded *Poltergeist* was made in between filming of *E.T.*, the first movie Spielberg made without his usual storyboards. *Poltergeist* may be trite, but it's also a splendid horror-film farce that's often delightfully amusing. When Zelda Rubinstein appears in the story as Tangina, a spiritual medium, she enters from the background and overtakes the foreground.

"What side of the rainbow are we working tonight?" Steve asks sarcastically, evoking another pop cult memory of *The Wizard of Oz* (1939) Munchkins. "This house has many hearts." "I just don't like trick answers." Tangina talks about "life force," "There is no death, there is only a transition to a different sphere of consciousness," "Will you do anything I ask even if it comes contrary to your beliefs as a human being and as a Christian?" and "the real light," Spielberg has fun with his own sentimentality. Tangina speaks of Carol Ann's "Light that implies memories of love and home," the ideals that inspire so many Spielberg narratives from slavery and World War II immigrants to stateless migrants and 9/11-era dystopians.

It matters that Spielberg films Tangina's monologue, respecting her dwarf height so that her wisdom comes through poignantly: "They are not a part of consciousness as we know it; they linger in a perpetual dream state. Inside this spectral light is salvation." Here, in this ratty contest is the source of Spielberg's ecumenical grace that Spielberg first expressed in his greatest film *Close Encounters*. Spielberg isn't necessarily a dogmatic believer but as a popular culture maestro, he respects the widespread belief in goodness and faith. *Poltergeist* doesn't work at that level of a hermeneutic pursuit, any more than one can examine Cecil B. DeMille's quasi-Biblical epics *Samson and Delilah* (1949) and *The Ten Commandments* for religious faith, but its colorful, witty gamesmanship displays Spielberg's unfettered craft in a brief dream/nightmare phase.

# E.T. THE EXTRA-TERRESTRIAL (1982)

## E.T. vs Resident Evil

A RADICAL NOTION: STEVEN Spielberg's movies are not meant for children. This week's reissue of his 1982 *E.T. the Extra-Terrestrial* may remind some people of a Walt Disney perennial re-released at seven-year intervals, but such cynical thinking always misleads Spielberg's fans—and his debunkers. Their primary mistake is to take the film's premise—a boy's encounter with an alien unleashes deep-seated imaginings—as the limit of its meaning. The movie's universal fascination certainly includes children, but the full appreciation of Spielberg's imaginings—and of his filmmaking quest—requires an adult sensibility that perhaps now, 20 years later, more people ought to recognize.

*E.T.*'s zeitgeist popularity was the kind of phenomenon that usually happens once in a pop artist's career, but Spielberg has entranced a mass audience and revolutionized the workings of the entire film industry on several occasions: *Jaws*, the Indiana Jones series, *The Color Purple*, *Jurassic Park*, *Schindler's List*, *Saving Private Ryan*. Spielberg's filmography is as full of world-historical landmarks as the Beatles' discography. Not through catering to the lowest common denominator, but because he has two extraordinary gifts: direct emotional access and absolute visual panache. Only D.W. Griffith has comparably commanded movie culture and the art form itself simultaneously. To deny this about Spielberg is to lie. Yet some people would rather pretend to themselves than reject the cynical trend of contemporary film culture by acknowledging that cinema (and Spielberg's films in particular) has a humane essence.

In the modern era, only *The Godfather* has been as popular and profound as *E.T.* (*Titanic*? Ha!) But *E.T.* never received proper commendation. In 1982 the New York Film Critics Circle gave Best Picture to *Gandhi* (1982) and Best Director to Sydney Pollack for *Tootsie* (1982). By now, everyone knows that was arrogant ignorance. Critics, like many viewers, are unable to appreciate the precious solemnity of human experience that Spielberg found in the tale of Elliott (Henry Thomas) assuaging his loneliness. Condescension to Spielberg's art even included the great Pauline Kael—Spielberg's most astute '70s critic—who hailed *E.T.* by originally comparing it to the children's book *The Wind in the Willows*. That faint praise missed what really goes on in the film, and what's central to Spielberg's imagination. He has always been after an understanding of spiritual communication. That's the point of young earthling Elliott relating to the extraterrestrial. It can now be seen as the emotional basis of how the African slaves interacted with white American abolitionists in *Amistad*. Seeing *E.T.* again allows us to correct even the best-intended misreadings of 20 years ago, the diminutions that have become standard notions of what Spielberg's art is designed to reveal.

First, Spielberg appeals to the child (the uncorrupted viewer) in us, but transcends childishness by touching on the

Divine. Think about it: Does the film's final F/X—a rainbow—belong to the vocabulary of children's fiction or does it evoke a greater message?

Spielberg's view of childhood experience has such purity and concentration that some people cannot see its artistry. (Hacks as crude as Ron Howard, Stephen Daldry and John Badham have based careers on poorly imitating Spielberg's touch.) The opposite problem occurred with *A.I. Artificial Intelligence*, which is as emotionally authentic as *E.T.*, yet critics couldn't grasp how that film spoke to the human essence—that the robot David, like the real boy Elliott, embodied a distillation of human thought and spiritual aspiration.

Genre—the commercial classification of storylines—is the problem. People take their market forms literally, without interpreting them. That's also why Spielberg's movies are not for childish adults (a position for which *The Village Voice*'s Spielbergphobia has become synonymous). The same war that the French New Wave waged 50 years ago against the denigration of American pop cinema (Hitchcock, Nicholas Ray, Sam Fuller) erupts again when one defends Spielberg's genre enhancements. Watching *E.T.* on the big screen—and not diminished on TV—restores the largeness of its concerns. "Why don't you grow up! Think how other people feel for a change," Michael (Robert MacNaughton) says to his little brother Elliott. It's the basis of Elliott's evolution toward sensitivity—his empathy is comically represented by the contagious yawn he communicates to E.T. (A marvelous memory of childhood for me—and for how many others?) The lessons parents hope storybooks will impart to their offspring are not different from what adults want from art. Spielberg perpetuates Griffith's non-condescending faith in how movies can instruct and nourish. Oddly, critics belittle this aspect of *E.T.* and would arrest Spielberg at only this kindergarten stage of development. Yes, *E.T.* suffices as a child's entertainment, but it reaches for more.

As his first astonishing feat, E.T. demonstrates where he came from by levitating clay balls and making them orbit in a miniature solar system. Spielberg's trope anticipates Bela Tarr's sublime rotating-people dance that begins the metaphysical parallels in *Werckmeister Harmonies* (2001). Elitists will scoff at that comparison, but that's just middlebrow—and middle-aged—snobbery. Tarr evokes folk ritual with the same legitimate purpose with which Spielberg evokes childhood play—touching on fundamental behavior. Some prefer thinking Spielberg frivolous, but after *The Color Purple* it wasn't his sensibility that was problematic. Instead, many people's traditional movie responses went rigid at his ethnic, spiritual transformation of genre. (Though it's always worth noting that the popular audience embraced *The Color Purple*; only snobs balked.) A movie about Black lesbians was radical in 1985— and still is. You'd think Spielberg was Reagan Incarnate given the way even liberal critics went off after him after *The Color Purple*. His humanism has only gotten deeper and richer, yet they deny Spielberg's art as craven sentimentality.

This perverse defensiveness presaged the *Pulp Fiction* (1994) era in which cynicism became the most prized movie ethos. It's currently represented by the thriller *Resident Evil* (2002), a *Matrix/Alien* hybrid done in the peculiarly heartless style of video games (it's based on the bestselling Capcom game). This appeal to dread is no more legitimate than any other gimmick, and it's a fallacy to think it is more mature. Yet Spielberg's unfashionable agape exposes the preference for pessimism and misanthropy over truth and emotional realism. *Resident Evil*'s director, Paul W.S. Anderson, owes his headlong pace and high-decibel sound F/X to Spielberg's rejuvenation of the action movie in *Jaws*, but none of these spectacular killings or Milla Jovovich's tomgirl elegance (including some emotive, erotic flashbacks) match Spielberg's exhilaration. It's really for children. Exhausting and insensitive—especially about death.

*E.T.* deals persuasively with loss when Elliott's friend dies. It's the only work of film art to treat resurrection since Carl Dreyer's *Ordet* (1955), but it's distinguished by Spielberg's wonderment—an amplitude of passion and mystery, even in a suburban setting. ("There are no goodbyes," Michael tells Gertie.) Spielberg supersedes the haunted-house horrors of *Resident Evil* or bad-vibe hits like *The Silence of the Lambs* (1991) or *Seven* (1995), knowing it's naive to consider dark moods more serious than optimism and that it takes maturity to understand why. Elliott, the wise child—in the final image— is the fulfillment of that maturity. Still ponderable two decades later, Elliott's close-up (evoking Truffaut's *The Wild Child* (1970) verging on enlightenment) conveys Spielberg's concept of human experience—an openness to belief not limited to fairytales but accessible through the greatest of the popular arts. Critics cynically misread the scene in *A.I.* where David prays to the Blue Fairy, probably because they are philosophically opposed to what the scene represented (innocence and prayerful devotion). The same obstinacy stymies their response to *E.T.*'s commingling of fairytales and sci-fi with something immanent. When Elliott insists, "This is reality!" he's asserting Faith, acting upon an answered prayer.

Elevated pop sensibility is the simple reason *E.T.*'s iconographic bike chases are so magnificent. They adduce the trifles of American youth in moments of existential suspense so that the taken-for-granted pleasure of a toy becomes a means of transcendence—a ride full of spirit toward the spiritual. Common childhood delight has never been more exactly portrayed than when Elliott and E.T. take flight. But to indulge the sense of escape—from suburban conformity, from the mundane—and then dismiss it denies how deeply Spielberg's vision has probed. It forgets the intensity of one's own purest desires. That ride across the face of the moon has a psychic impact that can't be laughed away. It's powerfully wonderful. And afterward, you must consider the significance of that rainbow E.T. leaves behind. A kid viewer might feel it, but you shouldn't necessarily expect him to get it.

*New York Press*
March 2002

# TWILIGHT ZONE: THE MOVIE (1983)

## *A Boomer-rang Remake*

*T*WILIGHT ZONE: THE *Movie* remakes the famous 1960s
Rod Serling TV mystery series through four contemporary
filmmakers: John Landis, Steven Spielberg, Joe Dante
and George Miller. Each director differs from the fantastic
sensibility that Serling used in short stories that addressed
social issues and psychological obsessions, but each man brings
his own particular panache to the short story form. The results
are mixed.

A prologue and first episode, both from Landis, start
with horror comedy, like Landis's hit *An American Werewolf in
London* (1981); these feature Albert Brooks and Dan Aykroyd
in a buddy-movie shocker and then move to a moral tale starring
Vic Morrow as an American bigot who confronts his racial
prejudices in an otherworldly replay of the Vietnam war. The
opening short is funny, if extreme, while the longer narrative
suffers from being obvious. (Our knowledge of the real-life
tragedy that occurred during the making of this segment casts
a pall that is never exorcised by Landis' lack of finesse.)

That awkward beginning leads to an ultra-sentimental
segue. Spielberg's "Kick the Can" stars Scatman Crothers

(the shock-victim of Kubrick's *The Shining* (1980)) in a story about rest home seniors who are tempted by the possibility of forestalling death by returning to their childhood through playing a game of Kick the Can. This is the first episode to actually remake Serling's program yet it has the hallmarks of Spielberg's childlike agape and otherworldly humanism. When the elderly actors are replaced by child performers who speak in the idiom of ethnic old-timers, the magical *Peter Pan* affectation recalls the begrudging criticisms that *E.T.* was cloying. Yet, Spielberg's smooth, dreamlike venture into the occult is kindlier than his production of last year's *Poltergeist*. "Kick the Can" touches on the ineffable when Crothers sings the song lyric "age doesn't matter" which suggests an existential sense of life, eternity and the after-life. It's largely saccharine and surprisingly, profoundly touching.

Dante's "It's a Good Life" fulfills the promise of this omnibus movie. Not only does a director of the American Renaissance bring aesthetic daring—and dazzle—to conventional storytelling, but Dante also exhibits fondness for his pop culture heritage. The story of a child who intimidates adults by forcing them to submit to his will (or else suffer the punishment of cartoon surrealism and adolescent hostility) comes across powerfully through Dante's—and cinematographer John Hora's—exaggerated colors, bizarrely angled compositions and frightening homage to TV hysteria. Its scariest scenes are like an update of *The Cabinet of Dr. Caligari* (1920). In cinematic terms it's more intense than anything Serling ever achieved on television and brings the ambitions of this entire film to an exhilarating high point.

Miller has a go at "The Terror at 50,000 Feet," perhaps the most famous of the *Twilight Zone* episodes, showing off the panache that made his *Mad Max* films, especially *The Road Warrior* (1982), box-office sensations. John Lithgow plays the airplane traveler who looks out the window of his passenger seat and sees a creature on the wing of his airborne plane. It is only he who sees the beast. As he goes from unbelieving to horrified to frightened, his shocked realization grows into fear. The creature goes from prankish to teasing to threatening; its fiendishness matches Lithgow's wide-eyed, open-mouthed hysteria. Miller's one-note tour de force (increasing only in dynamic intensity) suffers from obviousness. It feels more like a programmer rather than a genuinely brain-twisting, unnerving and scary *Twilight Zone* classic. Dante takes the prize, meaning his TV satire lives up to true Rod Serling wit. It's a new classic.

# INDIANA JONES AND THE TEMPLE OF DOOM (1984)

## *Temple of Gremlins*

**A**FTER THE PHENOMENAL successes of *Jaws*, *Close Encounters*, *E.T.* and *Raiders of the Lost Ark*, Steven Spielberg, at age 37, has both the financial means and the talent to do anything he wants. What he wants—to judge from his current film *Indiana Jones and the Temple of Doom* and his production of Joe Dante's *Gremlins* (1984)—is simply to build a better mousetrap, a machine to ensnare a mindless audience.

The tandem release of *Temple of Doom* and *Gremlins*, two highly self-conscious, movie-fixated films, seems to close the circle on the most recent great movement in movie history: The American Renaissance that began with *Bonnie and Clyde* in 1967 that flared and gleamed throughout the '70s when many, including young, filmmakers remade such Hollywood genres as Westerns (*The Wild Bunch* (1969)), sci-fi (*Invasion of the Body Snatchers* (1978)), detective films (*Chinatown* (1974)), musicals (*Nashville* (1975)), service comedies (*M\*A\*S\*H*), film noir (*Point Blank* (1967), *Taxi Driver* (1976)) and horror films (*Carrie* (1976)) in terms of their own contemporary social observation. Movies changed because the most alert, committed people making them in this period sought to close the gap between the product made by the Hollywood factory and the audience's real and fantasy life as affected by that product. New movies became much more technically sophisticated, extravagant, their effects more intense and their concern with other movies more pronounced.

The intoxicating elation of a film by Altman, De Palma, Spielberg, Scorsese, Walter Hill, Coppola was in the richness of their style. Watching pictures like *The Godfather Part II* (1974), *McCabe & Mrs. Miller, Taxi Driver, The Fury, The Long Riders* (1980), *Close Encounters* was like having new eyes, acquiring new insight. For the film generation of the '70s, movies were better than ever because they were never before so movieish, so fast, so colorful, so full of incident, detail, or so up to date. Standard sentiment and piety was often countered with impudence, irreverence and when necessary, pity and horror. These movies had a new aesthetic and, it seemed, a new truth. All this, just from filmmakers questioning and reexamining the conventional structures and techniques and assumptions of movies.

*Gremlins* and *Temple of Doom* show a similarly sophisticated approach but they produce a powerful depression (the exact opposition of elation). The heightened spectacle in *Temple of Doom* and the cynical inversion of shtick and audience expectation in *Gremlins* serves little apparent purpose aside from exercises in extreme manipulation. In both of these pictures, enjoyment is either drained out or made distant because the elaborate, complicated effects relate to no sustained meaning. The films grab your attention—and never let go—while you are subjected to a barrage of stunts and jokes. The idea is the same as those that flourished in the '70s: our responses to movies don't shut off when the projector does; the junk and fairy tales in our subconscious may be more primary than we believe (or allow ourselves to believe). But in the '70s the idea was to reveal how the movie-watching and fantasizing process was complexly intermingled with ideas about politics and sexuality and history as well as ideas about art (movies).

All *Gremlins* does is present a purely fictive world and circumstance: a jovial Santa Claus of a father (Hoyt Axton) presents his son Billy with an early Christmas gift: a "mogwai" pet/creature. Inadvertently, the pet multiples and these mischievous offspring—gremlins—lay waste to Kingstone Falls where the film is set. This subversive Christmas story, involved so obsessively with the benign characters and trivial situations of movie pastiche, tackles a subject that, to say the least, is soft and safe. As Billy Peltzer (Zach Galligan) and the citizens of the tiny town are besieged and fight back, the movie becomes a ridiculous guerilla handbook on pet warfare; through knives, bombs, food processors, a microwave oven and sunlight. Dante involves himself with beating a dead gremlin. All the impacted movie lore and cult humor go nowhere. The movie devours itself and not with the result of liberating the viewer's imagination as Brian De Palma did in *The Fury* where he followed the logic of movie thrillers to its wildest extremes. The action in *Gremlins* never builds; it's repetitive, often incoherent, with no basis to explain the gremlins' transformation or even the fates of various characters. By sealing-up the convoluted mayhem with a combination fortune cookie/greeting card ending, the movie withdraws itself from our understanding or relevance. It is, like *Temple of Doom*, a self-contained work-out, frighteningly oblivious of the audience's need to assimilate what it has seen.

*Gremlins* is too poorly conceived and structured to be able to argue about its moral viewpoint—it lacks one. Dante's anarchic, Creature Feature universe vitiates all the rules of monster movies and satire to the extent that he cancels out his own jokes and his own scares. He's like a talented David Cronenberg—too smart to believe the junk he's suited for. But Dante could not have anticipated that the result of his all-stops-out trash movie jamboree would be this irritating and tiresome—the whole film suggests a junk movie equivalent of the hamburger-and-peanut-butter junk food gross-out featured in Dante's brilliant episode of last year's *Twilight Zone: The Movie* (1983). It's a childish indulgence, a pointless extravagance, in which Dante reveals the nothing he got from trashy films, the dumpster mind Hollywood has left him.

Unlike De Palma and Hill, or Bernardo Bertolucci and Andre Techine in Europe, Dante only mimics what he's seen, without transforming or informing it. It's all nonsense. We're thrown everything we never cared about in movies only to see how worthless it all is. A junkyard of jerry-built mechanisms with no story to tell, and nothing to say, *Gremlins* traduces even the mechanisms that, before, seemed magical; like Spielberg's recreation of a child's universe and the Disney-like anthropomorphic affection toward puppets and the animal world. Dante's problem is not that he doesn't believe in movie magic just that he isn't capable of it when it counts; when he needs to understand and respect the audience's threshold for beauty and fantasy no matter how whimsical or inane. That's why this smarty-pants thriller contains a stupefyingly trite sequence of gremlins behaving like rowdy, uncouth movie patrons, talking, eating, jiving, drinking, flashing. This sequence has the sour, hateful attitude of a filmmaker criticizing the public for the tricks he's able to play on it. Its ugliness is like that of the spring snapping on a mousetrap.

Spielberg's *Temple of Doom* is all funny, fast-springing traps, full of belief-defying feats that should, ideally, be a constant, zingy delight. The problem is that in making the most extravagant, seamless, best-directed adventure movie in Hollywood history, Spielberg has not really brought it up to date. The picture's sophistication is all external. He has revved-up the adventure genre without renewing it or altering its ideas or possibilities. There are two major, unfortunate results:

First, that Spielberg's intrepid Great White Hero's exploits in the Third World still have the xenophobic racist and macho sexist pieties of the less enlightened Hollywood films of 50 years ago; Indy drags with him an oriental orphan (the only male his equal) and a screeching hysterical woman. (*Gremlins*, too, has its racist overtones in the fracas made by those critters with stereotype ethnic characteristics like breakdancing, etc.) *Indiana Jones* takes place in the make-believe world of no politics, the world of generic lies and conveniences that most people have been fighting to resist, to expunge from the recesses of their minds, since Watergate and Vietnam when the political and sexual promises and assumptions of popular culture were exposed as impossible and false.

Secondly, by ignoring modern sensibility, Spielberg's movie-making regresses to the old-fashioned, thrill-a-minute sort that contemptuously condescended to the public, controlling an audience's reactions and responses, leaving no room to breathe, even to think. Not since *Jaws* has Spielberg practiced such all-out, shameless manipulation of motor responses and left our minds alone, starved. Jean Renoir once remarked that his own films were not complete without an audience to interact with them. Spielberg's movie does everything itself; it doesn't need an audience—which may be why its acceptance has been so widespread. The film makes no demands on anyone. Strangely, people have taken more offense at this graphically cartoonish film's supposedly "excessive" or "intense" action than at the insult of its neglecting a viewer's emotional, reflective needs.

Of course, *Temple of Doom* is superior to *Gremlins*, in its bizarre banquet scene alone: the meal that includes chilled monkey brains and eyeball soup elevates the gross delights of childhood to the level of hilarious fable. The writing and staging of this scene show Spielberg's gift for the wonder of innocent trash. He polishes his special quirkiness and humor, capturing it for all time. Dante misses that almost entirely in *Gremlins*. His own gift (as seen in *The Howling* (1981) and *The Twilight Zone*) is to show the psychological dread beneath basic, primitive fantasy—he goes to dark where Spielberg goes to light (De Palma in movies like *The Fury* does both). But there's so much confusion and overkill in *Gremlins* that Dante's possible dark insight is murky.

A new German production, Wolfgang Petersen's *The NeverEnding Story* (1984) maintains a sure grasp of fantasy storytelling. This is its subject as a little boy reads a storybook and imagines himself in the place of its characters where a planet is dying, being enveloped by a void ("The Nothing") because its inhabitants lack imagination—a great metaphor for movie culture in 1984. Like his schoolboy hero, Wolfgang Petersen restores fantasy and imagination where it has been lost, to the kind of moviemaking which Spielberg and Dante and that pop culture guru George Lucas have obliterated. *The NeverEnding Story* is a bit wan and genteel compared to American films of its ilk but this summer even the best American filmmakers seem to have lost sight of those essential fantasy film qualities of reflection, rumination or illuminating the connection between pop ideas and myth. (It seemed a puzzling omission in *Splash* (1984) when the mermaid's story is connected to Crazy Eddie but never to Hans Christian Andersen.)

It isn't necessary for movies in a non-literate age to defer to literature or become literary; the greatest filmmaking the '70s sought to move people simply through the contemporary relevance of their imaginings, by making them understand their part in this voluntary mythmaking process of movie watching. The overbearing pyrotechnics of *Temple of Doom* and *Gremlins*, which represent the most advanced state of current filmmaking, ride roughshod over all that. Neither picture does much to reveal our yearnings or susceptibilities for narrative inventions. These movies burn out the brain cells, and they demand victims.

*Films in Review*
Summer 1984

# THE COLOR PURPLE (1985)

## Rethinking Hollywood Archetypes

*T*HE *COLOR PURPLE* is the best movie of 1985—and the strangest. Steven Spielberg adapts Alice Walker's popular tear-jerking novel with gleeful effervescence. He doesn't pretend to identify with the sorrowful story of Southern Black women's struggle in the first third of this century: we might be intrinsically skeptical if he did. Instead, Spielberg shows the same simple, optimistic, childlike perspective of his other films. He brings out the feminist fairy-tale essence of Walker's novel, more than ever confounding and expanding one's view of pop art.

Spielberg's movie recalls a pop tradition so vast it includes D.W. Griffith silents, Lana Turner soap operas, Picasso sculptures, Ntozake Shange plays, rhythm-and-blues and gospel records, Charles Dickens serials, faux-naif Black musicals, liberal-social melodramas and John Ford Westerns. The film constantly shifts moods and effects and suggests other movies as Spielberg recreates Walker's fiction out of his own pop-culture syntheses.

Arguably this is the only measure of life that he knows, thus it's also an honest approach. Such a synthesis happens to bring Hollywood further up to date on feminist and racial issues than the critical establishment may be ready to admit or accept.

For better or worse, *The Color Purple* is a genuine state-of-pop-consciousness movie. Its deft, undeniably effective emotional displays amid frequent, heavy-handed manipulations force a viewer to understand the artifice of which movie fiction is made and the visual, poetic codes from which Black people and Black experience have been almost permanently segregated but that Spielberg now restores.

Because of Walker's feminist preoccupation that places racial discrimination second to the oppression of women, the filmmakers (including Dutch screenwriter Menno Meyjes) don't get hung up on the same old fairness bug that prescribed all previous movies about Blacks. Watching this film is like returning to your own reflection in a mirror—you don't notice what others may see, you recognize traits distinctly familiar to yourself, perhaps marveling at their form and substance.

*The Color Purple* feels like the first insider's movie about Black Americans to come out of Hollywood because the characters aren't defined by their relation to the white world or created through a white artist's sympathetic condescension. These are new Black archetypes; as fictional creations they are so free of political justification that the whole issue of "correctness" is zapped. The actors are simply wonderful to behold (in part because of Spielberg and cinematographer Allen Daviau's determined prettiness). Here, at last, is a vivid panoply of Black faces, well lighted and without exoticism, treated as natural screen images just as white faces always have been.

Because of Spielberg's famous sci-fi benevolence, you could call this "loving the alien" (he automatically transcends those do-good racial allegories *The Brother from Another Planet* (1984) and *Enemy Mine* (1985)). He has made the real advance of treating Black people (characters) as any other. Spielberg's consciousness here is so heightened, it's giddy; he floats about the earthbound particulars that snag other filmmakers who emphasize conventional Black dialects and ghetto atmosphere. Like Walker, who freely accepted these things (she knew that Black and Southern didn't always mean impoverished), he works to convey a spiritual, emotional quality instead.

Not only have reviewers who have compared *The Color Purple* to Disney's *Song of the South* (1946) misunderstood Spielberg's ingenuousness, they've read it wrong. The film's characters are not carefree, inhuman or dimensionless. The struggle toward self-respect by the protagonist Celie may be predetermined, but it's neither shallow nor simplistic. Spielberg and Meyjes string together the most telling events of Celie's sojourn: from submissive self-deception (Celie's advising a man to beat his wife may be the most succinct, multileveled illustration of Uncle Tomism on film) to her developing wiles in a round of pathetic-comic-ironic-then-defiant servant scenes. Each increment of her emotional climb is fleet and dramatically potent.

Profundity has only possessed Spielberg in relation to toys (*E.T.*, *Close Encounters*, or the climax of *The Sugarland Express*, where a teddy bear bounces along a road). He's shown amazing depth in ways other "mature" filmmakers could not, such as the moment in *Sugarland* that wove a man's despair into a few stolen seconds of a Road Runner cartoon. Spielberg's snappy, head-on visual style is risky and arch for drama. It's what always kept people from taking him seriously, and *The Color Purple* often veers into the stylized hyperbole of Frank Tashlin farces and Byron Haskin adventure films.

But this cartoon sensibility is not subtle enough for the few scenes of Black-white interaction—as when Miss Milly (Dana Ivey), a victim of white male supremacy, vents her helplessness in paranoid hysterics. Yet the problem may actually be that Ivey, an expert stage comedienne (*Driving Miss Daisy*), lacks the emotional resonance of the Black actors. But it is nonsense to complain about Spielberg's facility. The precision of any one scene, such as a young widow admitting that her husband died "on top of me," packs an ideological wallop greater than Jill Clayburgh's whole bra-burning career.

The most common dispute with the film regards Spielberg working in broad inappropriate slapstick for fear of alienating his audience. This has invited a backlash long-brewing since such loud, blunt, even racist Spielberg productions as *Gremlins*, *Indiana Jones and the Temple of Doom* and *The Goonies* (1985). It's unfortunate that this rancor has erupted with *The Color Purple*, because this film should redeem Spielberg's "genius." His instincts for the entertaining effect here transform Hollywood's entire racist legacy.

Racism in Hollywood films was usually subtle and select— the industry regularly chose not to give fictional validation to the Black experience or to include it only when comically expedient. Post-World War II filmmakers were stumped by the need for revision, and in the Civil Rights Era it was necessary for filmmakers to depict Black characters solely in terms of social transition. The filmmakers could not relax their views, and audiences have been tense ever since. Today, the only Black performer regularly involved in recognizable moral dilemmas is a human cartoon (Mr. T); Broadway maintains the minstrel-show façade of Black life through pastiche shows like *Sophisticated Ladies*, *Ain't Misbehavin'*, *Grind* and *Dreamgirls*, and the highest-rated TV show in the land is Bill Cosby's pallid Black retread of *Make Room for Daddy*. In this context the need for large-scale Black mythical figures—a distilled essence of human experience in black—is greater than ever before.

The first half hour of *The Color Purple* forms the basis of Spielberg's vision of childhood desire and euphoria—a precious but genuine humanist link—and it's miraculous: in a series of classic vignettes Celie is sexually abused by her "Pa," gives birth to two children who are taken from her, and is married off to Mr. (Danny Glover), who finally separates her from her sister Nettie (Akosua Busia). As the young Celie, Desreta Jackson gives the most lucid, affecting child performance since Henry Thomas in *E.T.* She has the emotional transparency of legendary film actresses and, when she is paired with pert, doll-like Busia, the two recall Lillian and Dorothy Gish in *Orphans of the Storm*, D.W. Griffith's 1921 epic about two lost sisters reunited after the French Revolution. Spielberg stages the scenes of Celie and Nettie's separation with a raw, mythic power equal to Griffith's. And if his audacity has the old master, who also directed the Ku Klux Klan romance, *The Birth of a Nation* (1915), spinning in his racist grave, it's just! This is the birth of effective Black screen fantasy—not a story of Black people who behave like whites or who finally inherit the kingdom of heaven, as in Marc Connolly's scandalous yet popular insult, *The Green Pastures* (1936). It's a vision of Black life that answers strictly emotional imperatives and is the first since King Vidor's unjustly neglected *Hallelujah!* in 1929.

Spielberg's art fills in the gap that has existed between the invention of film fiction and acceptable Black screen portraiture. The narrative here is heroically simple because, as the film's Griffith and Dickens parallels suggest, the political implications don't need to be spelled out; we can intuit them, and in the remarkable teaching scene between Celie and Nettie, Spielberg adds his own sweet structuralist-linguistic flourishes.

Whoopi Goldberg as the adult Celie brings a crucial shrewdness to the film, acting out the character's secret intelligence and at the same time a demonstration of the Black survivalist's bag of tricks. Her childlike playfulness makes the performance more than clever. When Celie blooms under the loving attention of the bisexual blues singer Shug (Margaret Avery), her joyfulness betrays a perfect emotional empathy between actress and director. There is no movie scene this decade better performed and directed than the discovery and reading of letters between Celie and Shug.

The actors carry us through Spielberg's Black remake of pop and movie history—from Shug's Bessie Smith-style dress and singing to the politicization of the Big Mama myth by Oprah Winfrey as Sofia. It also places Walker's tale properly in the tradition of popular women's fiction. We see how *The Color Purple* answers the specific needs of modern women to shape their own triumphant fantasies, as once provided by the books of Edna Ferber and Fannie Hurst and not just *For Colored Girls...* either. In *The Color Purple* one feels a continuity between such early feminist-race relations classics as Ferber's *Show Boat* and Hurst's *Imitation of Life* that also provided the staples of Hollywood melodrama about women who struggled free of dependency on men.

Spielberg somehow manages both the exuberance of *Show Boat* and the emotional punch of *Imitation of Life*; *The Color Purple* should prove as endurably enjoyable as both. This film fails in one aspect only: It doesn't sufficiently rectify Walker's hatred of men. Spielberg almost gets out of this because Glover—who suddenly and terrifically has become the most important Black male actor since Poitier—has a charming, intelligent presence that enriches the hard-hearted character of Mr., but the script neglects his turnabout. It's stupid to take this as a critique of Black men in particular; the scenes between Glover and Adolph Caesar as his father and Willard E. Pugh as his son construct a system of oppression that explains machismo as tradition outside race. Anything more would have significantly changed the material, which was conceived in terms of how women sustain each other—exaggerated to the point of idealizing sisterhood as lesbianism (and at the other end projecting machismo into incestuous rape). Spielberg isn't up to rethinking these kinds of literary tricks. He tries expanding himself by crosscutting between Celie in Georgia and her sister in Africa; Shug at the juke joint and her father in church. He does a technically superb shuffle and condensation of various ideological and plot information but not much more (Quincy Jones' overripe score blends themes more effectively).

All this means is that there are limits to Spielberg's artistry and that it's on ground that no other mainstream filmmaker has finessed or even dared. There's much to think about, to feel, much that matters, in *The Color Purple*. It's a flawed movie but possibly a great one because it's so vital.

*The City Sun*
January 1986

# National Board of Review:
## Best Film, Best Director

A S A POPULAR filmmaker, Steven Spielberg has often sacrificed subtlety for the sure-fire effect, as in the startling proficiency that made *Jaws* a comic horror movie. But because he is also a great filmmaker—an artist—there is a precision, wit and inspiration in the way he manipulates the medium. Now he's gone deeper. The ideas and emotions viewed in *The Color Purple* are so direct and potent that it is the rare humanist movie on social topics that does not preach a message.

The strong, sophisticated concept of Alice Walker's novel (about a woman's delivery from the tyranny of male-dominated society through an elaborate and loving network of sisterhood) plays like an exhilaratingly lucid fable. Celie (Whoopi Goldberg) grows from subjugation and ignorance to independence and self-respect. She achieves her full human heritage as a friend, lover and parent. The details of the setting in the rural Black South from 1909 to 1937 are only incidental to the story's outline. Through the intelligent social critique of Alice Walker's feminism (smartly adapted by screenwriter Menno Meyjes), Spielberg has made the first true racial crossover movie. The film is about the individual and communal triumph over a constricting ideology each character lives by that isolates and oppresses all sexes and races more than it is about race conflict.

The story is specific but it's told in mythic, general terms. Spielberg has the popular artist's remarkable gift for one-to-one identification between the moviegoers and the figures on screen.

He doesn't plead the case of his characters as do conventional liberal filmmakers Stanley Kramer and Sidney Lumet. As always, Spielberg appeals to fundamental, childlike emotions, so that his film makes direct contact with the audience.

*The Color Purple* will be controversial for the simplicity with which Spielberg treats Walker's themes. Certainly the villainous side of the male characters is cartoonish and the visualization of Celie's childhood will startle readers of the book who imagined a wizened, less youthful figure. But there is genius in this. Spielberg conveys the emotions of fear and innocence utterly without complication. His plainness contains the richness of Walker's themes without overstatement, except perhaps in Quincy Jones' fine, if emphatic music score.

Who would have predicted that Spielberg's innocent point of view could serve so wisely a story of a woman's life? Or that Spielberg of all people would make the most politically astute feminist film to emerge out of the Hollywood mainstream? The enduring beauty of this movie lies in Spielberg's unsentimental and profound acceptance of the childlike needs of the characters; he respects the essence of humanity. Spielberg's own themes of love, faith and homecoming (expressed at the peaks of *Close Encounters* and *E.T.*) are now deeper than ever. This is the fulfillment of his "cry-for-happiness" aesthetic.

Spielberg's work here is similar to D.W. Griffith's instinctive graphic skill, use of cross-cutting and powerful emotionalism in films like *Orphans of the Storm* and *Way Down East* (1920). The allusions to Dickens' *Oliver Twist* recall the basic pleasure of movie narratives begun with Griffith's Victorian method of telling long, rounded tales. Even the cast shows the same remarkable range of feelings as in a Griffith movie. From Goldberg's sly, original interpretation on, this is the best-acted American film of the year with especially memorable performances from Margaret Avery, Oprah Winfrey, Danny Glover and Desreta Jackson as the young Celie. This is a serious movie but its style is deft, light and emotional, not ponderous. It's a pop feminist epic and the strongest film of the decade thus far.

*Films in Review*
February 1986

# The Black Image A.C.P.

**R** OLL OVER D.W. Griffith, and tell George Gershwin the news. The depiction of Black people in popular culture, especially the movies, has entered a new phase of diversity, originality and artistic and emotional impact.

Stereotypes inherited from Griffith's anti-Black 1915 *The Birth of a Nation* and Gershwin's patronizing *Porgy and Bess* (composed in 1935, filmed in 1959) are being counterbalanced by a variety of Black artists and performers who have recently participated in pop culture through movies, music videos and TV programming.

Call this period A.C.P.—after *The Color Purple*—for the way Whoopi Goldberg, Oprah Winfrey, Spike Lee, Whitney Houston, Janet Jackson and Bill Cosby have seized the public's imagination and become household names. Most importantly, they all have follow-up projects on the boards, thus establishing a base for continued work and future accomplishments instead of one-shot glory.

The recent return engagement of Steven Spielberg's *The Color Purple* joins in by reasserting the Black ethnic presence in pop. The film's re-release may not signal a movie tradition but one year and $100 million after its first opening, it certainly looks like a Hollywood landmark.

*The Color Purple*'s success went beyond the box office, reversing the industry's resistance to ethnic drama since Sidney Poitier stopped acting in the mid-'70s. In addition to creating new stars, *The Color Purple* may well have inspired Poitier's return to film acting this year in the upcoming spy thriller

*Little Nikita* (1988) (he doesn't have to hold up the banner alone anymore). It also seems connected to the Walt Disney company's holiday reissue of *Song of the South*, the 1946 film-with-animation version of Uncle Remus stories.

The Spielberg/Disney parallels that began when reviewers cited the emotional and fantasy aspects of *Close Encounters* and *E.T.* made *Song of the South* a major A.C.P. event. Audiences could accurately judge the similarities in whimsy. But the re-release also made clear the improvement in Hollywood's racial awareness over the past 30 years—as shown in the differences between Uncle Remus' (James Baskett) effort to be liked for his storytelling and Celie's (Whoopi Goldberg) struggle to sustain herself in her own family and community.

Away from the double-barreled controversy that criticized Spielberg's characterization of Black men or ridiculed his "softening" of Alice Walker's Pulitzer Prize-winning novel, *The Color Purple* now seems as classical, as one-of-a-kind, as *Song of the South*. It's a melodrama (a pejorative term these days) but a Black, feminist, politically advanced melodrama.

Spielberg, the master-craftsman of the tear-jerker, gave the mass movie audience a purely emotional connection to the Black experience in America. This created an interest stronger and more curiosity-provoking than the reactionary militancy of '70s Blaxploitation, the telecast of the *Roots* (1977) miniseries, or the morals and homilies of Civil Rights Era films like *Lilies of the Field* (1963) or *Guess Who's Coming to Dinner?* (1967).

Every Black media figure looks different after *The Color Purple*—the same miracle Spielberg worked with machines and toys in *Close Encounters*, bicycles and childhood in *E.T.* Realism is not what did it but Hollywood's most elusive, "magical" ingredient: myth.

The characters in *The Color Purple* were written, photographed and performed to show the beauty of a fictional creation. Celie's first blossoming friendship with Shug (Margaret Avery) and Sofia's (Oprah Winfrey) Christmas homecoming conveyed the women's emotional essence and, so, their mythic, universal appeal.

The A.C.P. era is distinguished by Black performers who don't have to excuse or explain their appearance. *The Color Purple* proved Black actors' validity as heroic cultural icons as well as human beings. (The old butler and maid stereotypes implied real difference that went further than economic class stratification.) Oprah Winfrey's leap from actress to prosperous and trusted talk show host seems a logical result.

In the wake of Spielberg's revised big-screen conventions, the previous multimedia advances of such performers as Prince, Eddie Murphy, Bill Cosby and Richard Pryor have come together to form a period of cultural enlightenment.

In television, the Black middle-class family of *The Cosby Show* continues the reorienting effect of *The Color Purple*. It functions as an obvious means of acquainting America with the practices, goals and virtues its people cherish in common. This is a major but subtle change in emphasis from Norman Lear's '70s sitcom satires. *Good Times* and *The Jeffersons* were just equal-time comedies that made a joke of ethnic differences— the shows were still tied to a white point of view of Blacks as aliens. *The Cosby Show*, *227*, and *Gimme a Break* give their characters an individuality that lets their ethnicity go without saying.

Sometimes it's best said subtly, as on last year's episode of *The Cosby Show* that was aired to coincide with Martin Luther King Jr.'s birth: for two full minutes the doctor and family, one by one, gave their silent attention to a broadcast of a King speech. The subtle pride of last year's independent sleeper, *She's Gotta Have It* (1986), came from the producer-writer-director Spike Lee, a graduate of NYU's film school. Made for $175,000, the film has so far grossed close to $10 million nationwide. It is the surest sign since *The Color Purple* of the moviegoing public's eagerness for Black screen stories.

Filmmakers have responded to this need so regularly in the past year that the rhetorical selling point Lee made during interviews—"When was the last time you saw a Black man and woman kissing on screen?"—seemed just another Hollywood hucksterism. Richard Pryor's directorial debut, *Jo Jo Dancer, Your Life is Calling* (1986), had featured that display and more only a few months earlier.

From the music-video branch of pop, singers Whitney Houston, Janet Jackson, Aretha Franklin and Anita Baker have provided more star-worthy images of glamour and romance than Hollywood seems capable of right now. Jackson's popularly choreographed videos *When I Think of You*, *Nasty* and *What Have You Done For Me Lately* virtually revitalized the movie musical in miniature.

In *Jumpin' Jack Flash* (1986), Goldberg summed up the mass media's tradition of Black female exploitation and the pressure to imitate white beauty standards. The humor was on Goldberg's terms and she emerged, integrity intact, as the first Black female movie star—with dreadlocks.

The prominence of the Black Vietnam soldiers in *Platoon* (1986) epitomizes the more inclusive view of Blacks in current films. Richard Wright's novel, *Native Son*, came to theaters rather than PBS' *American Playhouse* only after the proven example of *The Color Purple*. Blacks provide the social background of *Something Wild* (1986), the revolutionary heart in the last scene of *Sid and Nancy* (1986), and were the focus of last year's nostalgic *Round Midnight* (1986) starring saxophonist Dexter Gordon.

The Black artist's responsibility to control his screen image is the subject of a new comedy *Hollywood Shuffle* (1987) written, produced and starring comedian Robert Townsend. Touted as the funniest debut since Woody Allen's *Take the Money and Run* (1969), *Hollywood Shuffle* speaks out and laughs about the temptations, stereotypes and struggle associated with the portrayals of Black people in movies and TV. It's a witty, spirited gloss on the social and cultural awareness that *The Color Purple* embodied and turned around.

The enlightenment is spreading. Carol Black, the white producer of TV's *Family Ties* series, came up with last year's controversial *Soul Man* (1986). Black's sitcom premise—*Black Like Me* (1964) updated through *Tootsie*—was neither offensive nor ahead of its time for the people who actually saw it. Its several good jokes kept pace with the changed attitude about ethnic humor, ridiculing naive stereotypes about Black behavior.

Protests against *Soul Man*, like the NAACP protests against *The Color Purple* that preceded the film wining three NAACP Image Awards, indicate how radical this era of enlightenment is. Not everyone is comfortable with it, but the erasing of Black screen stereotypes continues apace.

*The City Sun*
February 1987

# Fiction into Film: Best Adaptations

**WAY DOWN EAST (D. W. Griffith, 1920)** Made when people were still alive to the novel as a popular melodramatic form, Griffith's loose adaptation of Thomas Hardy's *Tess of the d'Urbervilles* is a tribute to the possibilities of taking fiction to heart and a lesson in how literature can become cinema with a sense of visual immediacy and aesthetic freedom.

**THE MAGNIFICENT AMBERSONS (Orson Welles, 1942)** Welles had done a radio version of Booth Tarkington's novel, but this film has the freshness of something newly inspired. Visually, the richest movie I know—it gives the same pleasure as written language and the same depth as kinetic art.

**VIVRE SA VIE (Jean-Luc Godard, 1962)** Godard's most gothic movie takes Edgar Allan Poe's story "The Oval Portrait" and makes it uniquely modern. The director even recites the text—a literal adaptation—in the middle of this Parisian story of a prostitute's travails, which also becomes a confession about Godard and his wife, actress Anna Karina, thus enlarging Poe's relevance exponentially.

**MASCULIN FÉMININ (Jean-Luc Godard, 1966)** Godard again, breaking unwritten rules with a documentary-style feature on the political and romantic habits of youth in the Pop era. Fact is, it's based on Guy du Maupassant's short story "Paul's Mistress" and is perhaps the ultimate proof that adaptations need not be dull-wittedly slavish.

**THE COLOR PURPLE (Steven Spielberg, 1985)** Spielberg's bildungsroman and still the only Hollywood movie about a black lesbian, pan-Africanism, and the legacies of Griffith, Fannie Hurst, Zora Neale Hurston, Douglas Sirk, John Ford, and, of course, novelist Alice Walker—all in one postmodern package.

*Bookforum*
June-August 2007

# Hollywood's Greatest Gay Film

**"O**VERRIPE," THE TERM *The New York Times*' Ben Brantley recently used to describe the 1985 film *The Color Purple*, is a way of staving off the emotional power of Hollywood's greatest gay film. "Overripe" belittles the same way words like "sensitive" and "severe" were once euphemisms that stereotyped gay men and lesbians. Even now, in the *Times*' current review of John Doyle's new Broadway revival of the musical stage version of Alice Walker's best-selling novel, Steven Spielberg's groundbreaking movie is still patronized.

This year marks *The Color Purple*'s 30th anniversary, which ought to be respected as a landmark in motion picture history. Spielberg's visually lush and dramatically potent tale put a lesbian relationship up-front and center in a mainstream American movie when nobody dreamed such a thing was possible. And, over the decades, millions of viewers have responded with affection and enthusiasm. (The film received 11 Oscar nominations, yet won none.)

Walker fashioned the story of Celie, a Black teenage girl in 1930s Georgia, who is raped, gives birth to two children soon taken away from her, and is separated from her sister Nettie, then traded off to an abusive man (symbolically titled Mr.). Unlike most feminist pop fiction, *The Color Purple* was a melodrama with links to Black gospel tradition. (Celie voices her plight to God.) Before identity-politics masochism promoted such lesbian hysteria like *Precious* (2009), Spielberg depicted Celie's restoration and family reunion as a triumph. Its spiritual and historical reclamation was based on recognition of Celie's gay humanity.

The credit denied *The Color Purple* may be linked to the overpraise accorded such later films as *Brokeback Mountain* (2005) and this year's *Carol* (2015), both starting with cautious, covert implications of gayness represented by white characters—as if Spielberg and Walker had not already broken-through popular resistance.

Even Doyle's new, minimalist staging of the musical gets its license from *The Color Purple*'s modern development of gay identity. Walker conjugated the term "lavender" from the days of the Mattachine Society when it was code for gay passion as "different" from conventional romantic hues—she moved across the spectrum of affection (now symbolized in the pride flag) from same-sex attraction, opposite-sex attraction, both-sex attraction. Lavender-to-Purple charts Celie's sexual experience throughout her hardship. ("I might be Black, a woman, I might even be ugly. But I'm here!") Plus, Walker and Spielberg explicitly link "purple" to an appreciation of life and God's wonders. "I think it pisses God off when you don't notice the color purple!" says blues songstress and Celie's lover, Shug Avery.

Perhaps this normalization of the humane in spiritual terms is what "intellectuals" object to as "overripe." It pisses some people off when gayness is seen as something other/more than a social principle or represented in terms that don't comply with secular convention—or when idealized by figures who don't come from society's dominant class.

The *Times* review praised Doyle's show with racialized clichés "Hallelujah," "born again," "glory to behold" and "gospel-flavored" as if we were back in the days of *faux naïf* Harlem Renaissance knock-offs. (The show's songwriters Allee Willis, Stephen Bray, and Brenda Russell rigorously refrain from indulging gospel excesses.) Doyle may strip Walker's story "to its essence," but Spielberg's movie moves audiences by giving the Black gay female experience the same cinematic richness that Hollywood had long reserved for Joan Crawford, Jane Wyman, and Lana Turner melodramas about middle-class heterosexual white women. *Carol* repeats that prejudice, minus the aesthetic richness.

The Color Purple teaches enlightened audiences to boldly accept gay emotion. Doyle downplays Celie and Shug's attraction (presenting a leg-spread Shug is coarse) whereas, on film, Whoopi Goldberg and Margaret Avery found understanding despite their characters' contrasts. (The letter-reading scene should be as hallowed as Brando-Steiger's cab scene in *On the Waterfront* (1954).) Their emotional rapport makes the moment of Celie and Shug's first kiss more deeply convincing than the entirety of *Carol* where Rooney Mara and Cate Blanchett show no rapport—as also noted by critic Peter Rainer. In the musical's biggest miscalculation, Shug Avery's number "Push the Button" reduces female sexuality to neurological sensation, whereas the hummable song "Ms. Celie's Blues (Sister)" in *The Color Purple* film (lip-synched by Avery but sung by Tata Vega) conveyed Bessie Smith-style ribaldry while celebrating feminist solidarity. It's the moment Celie's social liberation (her emotional outing) begins—and there's nothing in *Brokeback Mountain* or *Carol* that equals it.

That a film as bold and great as *The Color Purple* continues to be marginalized by the false sophistication of "good taste" amounts to deprivation. Gay audiences get shamed of their emotions and straight audiences get shamed of their affiliation and empathy. In a masterstroke, Spielberg concluded his finest love story with Celie and Nettie reunited: aged yet playing childhood patty-cake. Doyle preserves this phenomenon in the closing title song ("I don't think us feel old at all. I think this is the youngest us ever felt.") Thirty years ago, before it became fashionable, Spielberg understood that ritual as a direct correlative to gay folks' joy.

*Out*
December 2015

PART TWO

# A.C.P.

# EMPIRE OF THE SUN (1987)

## Spielberg Strikes Again

**E**ARLY IN *EMPIRE of the Sun*, Steven Spielberg directs an astute confrontation between Jim (Christian Bale), an 11-year-old English boy born and raised in the pampered life of English colonials in Shanghai, China, and a Chinese housemaid (Naishe Zhai).

The maid, attempting to appease the arrogant little scion, struggles to speak phrases in the difficult English language that has been forced upon her by cultural acquiescence and imperialism. The maid's resentment and the boy's snideness are simple and clear without undue emphasis.

Spielberg—whose last film was *The Color Purple*— is sensitive to the scene's Third World political subtext. It's doubtful if any other filmmaker in Hollywood history (or Spielberg himself before *The Color Purple*) would have dared upset the white Western perspective of a movie by even suggesting that there might be another to consider.

Because this is essentially a white boy's story set on the brink of WWII, it is important that the first Chinese person we meet is not the usual meek, comical, smoothly integrated slavey. Spielberg's honesty deepens his film's meaning and widens our perspective with this insight into personal political tension.

Although it occurs in a big-budget epic, the scene is remarkable as a depiction of a kind of pre-myth: it gives us a hint of the imperialist reality that our filmmakers regularly skip over as irrelevant to the needs and interests of the white Western society that bankrolls Hollywood. Later, when the Japanese forces invade China, imprisoning the British and Americans there, Jim's halcyon world is overturned. Reality and the force of Asian destiny slap him in the face—literally so, as done by the now liberated housemaid in a chaotic moment of strangely satisfying revenge.

That slap is not just a humiliated empire striking back; it's the adult world asserting itself to an unprepared child.

In the mainland melee that follows the bombing of Pearl Harbor, Jim is separated from his parents and spends most of the war on a tear, latching onto surrogate parents (John Malkovich, Miranda Richardson, Nigel Havers), sinking into his boyish fantasies about airplanes and flight. (There's a rapturous nighttime etude on technology and boyhood when the imprisoned Jim discovers a Japanese crew repairing their planes.)

This story of survival builds from the modern-day ecumenical appreciation for humanistic, technological and political progress; a sense of East-and-West commonality rather than past antipathy. Specifically, it is Spielberg's most unsettling vision of childhood (human) resilience. Not saccharine, the film presents a cool, awed view of a child's madness: Jim's delirious confrontation with life and his responses to war.

*Empire of the Sun* cuts deeper than John Boorman's recent, beautifully made but essentially insubstantial *Hope and Glory* (1987). Boorman's refreshed nostalgia (he opposed banal tradition by shooting the 1940s in clear light instead of a yellow haze) was a conventional effort. Spielberg stretches.

This story, based on the autobiography of sci-fi writer J.G. Ballard, contains suffering, violence and death but not in the orderly, manageable sequencing of Spielberg's other pictures. For Jim they cannot be wished away or blotted out, which presents a problem for an artist of Spielberg's benign nature. As with *The Color Purple*, he's had to reconceive the epic form and account for uneasy truths—this time not as a fable but as a challenge to his own recalcitrant optimism. You can sense Spielberg hanging on to the security blanket of the big-screen, David Lean-style craft in the picture's inflated length and slowed pace and repetition of incidents.

This uneasy reconciliation between old and new becomes explicit in an analogy to *Gone With the Wind* (1939) matching Jim to Scarlett O'Hara in a way that is too perfect—an allusion Spielberg can no longer really use but is driven to surpass. The film needs the quickened pace of *The Color Purple* and the buoyant dialogue of Spielberg's own writing in *Close Encounters*. In both cases, he discovered new territory; this script by British playwright Tom Stoppard offers a smart organization of hallucinatory WWII events but the skillful structure is confining.

This is Spielberg's first real-world movie since *The Sugarland Express*. He has practiced fantasy and folktale with rare purity because he has no dark side, no guile. It's plain now that he manipulated various Hollywood genres not in imitation of narrative tradition but always to improve them—politically, aesthetically—yet with an endearing sense of fun. Like Brian De Palma, Spielberg knows film form inside-out. Here he uses it *ironically*, to complete our sense of Jim's derangement.

Spielberg is not simply an underrated filmmaker, he's underestimated. His childlike benevolence does not preclude artistry of psychological complexity. It's a fallacy of Hollywood that, through movies, total sense can be made of the world and so be understood, condescended, escaped.

In *Empire*, the world that overwhelms a boy's senses is politically, mythically richer than Hollywood tradition allows. There's no cute comfort in this realization. The politics of war, race and sex haunts every phantasmagoric sight. Jim's peak experience—seeing the bombers he's dreamed about fly by and feeling their heat—is totally disorienting to him. It rattles the balance of sanity he has lived by. The movie ends when Jim closes his eyes at last. This way, Spielberg unforgettably draws the line between reality and the need for fantasy. This is a call every film artist will have to answer.

*The City Sun*
December 1987

# INDIANA JONES AND THE LAST CRUSADE (1989)

*Indiana Jones Makes History and Progress*

A MERICAN MOVIES ARE known for specializing in action but rarely for depth. In *Indiana Jones and the Last Crusade*, Steven Spielberg combines both. Of necessity he sacrifices the hot-foot pacing that led him disastrously into the careless racism of the previous Indiana Jones film, *Temple of Doom*. The result is the most intelligent "escapist" film to come out of the Hollywood ethos. It's a cultural landmark—the first American adventure movie to honestly confront the mythologizing of history.

What accounts for this change? Possibly *The Color Purple* in which Spielberg adapted Black experience and iconography to the visual styles and emotional structures of (white) Hollywood fiction. With new cautiousness, Spielberg continues the worldwide exploits of intrepid white archeologist Indiana Jones (Harrison Ford, back from the dead of *Working Girl* (1988)). It reflects Spielberg's respect for Third World cultures that *Temple of Doom* trampled over. Equally important is this film's peaceful resolve with the current political awareness of the West's dwindling superiority. It's literally a ride into the sunset.

**113**

Spielberg purveys his white American male hero's adventures almost objectively—certainly without the politically offensive egotism that has motivated American action movies from *Casablanca* (1982) to *Rambo* (1985). When the first Indy film *Raiders of the Lost Ark* appeared in 1981, it had the novelty of reviving the hellzapoppin' antics of old grade-Z serials for a wonderfully modernist, purely formal effect. Except for *Jaws*, it is the thinnest of Spielberg's films, more redolent of producer George Lucas' shallow pulp fantasies than Spielberg's poetic use of well-known movie tropes. *Raiders* inadvertently encapsulated the desperate American narcissism that was re-establishing itself in the Reagan era. Now Spielberg sensibly takes the time to assess what his rejuvenation of a tacky movie genre means. *The Last Crusade* comments on the imperialist tendencies of Hollywood moviemaking.

From the opening widescreen, full-color shots of Monument Valley—the Utah location made mythic in John Ford Westerns—*The Last Crusade* keeps audiences conscious of the tone and styles of movies that promote American heroism. Of all the Indy films this one is *enlightened*, Spielberg doesn't need to pace the action any faster because now everything that happens on screen is something to think about. He makes your mind race along with your heart.

This time the plot complications are witty rather than reassuringly familiar: Alison Doody as Indy's female sidekick shows a duplicity that takes on moral ambiguity. Bringing Indy's father (played by Sean Connery) along for the ride is, of course, a Freudian boost that includes an extremely adult father-like-son bit. This father figure helps make greater sense of Indy's compulsions. If Connery's casting seems inexplicably British, consider the significance of such a lineage—of the strapping young American taking over the global acquisitiveness of the British empire.

(Indy's recurring phrase "That belongs in a museum" is a joke on imperialism applicable to the Elgin Marbles as well as the pretend goodies juggled about in the film.)

Working from a story and script by Menno Meyjes and Jeffrey Boam, Spielberg rewrites the cultural fantasies heretofore identified with Ford and Rudyard Kipling. In the annals of popular culture that reveres those masters of pulp, their political defects are always ignored in favor of the "enjoyment" they provided. It is also assumed that subsequent masters of those same forms do not have to rectify the politics or the morality. Today, this insipid attitude judges Spielberg in terms of being emotionally swifter than Kipling and kinetically faster than Ford, but never admits the greater issue that racism and specious politics are organic to the beloved Kipling-Ford narrative styles.

Imperialist fantasies that are secure in their prejudices are not innocent kid's stuff but obscene. Spielberg shows that he understands that the form's subjectivity ought to, in fact, must be forsaken. Or, "let go" as Indy's father tells him when he maniacally reaches for the Holy Grail. The Grail is an emblem of sovereignty—an artifact not dissimilar to nationalistic movies that confer beauty, authority and divinity on the countries that produced them. (It's smart to equate the historical crusades with "modern" warfare.)

Part of the disease of Hollywood is that it has tricked generations of gullible viewers into thinking of its white, Western cultural biases as just. *The Last Crusade* shakes up this dubious confidence. The earth moves, cinematically speaking, but we always know where we stand. Progress, thy name is Spielberg.

*The City Sun*
May 1989

# Keeping Up with the Joneses

*"When the legend becomes fact, print the legend."*
—A HOLLYWOOD CURSE.

IVINERS OF POPULAR culture who once celebrated Steven Spielberg for his ingenious extension of the Hollywood film tradition ("A new generation's Howard Hawks") have deserted him when he needs them most. Spielberg's last three films—*The Color Purple*, *Empire of the Sun*, and *Indiana Jones and the Last Crusade*—are transitional landmarks in Hollywood's ethos. They attempt to expand the cultural awareness of commercial films, struggling with generic form while improving their political implications. This is nothing less than Hollywood glasnost, but reviewers expect aesthetic reform and cultural revision to come from Young Turk independents outside the official institution, or to be neatly differentiated by an acceptable passage of time— such as the generations that separate John Ford's sagebrush sentimentality from Sam Peckinpah's anti-Hollywood revisionism.

In *The Last Crusade* Spielberg repudiates the very genre conventions and moral infractions he himself perpetrated in the two previous films of this George Lucas-produced series. It was the thinnest material Spielberg worked on since *Jaws*. Complaints that this final, third installment lacks zest disregard the extraordinary enhancement Spielberg has effected. In place of the melodramatic Freudian suggestions that Irvin Kershner used to spike the pulpy *The Empire Strikes Back* (1980),

Spielberg makes a clean, funny, close-to-structuralist analysis of narrative practice. Insight about myth not speed, is now the series' point.

The sensational timing and stunt work in the second of the Indiana Jones trilogy, *Temple of Doom*, could not be praised as anything but a dispassionate exercise of craft; the increased speed and smoothness were at the expense of sensible, responsible cultural expression. It was an infantile jamboree. But there's no need to tolerate that misused virtuosity when films like *A Chinese Ghost Story* (1987) can, miracle by miracle, step on *Temple of Doom*'s feats, while offering an authentic picture of a foreign culture. *The Last Crusade* redresses the issues of culture and imperialism that Spielberg and Lucas previously ignored. This film doesn't need to be paced any faster, because, now, everything that happens around Indian Jones is something to think about. The mind races along with the heart.

This improvement is, doubtlessly, more instinctual than calculated, yet it's also a rare sign of folk-pop development in Hollywood. Spielberg's extraordinary mastery of formula and of narrative tropes seems, on its own, to tend toward cultural inclusion, a global egalitarianism—the opposite of "classical" Hollywood's aesthetics. Back then, the perfection of escapist forms was a systemic social reflex, an expression of the country's political ideology. Films like *Gunga Din* (1939), *Lives of a Bengal Lancer* (1935), *Drums Along the Mohawk* (1939), and *The Four Feathers* (1939) (and countless others) roused motor responses at the same time that they sanctioned belief in white superiority and Western imperialism.

After *E. T.*, the era's great popular film, Spielberg tackled two "minority" projects: *The Color Purple*, where he adapted Black American iconography to the Hollywood fantasy styles previously reserved for white fiction; and *Empire of the Sun*, where he showed absolute empathy for both the Chinese and Japanese positions in World War II. (It was, perhaps, less Sino-sympathy than Sony savvy.) These creative experiences must have sensitized Spielberg to the different, Third-World readings that a nonwhite viewer might give to Hollywood genre films—consideration that never occurred to old moguls who simply wanted to conquer world markets. The nationalist and racist biases in Hollywood cinema are appalling if viewed intelligently today. The entire history of Hollywood fantasy reveals its corruption in the persistence of white male heroism and Western domination. Yes, Spielberg should have known better when he began the Indiana Jones series but the general enthusiasm for *Temple of Doom*'s overwhelming kinetics and shoddy anthropology also proved that most critics neither knew better nor cared.

*The Last Crusade*'s full-color, wide-screen shots of Monument Valley in the opening sequence are brilliantly clever revisionism: the setting, familiar from John Ford Westerns, is the *locus classicus* of American cinema's solipsism. Spielberg sums up the process of patriotic indoctrination with a joke: the figures we see commanding this locale are horseback Boy Scout troops. The point: American action in the primeval West is, essentially, child's play. But movies that are proud of their national and racial biases are not kid's stuff, they're dangerous. *The Last Crusade* is knowingly constructed with allusions to the self-aggrandizing parochialism of the adventure film genre. There's a satirical element in seeing white male American derring-do writ so large. It becomes simultaneously tumid, neurotic, and comic. But unlike *Temple of Doom* and parts of *Raiders of the Lost Ark*, it's never insulting or oppressive.

Instead of presenting the opening sequence (with River Phoenix playing the teenage Indy) as a prologue, Spielberg compresses this antecedent information into the main story. Manipulating narrativity this way is the prerogative of a famous showman—he's tweaking the audience's awareness of storytelling by stoking the engine of his plot. The locomotive set-piece is a metaphor for narrative momentum, a visceral anecdote economically and humorously explaining the origins of Indy's mythic characteristics—his scarred chin, his fear of snakes, his dexterity with a bullwhip, and his trademark fedora. (Spielberg audaciously cast Richard Young, an actor who resembles himself and Harrison Ford, as Indy's amoral alternative role model.) This western-cum-circus-train sequence gives Indy his first quotable dialogue of the trilogy—"That belongs in a museum!" The phrase describes his motives and tenacity, but it also reverberates as a statement of Western acquisitiveness, applicable to the Elgin Marbles as to the pretend goodies—the Cross of Coronado and the Holy Grail—fought over in the film.

Linking American adventure movies to the Crusades shows a shrewd understanding of what adventure movies are designed to do culturally and politically. They're ideological war machines.

This makes good on the Joseph Campbell influence that Lucas botched in his *Star Wars* trilogy and in the little-people-as-the-Third-World-making-their-own-history in *Willow* (1988). The allusions to the big-screen history of the American West are connected to the Middle East pursuit of the Holy Grail by way of pre-Renaissance Italy. The global/historical sleight of hand is pure philological wit. We see the Grail as an artifact that, like Westerns and adventure movies, confers beauty, power and divinity upon its owner. These historical referents in the Menno Meyjes-Jeffrey Boam script expose the fascist, quasi-religious fervor that's been a part of the American adventure film from D.W. Griffith's *The Birth of a Nation* and John Ford's *The Iron Horse* (1924) to *Out of Africa* (1985) and *Mississippi Burning* (1988).

Spielberg's formal expertise makes *The Last Crusade*—a beautiful title, unlike *Temple of Doom*, which suggests an amusement park ride—into one of the most sophisticated adventure films ever made: its parts snap together with precise, dry cunning. It's the wised-up razzmatazz of an adult playing within the acceptable boundaries of world politics and subverts the globetrotter caprice that the Indy series revives. Finally, in *The Last Crusade*, the interplay between Indy's boyish spirit and (his father's) scholarly, political rectitude dramatizes the creative impulse threading its way through this era of dwindling western superiority. One response is to make a lovely but wan little myth study like Caleb Deschanel's smart revision of Daniel Defoe, *Crusoe* (1988). Spielberg's recent cinema, however, remains boldly fantastic while adjusting to global realities; his transitional films confront and rewrite historical fiction.

"Movies and TV programs like *The Jewel in the Crown* (1984) and *A Passage to India* (1984) are what I call 'Easterns'," Hanif Kureishi once told me, citing the European counterpart to the historical inaccuracies and political conceits of American Westerns. Kureishi was disgusted at the imperialist arrogance that only recognizes Third World cultures as things "that belong in a museum" for the first world's delectation. *The Last Crusade* is in agreement: as Indy maniacally reaches for the Holy Grail his archaeologist father cautions, "Let it go."

That advice, morally inspired, is also politically enlightened. And it gains significance coming from Sean Connery, who, fourteen years ago, in his best performance, as Danny Dravat in John Huston's *The Man Who Would Be King* (1975), acted out the racist-colonialist vanity of the British empire—the cultural tradition Indiana Jones inherited, via James Bond. Of course, Huston's film updated Rudyard Kipling by making it a working-class fantasy trapped inside the psychology of colonialism. Ultimately, the movie failed to break completely away from it. Spielberg distances himself by riding the genre into the sunset. He's not looking for a *Tequila Sunrise* (1988), the sour, decadent renewal of Hollywood's past.

This "letting go" upsets people who want to believe in John Wayne and the Raj and in the fast deployment of film technique without political consciousness. When the once "liberal" *Village Voice* recently printed film reviewer Georgia Brown's blithe admission of her antipathy to and impatience with films about people of color, it's clear that our film culture is mired in barely understood racism. Brown instead glossed over *The Last Crusade*'s political themes to make knee-jerk accusations of sexism—the only ethical issue most white critics seem to care about.

The most audacious moment in *The Last Crusade* deals impudently with the significance of history and myth: carrying his father's diary, Indy comes face-to-face with Adolf Hitler in the middle of a Nazi book-burning rally. Hitler—a media star and he knows it—autographs the diary rather than burning it. By inscribing the text that Indy has been using—almost religiously—as a reverent guide for survival, Hitler puts his mark on a historical record. This scene is worthy of E.L. Doctorow's *Ragtime*: Hitler's graffito intrudes on a subjective text; his existence is a type of uncomfortable truth that must

**121**

be dealt with in all our personal versions of history. The anti-Spielberg critics are all little Hitlers—cinema-burners—who don't want movies to tell the truth. Realizing how moviegoers turn legend into "fact," Spielberg will no longer simply film the legend people want to believe, because history is more complicated than movie myths allow.

Regarding the sexist charges: Unlike R*aiders'* Karen Allen or *Temple of Doom'*s Kate Capshaw, Alison Doody's Elsa is the series' first female who is not helplessly feminine. In the larger historical framework, her "villainy" is as ambiguous as Indy's "heroism." They're psychopolitical peers. The comic use of Nazis surpasses Ernst Lubitsch's *To Be or Not to Be* (1942). It's historically apt for Indy to say, "I hate those guys" matter-of-factly; the film eschews sentimentality on this subject, too, yet shows prescience (with the benefit of hindsight) in a closeup of an indestructible Nazi insignia. That shot forecasts the next probable development and final solution of the Indiana Jones saga: the War, which was only entertaining in the movies.

Born a Jew and consecrated a filmmaker who's taken on the task of entertaining the world, Spielberg has to maneuver between a personal political agenda and a respect for both Christian and non-Jewish, American and international cultures. Few men in the history of Hollywood have attempted this honestly. Spielberg closes off a racist film form with *The Last Crusade*, because today no one can conscientiously make movies the way they used to.

*Film Comment*
July 1989

# ALWAYS (1989)

## *The Spectacle of Always Recalled*

**"T**HESE THINGS ARE fragile!" Dorinda insists to Pete in Steven Spielberg's *Always*. She has raced toward the man she loves—on bike, on foot, then climbing up the perch of his airplane where he prepares for one more dangerous mission as an airborne firefighter. This rushed, impassioned confrontation addresses reality as ephemeral and summarizes why Spielberg's first romantic love story is extraordinary: The scene's precarious emotionalism—Holly Hunter's Dorinda urging Richard Dreyfuss' Pete toward spiritual awareness—defines one quick, fleeting but important instant during their mortal portion of eternity. (Pace Andrew Sarris on Eric Rohmer's *My Night at Maud's* (1969): "There is no greater spectacle in the cinema than a man and a woman talking away their share of eternity together.")

This is the most daring stage of Spielberg's movie brat exploration of various Hollywood genres. His adaptation of the 1943 *A Guy Named Joe*, a metaphysical World War II romance directed by Victor Fleming and starring Spencer Tracy and Irene Dunne as lovers whose dedication and sacrifice embolden the national war effort, shows Spielberg's conscious engagement with his Hollywood heritage. The modern peace-time setting among fire-fighters in the American Northwest using favored technology (an A-26 plane, PBY, flying water boats) surpasses Fleming's routine narrative with glancing references to the more personal expression of Howard Hawks' fly-boy classic *Only Angels Have Wings* (1939), which portrayed professionals' camaraderie in existential terms.

Better than Fleming's boiler-plate drama, Hawks' film combines screwball comedy with a meditation on mortality, and Pete and Dorinda's love combines both with updated awareness—the love story is triangulated through her post-mourning romance with the young airman Ted Baker (Brad Johnson), a stunt flier who comes into the story on "A Wing and a Prayer," the name of his telegram delivery company. He's another damn Hawksian professional hotshot, like Cary Grant and Richard Barthelmess, testing death and risk. Johnson's fabulously attractive Baker represents what Dorinda sums up as someone who "looks like I won him in a raffle." Yet Spielberg has described the essence of this triangle as a romance that spans two worlds: "one present and one over-present."

This is bolder than what even the sexually sophisticated Hawks would dare. The sexual-spiritual test of human experience that Hawks borrowed from Joseph von Sternberg (via Sternberg's screenwriter Jules Furthman) is put to work in this update.

Spielberg uses the aviation-duty premise to address the profound sense of death—of love transcending mortality—that substantiates his career-long preoccupation with WWII patriotic, spiritual experience (as seen in "The Mission," an episode of TV's *Amazing Stories*, the Indiana Jones series, *Empire of the Sun*, *Saving Private Ryan*). Transposing wartime stress into daily first-responder endeavor, Spielberg and screenwriter Jerry Belson (TV veteran from *The Dick Van Dyke Show*, *The Odd Couple* plus Michael Ritchie's *Smile* (1975)—and uncredited on *Close Encounters*) combine elements from Rodgers and Hammerstein's *Carousel* and Frank Borzage's *Liliom* (1930) to create a multi-dimensional moral farce.

*Always* is purely elemental cinema as signified, visually and kinetically, by Spielberg's concentration of Earth, Wind and Fire (Purgatory, Heaven and Hell) motifs. Cinematographer Mikael Salomon gives Spielberg an unparalleled presentation of nature and spirit by photographic emphasis on the film's terrestrial/celestial/inferno atmospherics. These optics make for an amazing existential study—pushing Michelangelo Antonioni's *Red Desert* (1964) to further, naturalistic degrees. Salomon's cinematography captures the "magic hour" of light intermixing with shadow, what Wes Anderson would call "crepuscular" or "friscalating" light. *Always* has the fresh air look of every day a new day. Salomon's shifts between light and reflection, dawn and dusk, capturing America's Northern and Midwestern states Montana and Washington, are also existential gestures.

Vision—and visual expression—is everything. The fantasy/realism balance is sustained throughout the narrative's shift from service comedy into musical comedy. Dorinda putting on the white dress Pete gives her for her birthday, explains the heightened concept: She doesn't mind that he got the date wrong because of what the dress signifies: "It's how you see me!" We then see a working-man's version of an Astaire-Rogers routine—dark, ashy grime cleaned up to ardent entreaty and paced to "Smoke Gets in Your Eyes." That 1933 Jerome Kern-Otto Harbach tear-jerking classic (Spielberg uses The Platters' resonant, immortal, 1958 boomer-era rendition) is the most perfectly existential of all songs about eternal romance.

**125**

After opening with a parody of *Jaws'* water-bound danger (just like *1941*), Spielberg revels in storytelling freedom. He conveys varieties of tragedy and despair as when Pete's return to Earth with telepathic ability carelessly plants a depressing idea into an airplane worker's mind. It is the start of Pete's moral lesson. He is instructed by an otherworldly angel, Hap (Audrey Hepburn in her last screen appearance), to rectify his mortal behavior. Cavalier Pete gets a second chance at redemption. The process of Pete exchanging his role in Dorinda's life reveals *Always* to be a key expression of Spielberg's own imaginative processes.

The impact of *A Guy Named Joe* lasted throughout his creative life as evident in the thematic motifs borrowed from his father's Second World War reminiscence and the son's projection of wartime action and agony and the specter of death (also popularized by *Here Comes Mr. Jordan* (1941)). Pauline Kael pinpointed this theme as anxiety about "the finality of death" in her review of *Always*. But Spielberg, detached from the immediacy of war anxiety, romanticizes those themes. Instead of simply repeating Fleming's morale-boosting perspective and screenwriter Dalton Trumbo's forced gaiety and metaphysical sophistication, Spielberg reworks *A Guy Named Joe* through his movie brat's imagination.

*Always* is most captivating when Spielberg is being characteristically expressive: Pete's co-piloting instruction to Dorinda speeds her through a *Magic Flute*-like hell of forest fire that prefigures the ancestors' faith like Cinque in *Amistad* pronounced. And the co-pilot sequence cut from fire-red to river-blue is a major emotional transition—like the cut to Sally Field's emotional shift in *Lincoln*. Next, the camera's upward tilt into the starry night sky offers images of the cosmos and eternity that both recall and anticipate some of the most metaphysical visions from *Close Encounters* to *A.I.*

Then, the sapphire-blue baptismal section, when Dorinda's plane submerges underwater, originates the recurrent resurrection idea when David is seated in the downed helicopter in *A.I.* These moments are prayerful and confessional as in Pete saying, "I can tell you now what I could never say: I love you, Dorinda."

*Always* distills the anxious, mournful romanticism of *A Guy Named Joe* when Hepburn's Hap, Pete's heaven-sent guide, advises: "The love we hold back is the only pain we carry with us." This is the boomer/movie brat's version of metaphysical ardor—faith as idealized for his generation in *Carousel* and *Liliom*. Pete's cry, "Hap, get me out of here!" is like the metaphysical distress in Thornton Wilder's plea, "I can't look at it hard enough" from *Our Town* and his confrontation with mortality in *The Bridge at San Luis Rey*. These cultural evocations mark *Always* as Spielberg's ultimate mixed-genre film.

In the sequence of a school bus driver's death after struggling to save the lives of his young passengers, his resurrection and conversation with Pete takes place on a road that has the existential clarity of a vast landscape (evoking *Sugarland*). Here's where cinematographer Salomon pins cosmic consciousness in reality. The expanses of Montana and Washington oppose Fleming's soundstage locations. These existential gestures capture the twilights of dawn and sunset in the distance that catches Dorinda's eye and keys her into fate and eternity and impels her desperate run toward Pete.

Through this fantasy, *Always* works out the lessons of Spielberg's movie-youth and his artistic adulthood. Pete learns to transfer his love for Dorinda as a rite of passage. It is the wisdom of Hepburn's Hap: "Anything you did for yourself is a waste of spirit. To gain your freedom you have to give it. So go find out."

A Wing and a Prayer also describes Spielberg's venture.

# HOOK (1991)

## *Hook Gives Serious Happiness Its Due*

***H***OOK IS AN art movie for the masses but not the first such achievement for Steven Spielberg. Since the 1982 release of *E.T. the Extra-Terrestrial*, the most popular film of the modern era, Spielberg has operated on a level of mass communication, pop fantasy and cultural awareness unknown to any other filmmaker since (perhaps) D.W. Griffith. Spielberg wins movie audiences while fundamentally revising the art form itself. His expressive terms—in such movies as *The Color Purple, Empire of the Sun* and *Always*—are popular (so popular that he is vastly misunderstood as a mere manipulator) but his methods are serious.

That explains the basis of *Hook*'s modernist investigation of Sir James Barrie's literary theater fantasy *Peter Pan*. This is not a remake, as many reviewers stupidly allege, but a sophisticated reconsideration of the ideas expressed in *Peter Pan*. Spielberg takes those ideas—faith, imagination, maturity, mortality—and makes them cohere with the constant themes and practices favored in his film career. *Hook* is a $70 million personal movie from the most accomplished auteur Hollywood has produced.

Spielberg's seriousness involves going radically beyond expectation. Instead of simply re-doing a familiar legend such as Barrie's stage play, he has earned the right to actually call on the public's knowledge of myth, then expand on their sense of fantasy. Spielberg doesn't just famously touch the heart; he reveals, in *Hook*, the philological process by which fantasy transfers from one medium to figure in real life. This parallels the experience adults learn when transferring the myths of their childhood to the next generation. (Spielberg only recently became a parent.) *Hook*, therefore, is not about Peter Pan, the boy who never grows up, but how the ideas of *Peter Pan*—the character, the original story and play and concept—can be seen in the modern lives of adults who think they outgrew the legend but whose children are a new reflection of it.

By aging Peter Pan himself into the businessman Peter Banning (played by Robin Williams), along with an elderly Wendy (Maggie Smith), and an up-to-the-minute cutie-pie incarnation of Pan's fairy sprite companion Tinker Bell (Julia Roberts), Spielberg uses the *Peter Pan* characters reflexively— to remind viewers that they are watching a fiction, sharing cultural recall. This expansion is not a sequel even though it links up with the genre revision and improvement that have marked the most outstanding sequels of the recent past—*The Godfather Part II* and *III* (1990), *RoboCop 2* (1990), *Gremlins 2: The New Batch* (1990), *The Empire Strikes Back, Another 48 Hrs.* (1990), and, of course, the Indiana Jones series.

As much as Griffith was concerned with creating a fictional form that encompassed the personal politics of his time, Spielberg's equally self-conscious concern in *Hook* advances public response from simple awe at Barrie's original concoction. Barrie made popular use of art devices (such as audience participation in restoring Tinker Bell, also used in the American musical theater adaptation) that subsequently became associated with high-art theatrical concepts. Spielberg additionally uses the mass audience's awareness of Victorian era art to set up a confrontation with modern real-life experience.

A husband and father distracted by work, Peter's maturity-parenthood is shown as a psychological condition. As Peter lapses into his past, his memory becomes the medium for a second intellectual movement: Spielberg's exploration of myth and the postmodern audience's engagement with fantasy.

Of course, this Spielberg film, like all his others, is immediately impressive for its visual wonder and emotional richness (Wendy's tribute scene is a moment of grace) but the use of a few $10 words here is to make plain the serious personal thinking within that lovely, heartrending moment made possible by Spielberg's audacious craftsmanship which many people (most film reviewers) take for granted.

It is important to establish the ideational credibility of this most gifted, seemingly intuitive filmmaker, against the critical mode that—post *E. T.*—recognizes "seriousness" only as the province of "adult" stories and humorless, literal-minded filmmaking. If critics regarded *Hook* with the same (literary) biases they bring to the inert *Prospero's Books* (1991) or *Naked Lunch* (1991), they'd be closer to understanding Spielberg's sophistication.

Spielberg reignites the old battle against genre and pop art that the French New Wave seemed to have won more than 20 years ago. The triumph Godard and Truffaut effected by transforming disreputable American genre films into intellectual comedies is the unrecognized basis for Spielberg's enlightened approach to fantasy and old-movie mythology. Never before has this kind of savvy and sheer movie-making ability been brought to bear on mainstream material.

Box office figures ($91 million gross to date) suggest that the public is ready for it—ready to continue the aesthetic advance that Spielberg commenced with *E.T.*—even if critics are not. With each film that followed *E.T.*, Spielberg has received a critical debunking even though his technical proficiency and the commitment to the emotions and ideas he was filming only has increased.

The snide attitude (as opposed to aesthetic principle) that reviewers hold against Spielberg seems to derive from the incredible success of *E.T.* He's getting paid back, resentfully, for being so young, talented and successful—mainly for bringing consciousness to pop in an unthoughtful era—and this is more emblematic of '80s-'90s politics than Spielberg's own idiosyncratic politically liberal films. While opening Hollywood mythology to include African-Americans (*The Color Purple*), proposing an internationalist view of humanism (*Empire of the Sun*), considering the meta-movie-physics of modern spirituality (the pre-*Ghost* (1990) *Always*) and kissing a short goodbye to Western imperialism (*Indiana Jones and the Last Crusade*), Spielberg has laid out the terms for a politically conscious, aesthetically advanced, multicultural pop cinema. Throughout the '80s his career has been quietly revolutionary, changing Hollywood myth from the inside whereas all reviewers see is the surface.

Typical critical myopia about *Hook* is the oft-repeated line that the Neverland set—where Peter encounters his past and his eternal nemesis Captain Hook, a spiritual alter-ego (given emotional/thematic weight as played by Dustin Hoffman)—looks like a theme park (even though critics prostrate themselves over the latest Disney product-and-soon-to-be-theme-park, *Beauty and the Beast* (1991)). The Neverland location is *Hook*'s central setting but it's also the film's different (past) tense. The real-world splendors of the opening sequence, in which Peter, his wife and children visit the aged Wendy in London, recede as Spielberg intentionally moves the film into a more fantasy-like realm.

Carping reviewers failed to notice the choice of John Napier—original designer of the stage production of *Cats*—as visual consultant; Napier, who also collaborated on Francis Coppola-Michael Jackson's Disney World feature *Captain EO* (1986), lends *Hook* theatrical environmentalism. Spielberg intends viewers to respond to Neverland with consciousness of its artifice and of entering fable. He, of all contemporary filmmakers, knows the difference between a cinematic representation of fantasy and less mimetic classical imaginative forms—the very forms seen in previous *Peter Pans* on Broadway and TV productions. Cinematographer Dean Cundey lights Neverland to evoke the kinds of theatrical pastiche that characterized the first era of family movie musicals (from *Lili* (1953) to *Tom Thumb* (1958) and *Mary Poppins* (1964), *Oliver!* (1968), *Chitty Chitty Bang Bang* (1968)). *Hook*'s look isn't stale, it's complex.

As the inheritor of Hollywood's narrative traditions, Spielberg presents this complexity as abundance. The richness of *Hook* includes the juxtaposition of the adult Peter's reality with the stylized fantasy-memory. Similarly—and most importantly—Hoffman's Captain Hook can be seen as a psychological projection; he's the doppelganger Barrie submerged in a Victorian-era split between good and evil that Spielberg now clarifies as the opposing impulses of one's nature: the id vs. rationality; the kid vs. the adult. No previous version of *Peter Pan* that I can think of had this kind of intellectual clarity, mostly because those versions sought to keep the story childish. Spielberg has a mature artist's interest in how individual will challenges destiny, so he takes Barrie's characters and, in mixing them, distills their crises. Captain Hook's antagonism with Peter is a struggle between Age and Youth; each man is desperate as he faces down his own mortality.

Spielberg keeps this existential dilemma afloat within the subject of rediscovered juvenescence. Peter's reacquaintance with the forgotten child inside himself prepares him to accept his position in the life cycle while Captain Hook illustrates more common, adult cynicism. The difference is apparent in the very acting style of the precisely mannered Hoffman and Williams' anarchic exuberance. Peter Pan is the perfect role for Williams' frenetic, improvisatory performing and this is his purest acting, especially in the scene where one of the Lost Boys (Peter Pan's band of juvenile comrade-delinquents who he departed without truly leaving behind) molds his facial features into a restored—recognizable—smile. Williams registers spontaneous happiness and that enthusiasm characterizes the Spielberg gestalt.

An emotion as profound as serious happiness embarrasses most adults. Knowing this, Spielberg has made *Hook* as a reconstructed fantasy that bypasses adulthood's protective, psychological layers to give serious happiness its due. People who expect to see old myth stay intact may be troubled by this project, but Spielberg updates myth smartly in the scene of the Lost Boys as wizened old men cherishing the memory of childhood and Lost Boys whose indulgences—skateboards, baseball, ninja fighting—keep childhood in modern flux. It is not insignificant that Spielberg enlarges the mythology to include non-white children. (Peter passes his sovereignty over Neverland on to a Black boy.) This kind of change is essential to making pop fantasy modern and providing a deeper understanding of myth.

*The City Sun*
February 1992

# JURASSIC PARK (1993)

---

## *In Jurassic Park, Spielberg Satirizes Capitalism*

I N T H E C A S E of Steven Spielberg, most critics and filmgoers feel they are superior to the man and the kinds of movies he makes. Despite *Jurassic Park* grossing almost $200 million in less than a month, its dismissal-as-junk- and praise-as-junk are examples of the dissolution of popular culture as a unifying social force. *Jurassic Park* is the first movie since *E.T.* to demonstrate across-the-board appeal, and yet people suspect this as corrupt and/or dumb. Moviegoing is now so cynical and ignorant that audiences who enjoy *Jurassic Park* can't see anything in it beyond the dinosaur special effects.

After the past demi-decade of violent, thrill-ride spectacles by Arnold, Bruce and Sly, few people are willing to recognize that *Jurassic Park* is first and foremost a witty, critical commentary on this loathsome development in pop. However, it is a criticism made by an artist in love with pop, so the film's statement is ambivalent, not contradictory and, scene by scene, remarkable.

The most misunderstood scene in *Jurassic Park* is Spielberg's cutaway during a sequence of theme park havoc after the dinosaurs break out of their fencing and go after the children stranded in the jungle grounds. To amplify the irony of the dinosaur attack and the park patrons' endangerment, Spielberg shows the theme park's souvenir stand. It's dark, deserted, a commentary on how *Jurassic Park* tie-in products stand insensible to the chaos that's going on in the world. "People are dying!" two of the film's characters cry, announcing the significance of human life that this era's moviegoers are encouraged to ignore.

The irony of the souvenir-stand scene points out the enormity of the capitalist dilemma in modern pop culture. *Jurassic Park* is certainly an exciting movie with dinosaurs, but its special art qualities can be seen in Spielberg's use of the story (from Michael Crichton's popular novel) to address the problem of creating art in a greed-intensive culture. Using the Jurassic Park theme park as the site of the story's ecological-evolutionary crisis is more original than the old-fashioned sci-fi Man-must-not-play-God theme. In fact, that whole tired way of thinking about sci-fi is satirized by Jeff Goldblum as a chaos-expert who explains the park's screwy logic: "God makes man, man makes dinosaur, man kills God, dinosaur kills man." The warning is a sophisticated joke on sophistication.

This has been Spielberg's natural mode. His knowledge of film craft and pop lore puts him ahead of most moviemakers—and viewers—when it comes to reviving plots and genres. There is a discouraging tendency in today's culture to try to make movies "innocent" or as "innocuous" as they were once thought to be. But Spielberg keeps pushing the medium past people's expectations. This means, as with *Hook*, furthering the thematic interest of certain genres and taking into account (perhaps unreasonably) a general, pre-existent cultural knowledge of the form. (One of the most amazing special effects in the movie is the Jurassic Park promotional film, where a genetics and evolution history lesson is cleverly "made easy" through an animated lecture on DNA and cloning. It's the start of the film's extremely ironic wit. Spielberg is giving audiences a "trite" version of the science that this genre normally disrespects while simultaneously making the most intelligent, scientific-fictional extrapolations yet on film.)

Simply put, Spielberg isn't just making another dinosaur movie—why should he? We've seen dozens of examples and people are bored with the narrative variations. But in *Jurassic Park*, Spielberg is able to use that familiarity as he did in *Hook* to address issues beyond the Nature-mustn't-be-tampered-with clichés. *Jurassic Park* is really about the very contemporary habit of accepting commercial, institutionalized entertainment (in the form of theme parks and films that function similarly) that essentially violates once universal standards of humane concern. Spielberg investigates a dilemma that very much concerns him as a modernist artist: How does one express the creative impulse in a capitalist environment that values exploitation over humanity?

Critics of *Jurassic Park* accuse Spielberg of hypocrisy—of making the same dumb entertainment he seems to be satirizing—without noticing how different *Jurassic Park* is from other dino-genre films. The modernist examination of compromised integrity extends to the remorse displayed by John Hammond (Richard Attenborough, the conceptualizer of Jurassic Park, the Walt Disney-Steven Spielberg stand-in, who learns the meaning of heartless exploitation when his own grandchildren are threatened by the dinosaurs). The theme is played out in the film through wonderful (perhaps too subtle for some) details such as the exploitation of the earth by archeologists. It's the tampering-with-nature idea but played out differently. Nature—in the form of dinosaurs—doesn't take its revenge on man, nature is an amoral force, but it is stronger than the capitalist impulse that seeks to manipulate it, and that is the point most compelling to a filmmaker interested in producing conscientious, moral art in this era.

*Jurassic Park* can reasonably, and pleasurably, be viewed as a movie about the human responses to nature and ingenuity and the conflict between the two. Spielberg, advancing from Crichton, who sketched out similar themes in the insipid 1973 film *Westworld*, narrates a satirical fantasy about technology overwhelming human instinct. This is a development of the middle-class-delusion-of-being-in-control theme Spielberg explored in *Jaws, Close Encounters* and *E. T.*, movies that people dismissed as banal indulgence of suburban assumptions. But Spielberg's most domestic art offers an understanding about Americans' fascination with technology, the spiritual ambition that gets expressed through machinery and, ironically, through the system of industry and capitalism that winds up exploiting it. To express these things in Hollywood entertainment product is not hypocritical or contradictory, just insightful and, often—when personally imagined—poetic.

In *Jurassic Park*, the expression can be uniquely moving. The dinosaurs themselves are a monumental conjuring of nature through technology that Spielberg's special-effects team represents with the perfect amount of elegance and grandeur and terror. The dinosaurs are not cuddly or vicious; they appear simply beyond control, like a dream—or nightmare—made real.

Consistent with this, Spielberg's staging of the action sequences reminds the world of the miraculous ability of cinema form to bring intelligent expression to kinetics. In the first dinosaur attack, Spielberg passionately upgrades the kind of action and movement that often is used for no meaning whatsoever, just thrills. These dinosaurs have an animalistic beauty, integrity and individuality, not Disneyesque cuteness. They are awesome figures of nature.

One of the most extraordinary scenes in *Jurassic Park* is the car-chase sequence. It's not what you think. Spielberg stages this car chase in a tree. Two generations of humanity, an adult and a child, attempt to come down out of the trees like their prehistoric ancestors, but they're pursued—not by the bear that began Chaplin's *The Gold Rush* (1925)—but by an automobile tossed into the trees by a Tyrannosaurus rex. The image is magnificent: A car, symbolizing modern technology, crashes down upon the evolution-minded man (Sam Neill) and science-minded boy. This makes the chase stunningly suspenseful and ideologically funny.

So is the great image of a T-Rex replacing a museum skeleton of a T-rex (a joking homage to the absent-minded scientist of *Bringing Up Baby* (1938)) that Spielberg ends with the final flourish of a banner floating to the ground as the T-rex roars out its terrifying awakening. The banner reads, WHEN DINOSAURS RULED THE EARTH, and its descent, before the staggering sight of nature revived, is a compounded movie reference that, as it falls, puts pop trivia and the political economy of Hollywood and all amusement industries in their place.

*The City Sun*
May 1993

# SCHINDLER'S LIST (1993)

## *Toward a Theory of Spielberg History*

### ONE

**"W**ITNESSING," A TERM repeated in the most doctrinaire reviews of *Schindler's List*, actually happens only once in the movie. Steven Spielberg "witnesses" the tribute he has arranged in which survivors of the WWII Holocaust file past the gravesite of Oskar Schindler. It is a perfectly situated affirmation of the gratitude and humanity that a group of people express toward a man who saved their lives. The profound optimism—the goodness—of human experience has always been the subject of Spielberg's greatest art: *Close Encounters of the Third Kind*, *The Color Purple*, *E.T.*—each an ebullient fantasy. But there's no awareness of this sensibility in the widespread hurrahs for his latest drama.

Typically far from the mark is David Denby's praise of Spielberg's "anger"—imputing a petty vengefulness to the motives of the most benevolent filmmaker of all time. The tendency to turn Spielberg into Moshe Dayan (a Scheherazade into a sabra) suggests other frightening reasons for the movie's praise. With *Schindler's List* critics have reduced Spielberg's art to a hegemonic tool for promoting mainstream historical interest—an implicit policy as pervasive as the refusal of white

**143**

critics to see the meaning in a Black story like *The Color Purple*. That film is Spielberg's most audacious feat of "witnessing"—a poetic act of revelation rather than partisan reportage. But the critical line on *Schindler's List* misrepresents Spielberg's artistry.

As a piece of witnessing, *Schindler's List* is almost as disingenuous as the Oscar-baiting statements Spielberg has made about growing up, expressing his Jewishness, etc. He gives in to contemporary social and historical mawkishness by pretending a special significance here. It's the typical middlebrow equation of solemnity with seriousness. Spielberg's skills see him through, but *Schindler's List* is weakest as history, strongest at evoking the emotionality of the events depicted. Of all the techniques he employs—fast cutting, chromatic shifts, emotive lighting—the most specious is the pretense toward documentary realism. It's a desperate, unoriginal tactic for a fabulist-stylist who became a legendary filmmaker by always surprising the audience, freighting a dinosaur theme park with ethical comment, putting irony into a kid's fascination with Mustang fighter planes.

Similarly, *Schindler's List* is a dream of the Holocaust. But its newsreel trope is too literal-minded; in the age of *Hard Copy*, audiences' need for an authenticating format can devolve into an ahistorical thirst for atrocity as spectacle. To look past the poetry in Spielberg's Holocaust is to see less in it. When Spielberg and cinematographer Janusz Kamiński chose to shoot in black and white, they conformed to a somewhat fallacious theory that this particular historical event could not be adequately rendered in color. Spielberg's claim, "I have no color reference for that period," forgets William A. Fraker's zesty re-creations in *1941* (1979) and Allen Daviau's luminous *Empire of the Sun* (1987) images in favor of newsreel "reality." Kaminsky's b&w, a superlatively achieved combination of documentary style, natural light, and dramatic stylization, actually serves a banal, reverential function. (Only the shifts to color for scenes of religious ritual, shots of the little girl in the red coat, and the final scene in Israel attest to Spielberg's postmodern interest in activating viewers' consciousness, and to his still-estimable creativity.)

If the film falters, if the director is anywhere untrue to his gifts, it's in the pretense to b&w realism. This confuses his private, inventive use of mythology with an absolute historical reality. Recreating the shock of genocide and discrimination, Spielberg adds nothing to the understanding about how pogroms happened within European political history. This may seem sufficient to those who simply want the fact of the Holocaust confirmed, but it is, *imaginatively*, a small accomplishment.

## TWO

Never forget that Steven Spielberg proved himself a serious artist long before he took 35mm b&w cameras to Poland for *Schindler's List*. *Indiana Jones and the Last Crusade* addressed history intelligently, elegantly: revisionism and fun in one. Crossing the glove with newfound respect for previously dominated cultures (Indy's Western belief in museum curatorship is opposed with his father's Faith), Spielberg opened up his viewfinder to wonder. He gave serious attention to the WWII era and the fascist thrall of Nazism in personal, original ways. Although critics have been reluctant to admit that the farcical tone of the Indiana Jones trilogy and *1941* were worthy of their admiration, those movies went to the heart of the pop imagination.

Spielberg accomplished a postwar, postmodern miracle in those films—criticizing the political gestalt of the virtuous, victorious, prosperous West with the pop ethos of Hollywood fantasy, the tradition of which he is the truest heir. *Schindler's List* may fulfill an obligation Spielberg felt as a Jewish-American—and tributes from industry Jews such as Billy Wilder suggest he has kept a faith with the Jewish founders of the industry. But that's a false, biased assumption. *1941's* devotion to the pre-WWII sense of pop culture as wild, racist, naive—unmandated except by the principles of capitalism and pleasure (i.e., Americanism; i.e., Hollywood)—shows Spielberg shrewdly deflating cultural sovereignty at every turn; indeed, he opens the film with an impious spoof of *Jaws*.

*1941* astutely turned homey, U.S. imperialism (and the world's subordination to it) into a satirical jamboree—a first, important step toward changing popular attitudes about Hollywood prerogative. Spielberg made the change memorable in *The Last Crusade's* inspired incident wherein Adolf Hitler autographs Indy's father's personal diary. It unexpectedly summed up the psychic, historical weight that the fascist legacy exerted on the pop imagination. (An indestructible Nazi insignia is a significant "Never Again" motif through the trilogy.) Such clever business didn't necessarily identify Spielberg as Jewish, or as a history scholar, but it evidenced the wit, the political preoccupation, and the sensibility of an auteur.

# THREE

Spielberg is the rare Hollywood plenipotentiary not to settle for the status quo practices of the industry—until now. That means *Schindler's List*, rather than being his greatest work, is actually, in some poignant, infuriating way, his most compromised.

Surely an artist who works unfettered—and magnificently—in the Hollywood system, who can portray an industrialist's saintliness (and dedicate that sacrifice to the late Warner Bros. president Steve Ross), is aesthetically at home in genres that define the emotional life in hugely popular, sentimental terms.

In fact, the terms by which *The Last Crusade* can be recognized as a great work of humane and artistic contemplation were explicated 30 years ago by Andrew Sarris' manifesto "Toward a Theory of Film History" in *The American Cinema*. Sarris' important distinction between expressive art and sociological entertainment is the kind of critical clarity that advocates of *Schindler's List* have almost completely muddled. Reviews of that film, whether pro or con, aggravate the current disaster of debased popular taste. As Sarris prophetically suggested, *Schindler's List* is being foisted upon us tendentiously. It's this decade's *Gandhi*.

It isn't only Spielberg's integrity that these *Schindler's List* reviews demean through he's-finally-grown-up cliché or he's-still-trivial myopia. *Schindler's List* itself has been misread, misunderstood, "appreciated" (which is to say, trivialized) for the wrong qualities. It's as if obviousness were an artistic advance. *The Nation* provided the best twist: "Spielberg has in fact converted his incapacity into the virtue of restraint." Can the man who directed the most splendid, heartfelt Hollywood entertainments of the past 20 years accept that praise, that dismissal of his life's work, as reasonable? Do critics who think Spielberg incapable of passion and intelligence genuinely credit *Schindler's List*'s historicity?

Answers may lie in that widely disapproved climax when Nazi businessman Oskar Schindler (Liam Neeson) has delivered 1,100 Jewish political prisoners to safety after protecting them under the ambivalent wing of capitalist patriarchy. He confounds the Nazi regime's extermination plan by insisting that his workers are essential to its wartime productivity. The ploy is expounded throughout the film in a number of deceptions and a series of last-minute rescues culminating, once the Allies reach Poland, with Schindler releasing his workers. In response, the grateful Jews with mostly middle-class skills who have toiled as laminators, machinists and foundry workers, forge a ring for Schindler out of their gold teeth-fillings and he accepts it with a tearful speech. Though the contrite language is plain, it's a Shakespearean cry of humility. It's also the most purely Spielbergian moment in the film.

Not to dismiss several memorable scenes that imaginatively convey surprise, shock, pathos, but Schindler's expression of gratitude transcends the familiar catalog of misery. It's a concretely plausible show of decency. Until then, Neeson's performance is rather opaque. Schindler's transformation is only revealed in this speech: materialist Schindler, a vain, devious man, holds to a bourgeois sense of reason, but his apology and self-accusation redeem it. Critics who reject this scene as overly sentimental fail to understand how it works *morally*—like the climaxes of all Spielberg's films. It is a spiritual moment. Spielberg avoids the insulting concept of a great man's *noblesse oblige*; Schindler's humbling becomes a sign of grace bestowed upon his beneficiaries and the audience of moviegoers who observe its reenactment.

For two decades now, Spielberg has explored the emotional, thus spiritual, essence of movie spectacle. Audiences have often been right there with him, recognizing and appreciating moments of grace. The box-office success of *The Color Purple* proved the public's readiness for advanced

Hollywood fiction—and Spielberg's radical deployment of generic tropes. Critics' aesthetic awareness should have been excited by this sign of the director fulfilling a fragmented public's hunger for unifying emotional revelation; making a successful Hollywood movie about a Black lesbian confirmed Spielberg's auteurist consistency as a crowd-pleaser par excellence.

Think back: A grown man's trepidation intercut with the slapstick tragedy of a drive-in Road Runner cartoon—*The Sugarland Express*; a panicked mother distilling her frustration through artful renditions of mountains—*Close Encounters*; a Japanese sailor weeping at the (mistaken) thought he has demolished Hollywood—*1941*; elderly sisters regaining paradise and innocence by playing patty-cake—*The Color Purple*; a lonesome boy's sensory remembrance of his father's aftershave lotion—*E.T.*; a woman's bicycle race to proclaim the fragility of her love without waiting for the (unseen) response in kind—*Always*; and a group of adult orphans finding themselves in the moment they pay tribute to a woman who cared for them—*Hook*. These scenes are among the many trenchant episodes in Spielberg's cinema that critics have rejected as fanciful. Lacking sensitive, imaginative eyes, they can't recognize Spielberg's poetic distillation of human experience, his respect for emotion as the evidence of spirituality. The plots that get dismissed as utopian optimism are sincere expressions of a generous sensibility that constantly redefines human experience in pop terms.

The Holocaust-movie concept of *Schindler's List* gets in the way of Spielberg's visionary expression; it keeps some from seeing Schindler's speech as remarkable. Despite epiphanic scenes directed with Spielberg's impeccable narrative rhythm (a boy's quick life-saving game with luggage left in a street), his experiential mystery (the unkillable factory worker), and multilayered visual splendor (the snowy-ashy nighttime arrival at Auschwitz), they fit into a construct that is, frankly, less compelling than Spielberg's usual working through fiction to claim the essence of a moment or expand its meaning.

# FOUR

No scene in *Schindler's List* is as great as the letters sequence of *The Color Purple*, which explored narrativity in popular dramatic, rather than academic terms. Working in montage, Spielberg combined the story's Southern U.S. setting with images of Africa that illustrate a series of letters sent to Celie (Whoopi Goldberg) by the sister, Nettie (Akosua Busia), from whom she has long been separated. One startling cut from Celie, in Georgia, looking behind her, to a shot of an elephant coming through the trees in Africa, conveys her engrossed, transported interest. The parallel construction is similar to the letters sequence of John Ford's *The Searchers* (1956) in the way the story moves forward in two directions at once, but it's more culturally and politically enlightened. *The Color Purple* serves a timely social function by metaphorically connecting Celie, an uprooted descendant of slaves, with a newly revealed heritage—a fresh and by no means common Hollywood endeavor. The letters sequence, a genuine act of deconstruction, was itself an auteur's demonstration of rare heroism. It showed how the dissemination of history— witnessing—involves practices of imaginative rendering as well as historical recall: a leap of faith as extraordinary as Oskar Schindler's.

This great sequence provides the movie with a modern, multicultural purpose; the action in the African scenes implies the historic intrusion of Western industry and Christianity. Crosscutting between African musicians and an American chain gang of Black prisoners chanting a work song sums up one of the American holocausts. Spielberg's transitions epitomize the social displacement and cultural continuity of diaspora. It may not be his personal story or that of white and Jewish film critics, but it is emotionally and historically comprehensive.

Advancing from the political conservatism of *The Searchers*, Spielberg explores the communication of ideas and history that is central to the modern awareness of ethnic representation and the uses of pop culture. His methods are so ecstatically vivid that critics mistook this for condescension. It was anything but. In *The Color Purple* Spielberg attempted a first—applying Hollywood's entire fictional apparatus to create a romance about African-Americans, all the while adhering to the pop-feminist politics that marked Alice Walker's novel as a modern work. *The Color Purple* is the most successful example of the Eighties' interest in cultural signs and signifiers of African-American and Hollywood history that there is in mainstream American cinema, and is the quintessential example of Spielberg's sophistication. He expanded on it in *The Last Crusade*'s self-reflexive, accordionlike compression of the Indiana Jones series' play with history, anthropology and colonialist lore (not for nothing do the recurrent religious rituals in *Schindler's List* involve play with light).

A degree of this postmodernism may inform *Schindler's List*, including the impulse to change American movies' anti-German conventions. But it has been further submerged

**151**

by hegemonic criticism that turns the director's vision of the Holocaust back into a more conventional, vague view of history. This is why the pseudo-documentary style—so less inspired than the pop didactics of *The Color Purple*— is suspicious. The b&w austerity claims an objective truth, whereas the Technicolor, symphonic *The Color Purple*—daring to present Black Southern life as something other than Walker Evans docutragedy—challenged audience preconceptions. At the top of his game Spielberg counteracts conventional social mythology through a revivifying of genre; the docudrama pretext of *Schindler's List* loses that narrative anchor.

Acclaim for *Schindler's List* presumes that only now does Spielberg show an interest in history; it still denies his interest in revisionism. In truth, reviewers are congratulating Spielberg for making a historical movie that, unlike *The Color Purple* and *The Last Crusade*, does not disturb their view of the past or upset their perspective on pop culture. The film's few detractors resent (as they resented *The Color Purple*) his powerful spiritual-political suasion.

## FIVE

For those who know Spielberg's work, *Schindler's List* seems less expressive than *Close Encounters, E.T., The Color Purple, The Last Crusade, 1941*, and *Empire of the Sun* because its story is circumscribed, not by the factual requirements of history or Thomas Keneally's book but by the culture industry that has accumulated around the subject of this century's European Holocaust. The surreal, visionary *Empire of the Sun* and the hellzapoppin' *1941* seemed more personal reimaginings of the Second World War partly because their child's-eye-view is Spielberg's unique, legitimate purchase on human experience.

Unfortunately, much of *Schindler's List* fits prescribed Holocaust lore, the kind of thinking Pauline Kael once ridiculed in the phrase "Nazi junkies." A pornography of suffering—and revenge—that sneaks into movies on this subject can be read between the lines of the film's rapturous notices. (Spielberg told the New York Film Critics Circle their reviews "were not like reviews, they were like personal essays.") Even the waterfall of acclaim for Ralph Fiennes' charismatic performance as Commandant Amon Goth smacks of Nazi-junkie masochism. Dreamy-eyed Fiennes could be one of the stars of the porn film *Mein Cock*, but his acting is not more skilled than Ben Kingsley's nuanced portrait of bookkeeper-listmaker Itzhak Stern.

Like *E. T.*, the other film on which Spielberg eschewed storyboarding, *Schindler's List* pares down the director's visual dynamics. Though this pleased his detractors, he ought to remember that their objection to his *style* is basically a distaste for what makes movies exciting. One moment in the film has a legitimate cinematic thrill: the sequence when mothers are separated from their children epitomizes Spielberg's genius for connecting emotional purpose to compositional vectors. As with the *Orphans of the Storm* separation of the sisters in *The Color Purple*, this scene recalls Griffith's command of primal emotions and narrative vigor. The Spielberg twist (and plus) comes with the very Hollywood principle of "proportion." A single mother separated from a child is usual. (It was acted definitively by Madge Sinclair and Leslie Uggams in *Roots* and has since been used as a bogus, dull cliché in *Sophie's Choice* (1982).) But 200 mothers running after their abducted children

**153**

belongs to a most powerful artistic vision. It's a moment in which Spielberg has successfully reimagined the terror of the Holocaust in an original way. In that scene, the literal rush of emotion kills you without the nicety of taste and "truth." It is passion made essential, kinetic, made into cinema.

Call that scene a magnanimous gesture. Its primacy is the kind of thing most Hollywood directors can't do or do badly, and so turn Hollywood filmmaking odious. Spielberg is often cursed by a critical establishment that can't see the difference between his élan and a hack's blatancy. Those mother-child emotions needn't be trivialized or disdained—Spielberg employs them honestly (familial emotions are not simply manipulated but well *understood*), and his sense of Hollywood inflation contains a sensible assessment of the Holocaust experience. He restores dignity to the undignifying effect of a pogrom wherein individuals are *reduced* to faceless numbers, routed en masse. Spielberg's insistence on primal emotions in this scene ranks with Gillo Pontecorvo's at the climax of *The Battle of Algiers* (1966); the masses become undeniably human despite the effort to dehumanize them.

Complaints such as Leon Wieseltier's in *The New Republic* and Frank Rich's op-ed in *The New York Times* that *Schindler's List* celebrates the 1,100 Jews Schindler saved without a thought for the six million killed is fatuous mathematics and narrowminded ethics. They miss the fundamental fact that the movie interprets the mass experience of Jewish oppression. It's not a story of individual suffering and Spielberg would be as fraudulent as Nazi Junkie Agnieszka Holland (*Europa Europa* (1991)) if he pretended to describe that torment singularly. He relays the Holocaust as it comes to him: as a people's tragedy. The little girl in the red coat who triggers Schindler's compassion is a perfect Spielberg symbol for humanity, but he reenacts "personal" Jewish history without specific differentiation. Schindler and Goeth stand apart as stylized, slightly awestruck visions of the German Other—angel and devil portrayed as ambivalent human extremes. But the Jews are ennobled when called upon, in the end, to display nobility as opposed to piously asserting it.

Not even Spielberg's personal Holocaust interpretation has satisfied those "Never Again" drumbeaters who want a movie that parcels out sanctimony and guilt. That's the other side of the hegemony Spielberg dangerously plays into when he affects "seriousness" and "realism." Such naive Holocaust politics beg to be misconstrued; *Schindler's List* might have been an even stronger movie if it clarified itself as a version of history rather than a document of the real thing. All those awards showered on the film but not on the man who made it directly show a higher regard for the subject than for the artistry.

But *Schindler's List* is best experienced as something other than a Holocaust history. Steven Zaillian's script is not nearly as politically sophisticated as the John Milius-Larry Gross outline of genocide and racism in Walter Hill's *Geronimo: An American Legend* (1993). Zaillian's lucid charting of events—from ghetto mandate to prison transport to Schindler's factory ruse—is substituted for any analysis of class or the dialectic of policy vs. experience that brings political history to life. Spielberg rivals Vittorio De Sica's *The Garden of the Finzi-Continis* (1971) in early scenes that show middle-class Jews shocked into awareness of their third-class status but the complexity of ethnic oppression is never focused except to be simplified as mundane evil, cut off from social/political design.

Certainly, the way Spielberg emphasizes emotion and morality is about as fine as Hollywood has ever managed on this subject. But it has led to some gross, polemical exaggerations. David Denby's claim that "rage brings out [Spielberg's] intelligence" projects the critic's own responses onto the film's political reticence; *Schindler's List* has nothing like Akira Kurosawa's informed, masterfully tempered anger in *Rhapsody in August* (1991)—a view of WWII that critics chose to ignore. Even *Swing Kids* (1993) was politically savvier: director Thomas Carter used the Third Reich era as an analogy to contemporary cultural racism. *Swing Kids* brought home to the era of hip-hop censorship the dilemma of fascism— politics as people commonly perceive and practice it—in terms *Schindler's List* achieves only once: when Nazi troops storm a Jewish apartment building, ransacking homes while one soldier sits at a piano and delights his comrades with his playing. "Bach? Is it Bach? No, Mozart!" Spielberg slyly mocks the Germanic tradition in that instant—a demonstration of the political uses of art, flirting with post-WWII skepticism without resorting to mere castigation. That brief, brilliant moment touches on the tension between culture and nationalism that is a guiding principle of Spielberg's creative intelligence.

# SIX

*Schindler's List* falls into the not-always-artful but often sanctified tradition of Holocaust movies even though Spielberg enhances that tradition by finding a story that is hopeful rather than accusatory and despairing. He returns the "favor" Spike Lee paid in *Malcolm X* (1992)—when the Ku Klux Klan rode off into a bright full *E. T.* moon—by emulating Lee's modern-day documentary coda. And as usual, Spielberg does the unexpected. The memorial sequence of Schindler Jews and their offspring laying stones on Schindler's grave carries the moral conviction Lee hoped to get from Nelson Mandela's appearance at the end of *Malcolm X.* Lee's polemicism failed because he never showed a simple connection between the living Mandela and the dead Malcolm X. However, *Schindler's List* is very much about the connection between a member of the Nazi party and his company of European Jews. Victims and victimizers all discovered a spiritual commonality. The European Holocaust was but one of history's atrocities, and Hollywood's dealt with it before. The real-life evidence of gratitude, of love given and returned, testified to in the coda is something new and overwhelming. Spielberg's intuitive dramatization of boundless ecumenical faith, hope and charity extends, as always, to the way he updates Hollywood genres to meet the most contemporary emotional needs.

Now that Spielberg has played his trump card, it will be interesting to see if critics respect him when he goes back to the subjects he knows best.

**Armond White would like to cite Hannah Arendt's little-known biography of Steven Spielberg, *The Banality of Evil Film Critics.***

*Film Comment*
March-April 1994

# My Schindler's List Problem—And Yours

## ONE

### NEWSFLASH: SPIKE LEE RESCINDS HIS CONDEMNATION OF STEVEN SPIELBERG

A T THE National Board of Review's February 28 awards ceremony, Spike Lee bestowed the Best Picture Prize on *Schindler's List*, confessing, "When they asked me to present this award I asked 'Why?' Maybe it has something to do with Black and Jewish relations. But I want to say this is the best film I saw all year. I'm a member of the Academy [of Motion Picture Arts and Sciences], and Steven and *Schindler's List* have my votes."

Since Spielberg is the filmmaker Lee slams most often (Woody Allen is the other) this change of heart was news. It was also depressing: It seemed that Lee swallowed the mainstream *Schindler's List* hype.

Probably, Lee responds better to *Schindler's List* than to Spielberg's other movies—especially *The Color Purple*—because of a commonplace but mistaken political notion that a filmmaker should make movies only about his own ethnic group. This foolishness is implicit in the widespread critical enthusiasm that praises *Schindler's List* as piece of "witnessing" or "memory." Such valorization leans toward favoring nationalist, ethnic isolation and political biases—the very things critics use to condemn the point of view in Spike Lee's own movies.

# TWO

*Schindler's List* has become a tool to advance the political interests of the mainstream media. For that reason, it is difficult to appreciate Spielberg's extraordinary artistry in this movie—it's a *very* good film, if short of the greatness that distinguishes *Close Encounters, The Color Purple* and *E. T.* Consider a seemingly innocuous piece of critical hyperbole that appeared in *The Wall Street Journal*:

> Filmed in black and white, [*Schindler's List*] has both the deep feeling and hypnotic beauty of the Italian neorealist films made after World War II, by filmmakers who had lived through the brutality of the war—the emotional truth of experience.

In complete disregard of Spielberg's phenomenal accomplishments as a creator of fantasy, *WSJ* imputes a special truth and integrity to his recreation of a historical subject. This opinion shows little knowledge of Spielberg's *art*, but—like Spike Lee—it makes a priority of *Schindler's List*'s political themes, confusing them with the moral imperatives of a visual poet. By extension, this confusion suggests that the Jewish Holocaust is a greater subject than any other—an idea with which Lee connects even as he fails to appreciate *The Color Purple* as an expression of the Black American holocaust. What *WSJ* calls "the emotional truth of experience" is what made *The Color Purple* a phenomenon; it reconceived Hollywood melodrama as a form to encompass the radical political sense of Black and feminist struggle.

Most reviewers fail to recognize a similar artistic method in *Schindler's List*. Literal-minded, they prefer Spielberg resorting to pseudodocumentary style; they won't countenance the fact that Spielberg is adding a brick to the mythological edifice Western culture has made from the Jewish Holocaust. (He identifies with Oskar Schindler as an entrepreneur but especially with Schindler's great, ironic deed: He took responsibility for the safety of over 1,100 Jews during the Nazi purge of World War II.) Instead, reviewers do something more superficial; they concede to the righteousness of Jewish suffering—recognizing the Jewish Holocaust as an issue that supersedes any formal narrative strategy. This explains how Spielberg can be hailed for "remembering" and "witnessing" events that took place before he was a zygote.

Doctrinaire praise for *Schindler's List* undermines Spielberg's conscientious humanism—the ecumenical view of human goodness consistent throughout *Close Encounters*, *The Color Purple*, *Empire of the Sun*, *Always*, *Hook*, even the great works of historical revision, *1941* and *Indiana Jones and the Last Crusade*. To redeem a D.W. Griffith phrase, Spielberg has evinced a "great heart." It is a terrible irony that *Schindler's List*, Spielberg's attempt at applying a specific ethnic—rather than personal—nuance to his filmography, should be used to dismiss his larger humane interests.

# THREE

*"Not the holocaust/I'm talkin' 'bout the one still goin' on"*
—PUBLIC ENEMY, "CAN'T TRUSS IT"

It is immoral to play Favorite Historical Atrocity, but the *Schindler's List* craze has put a new spin on pop culture hegemony. *WSJ*'s implication that Spielberg has, in some sense, "lived through the brutality of war" is the kind of political realization that non-white, non-European filmmakers have been struggling to impart. It's the same sociological understanding about life that many critics vigorously refused to show Spike Lee's *Do the Right Thing* (1989). That's how hegemony works—affirming some worldviews, denying others.

In *Time* magazine, the review of *Schindler's List* did not run under the heading Cinema, Arts, Culture, Ethnicity or even News, but in a special section titled Holocaust. Let's face it, the movie obviously is being used to aggrandize white political preferences.

# FOUR

When New Jersey Gov. Christine Todd Whitman advocated special screenings of *Schindler's List* near state college campuses for students and citizens, *The New York Times* reported on Whitman's "monthlong public school initiative to teach tolerance. She said the initiative was aimed at combating all forms of bigotry, not only the anti-Semitic attacks but also the attacks on other religions and homosexuals."

Whitman's propaganda was in response to recent controversy over Nation of Islam member Khalid Abdul Muhammad's speech at Kean College last November. The governor also was practicing Hollywood hype but at another, insulting level: She suggested that the best lesson against bigotry is taught through the symbolic example of white, mainstream (Jewish) oppression.

The governor's retreat to *Schindler's List* almost perfectly demonstrates an institutional incapacity to deal with the actual American conditions of racial bigotry. Whitman, like many film critics, doesn't respect how unempowered people "live through the brutality of war" in America. *Schindler's List* thus becomes a convenient piece of escapism. Whitman's critics suggested that her initiative should be balanced with such films as *Eyes on the Prize* and *Roots*; they pinpointed the historical views that the mainstream frequently disregards.

# FIVE

The *Schindler's List* celebrators avoid Spielberg's complex vision of morality. Despite the film's moving coda (derived from a failed strategy in Lee's *Malcolm X*), where the Schindler Jews pay tribute to the Nazi party member who saved their lives, critics rarely mention the emotional cost of humanism that Spielberg takes pains to emphasize throughout the movie.

*Schindler's List* is no more an "optimistic" view of World War II than *The Color Purple* was a Disney vision of African-American life. Spielberg and screenwriter Steven Zaillian create remarkable demonstrations of human feeling (the brief, ecstatic scene of revolt by a couple hundred mothers); existential mystery (the prisoner whom Nazi troops are unable to shoot); and moral-formal daring (the poignant color schemes used in moments of religious ritual and the sight of a girl in a red coat). The best moments in *Schindler's List* resemble *The Color Purple* in the way Spielberg directs viewer consciousness toward a morally active awareness of cinematic narrative and a rethinking of genre archetypes.

# SIX

*Schindler's List* isn't merely the best Hollywood movie on the Jewish Holocaust, but it's the most emotionally generous. There's none of the finger-pointing vengeance, breast-beating pathos (as in *The Diary of Anne Frank* (1959), *Sophie's Choice* or the late-'70s TV miniseries *Holocaust* (1978)), or the smug, artsy hindsight seen in Agnieszka Holland's *Europa Europa*. Spielberg replaces what Pauline Kael ridiculed as European masochism with a livelier, American sense of culture critique, as in the destruction of a Jewish home during a solo piano performance ("Is it Mozart?" The stormtroopers ask. "No, Bach.") Spielberg slyly mocks the Germanic tradition in that instant—a demonstration of the political uses of art, flirting with post-World War II skepticism without resorting to mere castigation. That brief, brilliant moment touches on the tension between culture and nationalism that is a guiding principle for Spielberg's creative intelligence.

Spielberg takes his revisionism further in the precarious positioning of his title character, Oskar Schindler (played by Liam Neeson). "I am a profiteer of slave labor," Schindler says, the industrialist criticizing himself with a candor and moral sense unusual in Hollywood productions. (The words "slave labor" rang no bells for white American critics.) The situation that allows him to keep more that 1,000 Polish Jews out of the Nazi death camps is a capitalist irony: For seven months, he employs/succors them in his metalworks factory, turning the formerly middle-class citizens into "models of non-production."

The film sets up a neat antagonism between Schindler and Amon Goeth (Ralph Fiennes), the charismatic Nazi commandant. They are angel and devil examples of human potential for good or evil, but the film emphasizes each man's complexity more than his idiosyncrasy. (Evil and atrocity are not the movie's point despite the plethora of misinterpretations that claim so.) The movie (and Neeson's performance) hinges on the moment Schindler articulates his conversion. His expression of humility also carries multimillionaire Spielberg's own unusual moral imperatives. It is this moral artist, this poet, who turns the best moments in *Schindler's List* into something greater than a history lesson:

- The Mozart-Bach scene contrasts a party's-over episode where Billie Holiday's "God Bless the Child" emotion-alizes the background.

- Spielberg dispenses with identifying intertitles during the Schindler Jews' arrival at Auschwitz, preferring to locate the audience in the nighttime scene's emotional complexity—ashes fall like snow, a visual image of despair mixed with hope.

All this is greater art than the herding into showers that provoked most critics' knee-jerk responses to the movie.

Such automatic pity is useless (besides, Spielberg created much more harrowing scenes in *Jurassic Park*'s T-Rex and Raptor attacks—nightmares of science and nature run wild where the terror is always clear, always close). If the subject of Jewish oppression means anything to Spielberg, he wants to get a fresher, more honest response.

When a group of Black and Latino Northern California public school students were taken on a field trip to see *Schindler's List* on the Martin Luther King Jr. holiday (more Whitman-style propaganda to disregard non-white history), the kids' fresh reactions ignited another flurry of Black-youth demonizing and Holocaust prioritizing. The kids, who were reported to laugh at the film's most violent scenes, were blamed for being insensitive even though American culture has raised them to enjoy the depiction of violence in pop media.

In New York, where the media feeds on instances that exacerbate Black-Jewish relations, those California students were portrayed as jackals. The less dogmatic West Coast press gave mitigating details: During a scene where Goeth shoots a woman in the head, one of the students remarked, "That's cold!" which elicited laugher from his classmates. That fresher response contains a full awareness of horror, but in terms the mainstream doesn't understand.

Incidentally, one of the key moments in movie hermeneutics was in Arthur Penn's 1958 *The Left-Handed Gun*: A little girl witnesses a man being shot on the western street, one boot left standing. She giggles—a natural nervous response—but is slapped into civilized hypocrisy by her mother.

It's good to remember that kids who grow up disenfranchised and disrespected by their society, yet who can still recognize as "cold" the bitter inhumanity of an on-screen act, are the best hope for honest cinema and an honest society. *Schindler's List* should not be used as another mainstream tool to further marginalize them; those kids may be the only audience that truly appreciates Spielberg's best efforts.

*The City Sun*
March 1994

# THE LOST WORLD: JURASSIC PARK (1997)

## *Dino and Might*

**W**ELCOMING STEVEN SPIELBERG back to the movies comes as part of enjoying *The Lost World: Jurassic Park.* It's a reaffirmation of wonder—you know, the reason you loved movies to begin with. Since Spielberg's 1993 double-header of *Jurassic Park* and *Schindler's List,* many terrible things have happened to film culture: juvenile crap (*Pulp Fiction*), urbane crap (*Leaving Las Vegas* (1995)), gentrified crap (*The English Patient* (1996)) and those other—countless—movies where people outrun fireballs. In the space of a few socially-stressed years, Hollywood has emanated blunt, numbing, trivial, putrid pacification. Politicians and consumers alike have mistaken this for "culture." And reviewers mistake it for fun. But most of the hits in Spielberg's absence offer little illumination, or report, on how people live or dream. A worldwide blockbuster like *Independence Day* (1996) suggests that even our dreams have become second-rate, unconnected to morality, history, psychology or craft.

Hollywood filmmakers used to know how to make entertainment that got under your skin by delighting the mind's eye. Now, not even that unreliable old institution, the Academy of Motion Picture Darts and Appliances can pretend such films as *Speed* (1994), *Batman Forever* (1995) or *Independence Day* are addressing the audience's subconscious the way a good movie can. Current emphasis on action and F/X has reduced cinema to widgets, the better to facilitate industry exploitation. The Almighty Disney Company has reimagined cinema as a mousetrap.

Spielberg takes the same springs, levers, computer graphics, puppetry and editing, but by applying them to a sense of the lost humane world—the bond of a father and daughter, Ian Malcolm and Kelly (Jeff Goldblum and Vanessa Lee Chester); the interests they share with a professional woman, Sarah Harding (Julianne Moore); the integrity of a young photographer (Vince Vaughn); and the ambivalent ingenuity of big business—he winds up with a funny-scary adventure movie that is also restorative.

InGen, a modern conglomerate that has taken over the artisan ambitions of Jurassic Park inventor John Hammond (Richard Attenborough), is this sequel's villain. As run by an odious young CEO (Arliss Howard), InGen intends to rehab Hammond's abandoned cloned species of prehistoric animals for no other reason than ruthless exploitation—corrupt ingenuity. The Jurassic creatures are stalked, then caged for exhibition in the U.S. Updating *King Kong* (1933) and *Hatari* (1962) reassesses our pop culture's foul practices. Spielberg shows that it's corporate impulse, disguised as mass culture, that's gone wild (responsible for what critic Robert Hughes simplified at this year's Columbia University commencement as "weightlessness and anti-idealism" in the arts). So while *The Lost World* is certainly a whiz-bang improvement on *Jurassic Park*, it is *necessary* to see it as Spielberg parodying heedless commerce in order to recover essential emotions and deep virtues that hypertechnological Hollywood has forgotten. No one else is better suited to such an ethics lesson.

Why *The Lost World* is a dinosaur movie par excellence comes from Spielberg's mighty respect for the concept of entertainment. He's always believed in the significance of storytelling and the morality of art-making (both are inherent to his standard of quality). He come from that '70s American Film Renaissance that sought to complicate "non-serious" genres with surprising, truth-revealing elements—a shark hunt that evokes war's timeless horror, a UFO watch that searches for God, a Black lesbian identity saga that reveres the great unorthodox Family.

No apologies are necessary for the good time *Jurassic Park* gave millions of viewers; so this sequel is less a cashing-in than a lest-we-forget. Its good guys—an anthropologist-greenie-scientist team—want to study, protect and get-the-hell-out-of-the-way-of the impulsive, earth-shaking anachronisms. Principles energize the action but Spielberg's no puritan; he prizes vitality (even the dinosaur's ruthless efficiency) and gives his morality tale motion. With action equaling character, he shoots InGen's capitalist warriors as vehemence itself; they're introduced like a matinee version of *Apocalypse Now*—planes and choppers swarm like a wasp attack, then jeeps and land cruisers rip through the jungle island's brush, careening toward a fervent and sorrowful dinosaur hunt. The way Spielberg pitches his audience into the fantastic injects excitement—just as a preceding scene of Sarah frolicking with some benign beasts, as if in a midsummer night's fairy dance, choreographs awe. *The Lost World* shows a deft touch for both sweetness and audacity. Repartee between Sarah, Malcolm and Kelly has a jaunty flow, and the visual wit of the many dinosaur attacks escalates terror and amazement as only one other filmmaker, Brian De Palma, can rival.

Spielberg shares De Palma's comic taste for scariness, treating dangerous situations as film-culture lark. You know an impossible situation will be manipulated for its incredulity and that the sight of it—the thrill—will open up another level of expectation. Spielberg then heightens suspense by phenomenal visual composition—Julianne Moore stretched across a windshield, staring through its weblike cracks at the abyss below—then, with sensational timing, adds: a dinosaur attack, a bus toppling over a cliff, a race in the mud to tie a lifeline to a tree trunk. The entire sequence has the clarity and dazzlement of a nightmare. Apocalyptic camera angles tease the possibility of death, and when it comes, pop art has the satisfaction of sexual release. Neither immoral nor heartless, the power of art—this big, this detailed, this beautiful— deeply exercises the imagination. Absolutely nothing among the recent, debased standards of the action-film genre (*Speed* (1994), *Independence Day* or *True Lies* (1994)) comes close.

Unfortunately, welcoming back Spielberg comes with a down side: the temerity of critics who'd rather see trash like *Anaconda* (1997) because they simply resent Spielberg's talent and success. But it's the human value Spielberg adds to his kinetic ability that makes his work extraordinary. This film's dinosaur designs bare a fascinating relation to human faces: Goldblum's dark, angular features, Moore's bright hair and abrupt profile, the dino hunter's (Pete Postlethwaite) shining dome and the genetic ranges suggested by Chester as Malcolm's daughter.

Chester's appearance certifies that in addition to *The Lost World*'s ecological faith, it has great political daring.

Casting a Black girl as the child of white-identified Goldblum, Spielberg challenges mass-movie clichés by confronting real-life stereotypes. Chester's presence universalizes the genre. Her entrance is Brechtian: She cheers, "Daddy, Daddy, Daddy!" "What took you so long?" Goldblum asks. "I couldn't get a cab," she offers. Spielberg and screenwriter David Koepp shrewdly situate their conceit in satire of a common social problem. This caprice of Spielberg's will change millions of people as effectively as Mike Leigh challenged considerably fewer through the white/Black parent/child trope of *Secrets & Lies* (1996). It's a bold use of Spielberg's pop-art privilege.

Malcolm, a hipster ethical culturalist, is the director's latest autobiographical figure. Here Goldblum adds physical dash to the character's braininess. That superb speech in *Jurassic Park* about "standing on the shoulders of greatness" and "asking if we should" was so out of the ordinary of the usual action-movie claptrap that people preferred ignoring it to appreciating its implications. But Malcolm's fatherly concern resonates better than the trite brotherhood bromides in *Volcano* (1997). He's a dad on a mission, like in *Hook* (a much more interesting aspect than the Peter Pan principle that dull critics keep looking for). Spielberg's major protagonists, from *Jaws* and *Always* (Richard Dreyfuss) to the nondenominational Indiana Jones (Harrison Ford), all respond to social conventions with eccentric, charismatic behavior. That personality is part of how Spielberg practices—and redeems—genre. It shows in the soft, verdant imagery (shot by Janusz Kamiński), which cleverly mixes nature with artifice to envision life's rich and threatening lushness. *The Last World* is no stingily-paced thriller like *The Relic* (1997); in the last third Spielberg takes his ethics to town, where InGen's final irresponsible gamble creates not-in-my-backyard pandemonium. (And nature teaches revenge to its young.)

For a lesser filmmaker it'd be overkill; for Spielberg, going from jungle nightmare to suburban dream brings incessant delights: from a dynamic ship crash to a lovely joke of Japanese-American moviegoers fleeing a T-Rex as if Godzilla came to life. Pay attention to an audacious, quick panning shot across San Diego's American border stop where Mexicans line up for clearance and interrogation while T-Rex, unleashed by rampant corporate greed, barges to the head of the line. Neither the NAFTA treaty nor California's Proposition 187 have had wittier, more significant rejoinders. When he's this good, Spielberg invests fun with significance and makes pop culture roar.

*New York Press*
June 1997

# AMISTAD (1997)

---

## *Titanic: Sinking*

"**W**HITE PEOPLE WOULD rather see themselves die than watch Black people live," I heard a film student surmise after he'd read numerous negations of *Amistad* and media hype for *Titanic* (1997). The coincidence of these maritime dramas appearing on the movie scene—but distinguished by contrasting critical response—naturally makes you wonder at the opposing purposes people bring to the cinema. *Amistad* revives history and politics; *Titanic* disdains history for pseudo-science and fantasy. By any sensible standards the junky, trite *Titanic* would be ridiculed next to the movingly humanist *Amistad*, but it is precisely the '90s perversion of what might be called film-student enthusiasm—the desire for enlightenment and awe distorted into mere motor reflexes—that allows critics to misjudge Steven Spielberg's intense reenactment of history while preferring James Cameron's exploitation of tragedy as big-screen extravaganza.

If it is a race thing—indeed, the predominantly white critical fraternity embraces *Titanic* as a propensity toward the safe, affectless mode of apolitical culture—then that film student's observation correctly pinpoints a dreaded development: modern movie aesthetics have become inescapably aligned solely with the desires of the empowered class that controls Hollywood and the media. It's the strange antipathy toward *Amistad* that makes enthusiasm for *Titanic* seem an urge toward denial—even to the point of death. Cameron's morally-blank disaster movie certainly makes a spectacle of death, but its only spectacle, not tragedy or loss, because it hasn't really got a plot. The boat sinks—you know that. (Critic Gregory Solman calls it "the most underdeveloped nearly four-hour story in the history of the cinema.") But American movie culture sinks along with it, cheering the fake technology as a distraction from the era's ocean of idiocy.

At least the actual *Titanic* was a genuine, scientific achievement—an advancing experiment in naval technology. Instead, Cameron, who on ABC's *Nightline* had the nerve to criticize Oliver Stone's interpretations of history as a misuse of film technology, seals our pop culture's fate by centralizing a dinghy-sized subplot (a teen-idol love story with the facile Leonardo DiCaprio and a miscast Kate Winslet). This decadent escapism avoids the social and ideational details braved by even *Titanic*, the current Broadway musical play. (It's one of the few times in cultural history a Broadway play has been more thoughtful and imaginative on a subject than a contemporary movie.) Composer-conceptualizer Maury Yeston sets out the class issues of the ship's different passengers along with an honest, lyrical expression of the Titanic designer's and owner's technological ambition and dreams. (The play's opening ship-boarding tableau ends with a boy holding a model sailboat before the gargantuan sea vessel—measuring man's dream against reality.) Cameron, devoid of imagination, only does things bigger, bigger and more insipidly. His approach fits the era of selfish, insensitive expenditure: hype surrounding the movie's financial cost and expensive effort is in sync with our all-about-the-Benjamins ideology.

Cameron has become an icon of the postmodern era—a dopey Kubrick moving from the director-as-superstar era to the director-as-supergeek. Fascinated by his electric toy set but numb to characterization, Cameron (since *The Terminator* in 1984) has shown an end-of-civilization self-consciousness and determination toward larger projects with diminishing content. Ironically, despite the hardware he deploys like a battlefield general, Cameron lacks craft. Not skill; he can turn it out and churn it up. But *Titanic* does not show the basic storytelling know-how of the *Jurassic Park* movies (Cameron stole—thus bowdlerizing—Spielberg's framing device of a high-tech exposition of the action to come), or the layered characterizations of such well-made films as *The Poseidon Adventure* (1972) and *The Towering Inferno*.

When the iceberg that crashes into the ship first sidles by the Titanic, where's the dream maker's impulse to have someone on deck reach out and touch an iceberg? Whoever has? Who, given the opportunity, would not? Wouldn't such a gesture make that experience real and wondrous? Compare it to the two ships passing at night in *Amistad* (one adrift with African slaves, high-living white Americans cruising by in the other) where the passengers can only stare at each other in shared disbelief. That's understanding your moment and exploring it imaginatively. Cameron can never do that. He thinks up noisy, repetitive violent gimmicks. (Axing off handcuffs, unlocking gates, wading through corridors of water.) Okay, seeing the ship rise up and sink has grandeur of a kind, but is it really different from those '50s movies that advertised a cast of thousands?

That's a camp effect. Any James Bond movie you can name offers a similar thrill—twice.

Cameron's *Titanic* is ambitious in the crudest way. BIG, LOUD, SENTIMENTAL—FALSE! He has no originality to scare off brick-headed viewers, so this turd (floating on a sea of critical bilge) is accorded even more respect than Michael Cimino's *Heaven's Gate* (1980), which—irrational pacing, obsessive details and all—is a better film, a more "impressive" entertainment and production feat, a serious art effort about history and individual desire. *Titanic*'s teenage love story has little to do with desire in any complicated, genuine way; it's a blatant commercial repeat of Baz Luhrmann's ridiculous *Romeo + Juliet* (1996)—and is equally calculated and condescending. And unromantic, despite the swoony Old Rose framing device. DiCaprio's moony earnestness as the working-class boy-artist flouncing around with wild-eyed upper-class Kate Winslet is kids' stuff (compare it to the currents of passion flowing between Daniel Day-Lewis and Emily Watson as lovers recalling their thwarted adolescence in *The Boxer* (1997)).

Cameron's contrived love story appeals to a generation suspicious of any credibly expressed sentiments. Some element of adult cynicism contributes to the dumbed-down, low-down acceptance of this romantic contrivance. Befitting a famously expensive movie, part of the bizarre attraction is located in Cameron's hackneyed treatment of female distress. Winslet, playing the Young Rose, is berated by a craven mother (Frances Fisher) and a rotting cad fiancé (Billy Zane), yet she's no more than a pampered gold digger—Alicia Silverstone must have, sensibly, turned down the role. Preferring this prototype skeezer, Cameron (who surely doesn't identify with the film's artist figure) belittles the likeliest female icon, the unsinkable Molly Brown (Kathy Bates). He smashes even the hope of Brown's unselfish human will (which may only have been heroic mythology) for something wimpier and even hateful—a *Bridges of Madison County* love affair that the emotionally stunted Winslet character clings to even as a nonagenarian. Major goof: the old lady narrator/survivor (played by Gloria Stuart) travels to the shipwreck site seeking a jewel she had in her possession all along. (To follow the story, she ends up killing her fiancé by not returning the jewel.)

What can explain tolerance for such foolishness? Buried beneath critical praise is the sucker's thought that if Cameron went to so much trouble so single-mindedly, then *Titanic* must be important and must be supported. This wish for the "old" Hollywood has shrunk critical expectation, returned it to the '60s habit when big-budget roadshow movies commanded industry-wide respect. In the '70s, disaster films were properly understood as junk, but now Cameron gets lauded for indulging violent and romantic nonsense.

Every critic who praises *Titanic* should lose his/her credibility, but I know liking inanity suits the times. (A different criterion held in the '70s, when critics who praised *Jaws* were responding to something radical—Spielberg's revitalization of forgotten silent-film aesthetics, along with a new, good-humored sensibility.) Cameron's rise—along with Schwarzenegger's, along with Reagan's—is clear proof of debased, imperially managed popular taste. Movies no longer simply entertain; they're meant to stave off consciousness, usually by exploitation of dread, and you can apply this same denial to the way the mainstream media misrepresents almost every social catastrophe—it's Cameron's specialty, "true lies."

Critics can be liars, too. After decrying stupid movies, they put on their "It's-Just-Entertainment" dunce caps and celebrate the stupidest movies around—*Speed*, *Men in Black* (1997), *Air Force One* (1997), *Con Air* (1997), *Titanic*! And it's not just the I-love-everything TV and radio guys; more pretentious types fall for it. One reviewer rejected as "fluff" the suggestion of seeing the Broadway *Titanic*. "I like avant-garde theater," she said. "The kind of theater they put on at Brooklyn Academy of Music's Next Wave festival." My response, "But *Titanic* is not a Next Wave kind of movie," was met with a clown's pantomime of the word, "What?!" A wave of idiocy.

Christmas 1974: Nobody mistook the two blockbusters *The Godfather Part II* and *The Towering Inferno* as comparable—interchangeable. We knew one was art and the other represented the contemporary studio system simply at its most competent. 1997 critics have forgotten the difference; they accept that Cameron, since *Terminator 2* (1991) and *True Lies*, has debased genre and made it more shrill, condescending and obvious. Today, critics are more pleased to be presented with an absolutely inessential, warped piece of Hollywood escapism rather than *Amistad*'s example of essential and invigorating art. And if it's not a race thing, it's certainly the return of the white elephant ruling the waves of idiocy.

*New York Press*
December 1997

# Bitter?

**S**PIKE LEE, ALWAYS throwing up opinion—most recently and noisily on *Amistad* and *Jackie Brown* (1997)— is not a film critic. But maybe he's auditioning for a new career. For almost a decade now Lee's been something less than a film*maker*; his last bunch of movies regurgitate calculated dyspepsia with a few pre-chewed nuggets of self-conscious "style." He thus forces the white critical establishment into patronizing acclaim that always dissipates by the end of the year. His latest piece of race-baiting *4 Little Girls* (1997), was praised excessively last summer as a major socio-cultural event, yet only came in third place for the New York Film Critics Circle's Best Non-Fiction Film prize behind the all-white, aggressively subjective *Fast, Cheap & Out of Control* (1997) and *Sick: The Life and Death of Bob Flanagan* (1997), which together garnered almost four times as many points. Lee's film was also overlooked by Los Angeles and Boston critics groups. In a snit, he rebounded by bushwhacking his now critically-softened (thus easily attackable) colleagues Steven Spielberg and Quentin Tarantino. Sour grapes, that's the taste of mo' bitter blues.

On ABC's *Nightline*, Lee joined a panel, speaking against *Amistad* producer Debbie Allen and *Glory* director Edward Zwick. He sang that old tune he used earlier this decade to knock Norman Jewison out of the directorial post of *Malcolm X*. Lee claimed only Black filmmakers, and not Spielberg, could properly tell a story of African-American history. (Allen defended her film with conviction and diplomacy. Zwick did

**179**

a liberal's shrink and deferred to Lee's arrogance.) Days later, in the print media, Lee fumed about the utterance of "the N word" in *Jackie Brown* as an offense perpetrated by Tarantino and Samuel L. Jackson, stars, respectively in his own movies *Girl 6* (1996) and *Jungle Fever* (1991).

It's rare that one filmmaker publicly attacks another—some code of empathy, borne out of struggle against industry stubbornness and backstabbing, usually keeps directors mum when differing with their peers. (Back in 1986, on Gil Noble's *Like It Is*, Melvin Van Peebles refused the bait by panelists feeding on *The Color Purple*. When asked if he thought a Black person should have directed the film, if it might have been better had *he* done the film, Van Peebles deflected racist implication and answered: "I only wish I could have directed it as well as Spielberg did.") But Lee, who rides a stunt car of racist outrage in our exploitive media circus, pretends a seriousness more important than politesse and makes a clown of himself—again.

Holding malice toward both *Amistad* and *Jackie Brown* is an untenable position—it suggests envy more than morality. Lee confuses the very issues of ethnic portraiture and historical perspective with which every American filmmaker and film critic worth a damn has to contend, and that both *Amistad* and *Jackie Brown* renew. Because those movies are expressions of such divergent social and moral vision, Lee's attack leaves the culture no way to deal sensibly with the issues and effects of race and politics and art—except through his absurd limited defense of racism: that only one group knows, only one group can, only one group should.

Earlier signs that Lee was off-kilter came in 1994 when after almost 10 years of bashing Spielberg for the great, history-making *The Color Purple*, he presented Spielberg with the National Board of Review Best Picture prize for *Schindler's List*. At that ceremony, Lee assured Spielberg of his personal Academy Awards vote. Worse than sucking up, this was the same crude misjudgment as Lee's *Amistad* denouncement; he was swilling to praise *Schindler's List* as an ethnic broadside, a typical misunderstanding of artistic intent. Lee, like a lot of film critics, has no real understanding of what Spielberg is about as a film artist; he mistakes Spielberg's uncanny popular touch and his broad cultural identity as a form of limited humanity. It recalls the way *New York*'s David Denby, the critic who fearfully predicted *Do the Right Thing* would cause riots, later commended *Schindler's List* as an expression of "Spielberg's anger" (as if to turn that complex moral examination into JDL propaganda). Captious Lee also throws prejudiced ballast behind his misinterpretation, relating Spielberg's work to his own brand of moral extortion.

Lee may have a point in thinking only an African-American has the right to feel a certain historically-based indignation on the subject of slavery, but he misses the point that makes *Amistad* extraordinary: Spielberg's understanding that slavery (like the Jewish Holocaust) wasn't the disgrace of only its immediate sufferers. Lee lacks Spielberg's greater awareness. He joins the pack of idiotic film critics who think any movie on these subjects must, automatically, repeat their own ignorance, thus perpetuate tales of victimization and guilt and hollow uplift. Lee thinks that way, even though he professes to tolerate none of it. The strange hallmark of his *Malcolm X* is that, despite Lee's effort at hagiography, it was essentially so resentful and down-putting. Rapper Ice Cube gave the film its ultimate summary when relating post-'92 rap's lack of politics to the exhaustion caused by Lee's movie. ("That [politics] all ended with *Malcolm X,"* Cube told a hip-hop magazine.)

To redirect the *Village Voice*'s strange but telling rave of *Malcolm X* in 1992: Lee works with "a poverty of means." I think that unfortunate phrase was intended to indict Lee's "paltry" $30 million budget as compared to typical Hollywood-epic price tags. It's worth realizing that in terms of 1997 dollars, Lee spent more on *Malcolm X* than Spielberg did on *Amistad* (reportedly $40 million), yet Lee's besmirching campaign is unaccountably cheap. He shows the same poverty of means as those critics who disregard the importance of *Amistad*'s subject. They confuse their own exacerbated responses to race and politics with Spielberg's modesty and tact and rather lovely suasion. (By comparison *Amistad*'s subtly-extended sea metaphors expose *The Sweet Hereafter*'s (1997) and *The Ice Storm*'s (1997) blatant symbolism as the work of hacks.)

It was bad politics when Lee complained to Forrest Sawyer: "How come the white guys always got to be the hero," forgetting that *Amistad* begins and ends with the Black African Cinque (Djimon Hounsou) and that the white characters throughout identify him as the center of the issue. Unable to cite actual examples of Spielberg's misrepresentation of Black humanity, Lee fell back on the errors of shabby, unserious historical distortions like *Mississippi Burning* and *Cry Freedom* (even though the latter starred his fave, Denzel Washington). What may forever keep Lee a minor filmmaker can be seen in this foolish campaign. He views society and history and art with a small heart.

And it's fake politics that Lee professes when attacking Tarantino in *Daily Variety.* "What does he want to be made— an honorary Black man?" Lee asked, holding the white man responsible for insensitivity of which the Black male star of *Jackie Brown* is also guilty. Tarantino's misjudgment pales next to Samuel L. Jackson's sulfurous self-contempt—a career path that began with Jackson's sodden crackhead in *Jungle Fever.* Yet Lee ignores Jackson's crime in favor of blaming Tarantino, allowing venality only when practiced by Blacks.

This relates, in some pitiful, desperate way, to the voguish regard for '70s Blaxploitation movies—the low-rent run-offs of a racist film industry—as if they were genuine folk art (as if B-movie director Jack Hill were an artist evoking human experience on the same level as genius pop composers/ producers Kenny Gamble and Leon Huff). Such insulting pop irony leads a facetious, shallow culture to produce a *Jackie Brown*, a Blaxploitation movie for white people. Tarantino approaches the same old racial gulf and attenuates it with the same glum visuals and dour characterizations. It also leads non-thinkers like Spike Lee to assume that the lack of artistic choice Black actors, directors and composers suffered during Blaxploitation did not hinder their best instincts, that only their ambition—not their work—mattered. He has carried that '70s adolescent infatuation with anger funneled into wretched junk over to our New Black Hollywood era, in which only Black careerism matters and must be defended at all costs against white filmmakers he views as encroachers.

But Tarantino and Spielberg are not to blame for Hollywood's usual rebuff of Black sensibility. (Both *Jackie*

**183**

*Brown* and *Amistad* evidence some definite—if different—respect for Black sensibility.) Reducing his industry fear to the bogus "N-word" complaint of hypocritical op-ed pundits, Lee avoids crucial matters of Black artists' intent. I attended a *Jackie Brown* press conference where Sam Jackson boasted, "I used the word 'nigger' five times in one sentence; that's hard to do." Not when you're deep into self-hatred. Same goes for Hazelle Goodman stumping the media trail for her role as a hooker in *Deconstructing Harry* (1997). In a sane world, Woody Allen should not have been able to find a Black woman who would play that part; he would, more interestingly and appropriately, then be forced to resort to D.W. Griffith's *The Birth of a Nation* ploy of having demeaning Blacks played by white actors in black face. And it would have been a more fascinating movie.

Lee reported to *Variety* that if he had used the word 'kike' 38 times in *Mo' Better Blues* (1990), "it would have been my last picture." He also tried an ethnic sucker-punch on *Nightline*, grousing that he would not be allowed to do a film about Golda Meir. But why would he want to do either? And in each case he assumes, like many bogus "independents," that Hollywood is the only filmmaking source.

By the tone of these brash arguments, Lee doesn't examine his own knee-jerk responses—neither do most critics. Their love affair with Samuel L. Jackson and his continually perpetrated evil is plain evidence that racial distance prevails in film culture and that critics prefer stigma to truth. It was only at that *Jackie Brown* press conference that I finally understood that Jackson's odiousness came from something more complicated than Tarantino's permissive racism. QT revealed that Jackson's Ordell Robbie was the film's character he most identified with, because, "I grew up around Black people. My mother dated

Black men. The man who was my father figure was a lot like that. Not as dangerous as what Sam Jackson plays but, uh, he was pretty shady." So while Jackson may be doing some private parody or mimesis of "Black" character, Tarantino is working out a deeply American Oedipal complex. Forget the homage to Pam Grier and '70s soul music, the word "nigger" is Tarantino's most important appropriation. He uses it so insistently because it stands in for "motherfucker."

Calling out name-calling is a diversionary tactic, especially for Spike Lee, whose Black and white characters are all stereotypes. Let Tarantino use it till he chokes on it; a more important criticism is that such language becomes the full extent of his characterization—Ordell Robbie is nothing. Less than human, he is simply the evilest "nigger" (as opposed to hip-hop's "nigga") one can imagine. He's as bad as Lee wants to be.

If Lee's rancor becomes a measure of contemporary ethical judgment, if it blends with the chorus of insensitivity and callousness that has applied critical censure to *Amistad*, then we're all in deep trouble—intolerant of good intentions and good movies but fired up with cynical certainty about bad ones. *Amistad* opens with a scene of uncannily sharp instinct that surely pays homage to Public Enemy's great slave narrative "Can't Truss It." ("Blood in the wood and it's mine.") The opening of *Do the Right Thing* wasn't nearly as provocative. And in the glorious "Welcome to the Terrordome," when PE cried "Who do you trust, man?" it wasn't a question about white or Black artists, but was, sensibly, a quote from the Brian De Palma-Oliver Stone *Scarface*. That kind of diverse pop sensibility one can trust.

*New York Press*
January 1998

# Emancipating Movie History

F ADING INTO A blue-black face, lightning illuminates the screen to flash a man's stress, sweat and determination. The scene is scored to sounds of breathing and scratching; its inner tension will reveal fingers prying a nail from broken grains of wood smeared with blood. More flashes of the man using that nail as a key. Breaking bondage. A wordless revolt begins in silhouettes more stark than certain. Black captives come above board using cane-cutters to overtake Spanish-speaking white men guiding the boat.

It's a kick-ass opening. If we don't know exactly what's going on, we still know what it means. These first images of Steven Spielberg's *Amistad* are primal—not elemental like the shark attack in *Jaws*—but born of the same American psychic armature Griffith instituted with his threatening Blacks in *The Birth of a Nation* (and that continues in modern Hollywood depictions of race when Robert De Niro glances to a Black Secret Service henchman to dispatch Dustin Hoffman in *Wag the Dog* (1997)).

*Amistad*'s nighttime shipboard revolt ignites a secret American spectacle—the threat of racial Armageddon comprised of Black necessity, white indifference—both locked in fear.

What follows is restorative—a deep, careful, deliberate investigation into the context of revolt. Spielberg's fearless admission of blood-letting is something the independent academic filmmaker Haile Gerima would not even dare in his slave epic *Sankofa* (1993) which only showed Black suffering and abuse, implying the need for revenge but shying away from the bloody horror of revolution. Spielberg's scene cannot be justified without a sober drama to explain it. Otherwise, it would be a trite, get-whitey tactic and while some may flinch at it as such, that's a shallow response. As Cinque (Djimon Hounsou) strides toward a Spanish sailor frantically loading a musket, his bare chest, square shoulders and unstoppable forward movement seems inevitable—righteous.

The sight of him burying a sword in the white-shirted body, its length going through and beneath the deck to the upward thrusts of more chained hands, justifies the necessity of vengeance in a single image. When the sword is slowly pulled out of the body, Spielberg's uptilted image is heroicizing, mythic (of course) but also analytical. The specter is defined, scrutinized. We can't pretend not to know the source of this vengeance or its reason and that horrid awareness isn't an anonymous thrill-ride, it can be named. It is history.

A typically subtle moment in *Amistad* shows two 1839 newspapers reporting the same event: MASSACRE AT SEA; A DIFFICULT SLAVE CASE says the mainstream press headline while the front page of the Abolitionist broadsheet *The Emancipator* declares FREEDOM FIGHT AT SEA. Central to the film's overlooked complexity is Spielberg's double consciousness of how mainstream media initiates a perspective—a biased discourse-that must be countered by a different more inquisitive understanding. *Amistad* speaks truth to power in the way it countermands mainstream cinema—the cultural apparatus Spielberg is expected to use as unselfconsciously as the hack Alan Parker did when manufacturing historical distortion in *Mississippi Burning*. Instead, Spielberg challenges reigning notions of history, humanism and cinema by making a movie about the slave trade—not Slavery, but the machinations of political power demonstrated in slavery's practice and its usual historical retelling.

In another subtly persuasive detail, Spielberg shows the child monarch Isabella II of Spain writing to influence President Martin Van Burn's interference in the trial of African slaves' freedom. "The business of great nations is to do business," she says, also a summary of how we understand media and movie industries to operate. She continues, "Power is their wealth. Speak words that protect that power. The African must never go free." That's a harsher historical statement—distilling imperialism to its racist core—than we get from most movies and some critics have been willing to dismiss it as dull agitprop rather than notice the way Spielberg streamlines political motives into a concise yet expansive drama of human initiative.

*Amistad*, a confrontation drama rather than a historical epic, compresses past events that Hollywood convention would draw out—as if length equaled gravity or importance. Screenwriter David Franzone (and unaccredited Steven Zaillian) combines the disparate intentions of Africans, Americans and Europeans, intensifying the complex issues of human rights struggle. The struggle is still misrepresented by contemporary media. In *USA Today* one political pundit led the effort to besmirch *Amistad*'s challenge, attacking the film (through the publicity study guide DreamWorks has made available to educators) as "warped" and "misleading." In advance of *Amistad*'s release, a benighted wag in the *New*

*York Daily News* panicked: "the inevitable pomposity and guilt-mongering [...] will follow." False prediction and bad thinking. As a result, *Amistad*—the most talk-worthy pop movie in years—is sinking from public discussion the way *Titanic* should have. Apparently, 34 years after the Civil Rights Act, exasperated Americans, white and Black, have learned to ignore or defend their prejudices against even Spielberg's seductive, confrontational skill.

By dramatizing the first civil rights victory in the United States—the 1839 struggle for autonomous recognition of 53 Africans abducted into slavery then fought over in court by various professed owners and punishers—Spielberg has taken a popular artist's boldest risk: telling a story most Americans don't want to understand (what many would confine as a Black story) in the belief it should be a shared experience. To wit: his proven entertainer's instincts have been amply defied by *Amistad*'s equivocal and hostile reviews and a few baffled viewers. They miss the film's immediate marvels—vivid recreations of history and simple elucidation of recondite legal maneuvers. Right off it's more serious than most mainstream movies dare to be—boldly reimagining history just as D.W. Griffith reinterpreted the Civil War (*The Birth of a Nation*), the Huguenot massacre (*Intolerance* (1916)) and the French Revolution (*Orphans of the Storm*).

Few contemporary filmmakers display the ability or the audacity to survey current concerns through a historical lens and Spielberg's effort is compounded by the contentious element of race—a political contrast, not a scientific fact—that he wastes no time arguing. Spielberg's personal response to this tale—his need to clarify the confusions of racial politics—makes it great. It is perhaps the only recent American movie to subvert the standard hegemonies of popular discourse for a transcendent p.o.v. (It isn't commonly understood that Spielberg's serious love of cinema diverges from standard Hollywood hegemony.) Refusing what Edward Said once called "the security blanket of history, literature and the humanities," Spielberg expresses a personal vision of man's struggle to free himself from ideological constraints—an endeavor of conscience, his (and Griffith's) great theme.

Griffith first realized cinema's ability to reconfigure historical perception and though the controversy has never ceased (ask Oliver Stone) audiences are still uncomfortable with such modernist challenges to orthodoxy. Many critics and viewers seem less sophisticated than Spielberg about distinguishing art from history. Both are retellings, both fabrications, but Spielberg aspires to emotional persuasion while historians pretend to control fact. This distinct artistic endeavor can sometimes grasp difficult, elusive truths; it keeps *The Birth of a Nation* relevant (the first great American movie; it opens significantly with a reenactment of the slave trade) while leaving *Amistad* (the first great American movie to signify a hero's distinct African origins) little appreciated.

Evoking other film legends, Spielberg's identification with *Amistad*'s history may be more intimate than *Schindler's List*. It proves a kind of American showbiz miracle (a spiritual leap of faith like the one Indiana Jones makes in *The Last Crusade*) that is also a political miracle. Nominally a white Jewish-American and a leading media broker, Spielberg is expected to function in the interest of self-identified groups and empowered peers—the casual point of reference commonly used in "socially aware" movies like *Quiz Show* (1994), *L.A. Confidential* (1997), *Dances with Wolves* (1990). But it's in the transmutation of ideas into expressive imagery and evocative drama, the interplay between Black and white consciousness, that *Amistad* is most powerful—and enduring. Its seriousness is inseparable from its kinetic effects, which include using courtroom theatrics (light streams from windows, mixed physiognomies) for the exposition of ethical issues buried in history and politics (court summaries as living, vibrant philosophy). *Amistad*'s images from the first shipboard scenes to the closing Supreme Court argument go from visceral climax to intellectual climax, two kinds of dynamism expressing a development of emotion—the African's mysterious revenge to the politician's equally mysterious (almost religious) patriotism. These contrasting night and day sequences bookend the film, reflecting the rights of self-defense and finding their basis in American constitutional principles. Spielberg's familiarly vibrant style grows here into an astounding lucidity. Beginning and ending sequences convey more than one point—in the manner of Griffith's multileveled *Intolerance* that trusted an earlier audience's intelligence and offered more ideas (more centers of interest) beyond its primary plot. As Godard has suggested, "Cinema was made to be thought about but that has been forgotten."

This exhilarating complexity arises from an artistic grandeur that David Denby in *New York Magazine*, resisting the emotional sway of the politically impassioned imagery, called "almost intolerable"—referring to the opening that Spielberg insists be appreciated more complexly than for shock value. Those who limit Spielberg to excitation disregard the import of *Amistad*'s opening scene—mistaking the energy and impact of stirring images with base motives or, in Denby's term, mere "monumentality."

Without fabricating documentary realism, Spielberg breaks through the charade of biased reporting. His stirred-up action evokes resources of subconscious knowledge, culturally-learned apprehension and stereotype (history's residue). In the political cybermag *Slate*, this scene of Cinque's colossus-stance was compared to *King Kong*—a highly subjective and dubious reading of Black oppression as racist anthropomorphism (mawkish "sympathy" favored by sanctimonious white liberals). But Spielberg's sequence can absorb such insensitivity by simply surpassing it. The opening is not a perverse, camp metaphor, but a vision of that very shock, the Black anger and revenge Griffith inculcated but would not permit. It has particular resonance in O.J. America utterly without *King Kong*'s aspect and that is part of its job. Spielberg goes past adolescent thrill and the superficial frisson of different races clashing; he realizes that recognizing the difference is a matter of putting one's own identity in context rather than holding it as the pretext for understanding.

"Slaves are not grateful for their freedom!" Black Hollywood actor Rex Ingram bellowed as the Djinn of the *Arabian Nights* in the 1940 *Thief of Bagdad*—released seven years before Spielberg was born but a beloved children's fantasy film ever since. Ingram's declaration evidently stuck with Spielberg who now repeats the Djinn's colossus stance, stouthearted exuberance and pride. That was a fabled image but Spielberg radicalizes his childhood awe, turning every moviegoer's affection for Ingram's Djinn—the genie who must grant his boyish master three wishes before gaining freedom—into a cultural appreciation. Cinque is endowed with the Black history and awareness Spielberg learned since first seeing *Thief of Bagdad*—this is not stereotyping, it's consciousness.

Morgan Freeman's abolitionist character Theodore Joadson (possibly named after Spielberg's adopted Black son) is one kind of hero—sage, circumspect with an unforgettable scene where the memory of slavery breaks his own confidence— but Cinque out-does Joadson. Existing in terms of pop art excitement, he represents honor, dignity, and heroism with sweet, sensual exhilaration. Cinque's image is the kind of thing a father may well think a contemporary young Black man may need to know—not a sop to hip-hop iconography but an enlightened pop myth. He's an exemplar of how to stand as tall as Rex Ingram's magisterial Djinn, how to hold himself upright and acquit himself justly. That image is part of the humane appreciation Spielberg believes is inextricable from the wonder and fascination of that great social art form, the movies. Going from the Djinn's benign spirit to Cinque's wrathful man demonstrates Spielberg's need to evolve film fantasy into serious truth. If you're with him, *Amistad* flies higher than a magic carpet.

How does a pop filmmaker return a democratic form to its democratic principles? *Amistad* engages that problem by addressing historical troubles with film art—truth and beauty on imaginative wings. Four years ago a critic said Spielberg was venting anger in *Schindler's List*—an absurd proposition that reveals the reviewer's particular animus. The most credible objections raised to *Amistad* have been by Black filmgoers who avoid seeing it because they "don't want to get angry." But the film's superb development of ideas and emotion works against superficial reflexes. John Singleton's trivializing race-riot history *Rosewood* (1997) gets you angry through the realistic abuse and fantastic revenge but *Amistad* does more than simply redress historical wrongs. Those white-Black handshakes at the end are not facile suggestions of brotherhood (nor anything so bland as detente) but a grown-up representation of the humane understanding Spielberg memorably explored in *E. T.*—for those who are themselves understanding.

Just as *Amistad*'s story moves from threat to promise, it is ambivalent enough to always infuse one with the other—the promise in Cinque's violent release at the beginning, threat in his unknowable voyage home at the end. There's no propaganda between those poles, but room enough—emotion enough—to recognize history's significance without claiming ownership.

*First of the Month*
February 1998

# *Against the Hollywood Grain*

**R**IGHTEOUS BLOOD-SPILLING—THE OPENING jolt of Steven Spielberg's *Amistad*—is less Biblical rage than a new kind of pop fury. You're gripped by the teasing master of *Jaws* and the *Indiana Jones* and *Jurassic Park* movies, but it's not a joke. This is the blood that esteemed independent filmmaker Haile Gerima wouldn't dare let flow in his slavery epic *Sankofa*—slaveholders' blood, white folks' blood. And the scene of Cinque, the abducted African played by Djimon Hounsou, digging a nail out of a ship floorboard to free himself evokes the most harrowing detail of "Can't Truss It," the Public Enemy rap song about slavery: "Blood in the wood and it's mine." But *Amistad*, which details the political machinations and spiritual urges surrounding an 1839 bloodbath, forgoes the anger expected when contemporary artists visit historical atrocity. These primal images are born of American racial psychic armature. When Cinque slowly pulls sword out of white-shirted body, Spielberg's uptilted image is heroicizing, mythic (of course), but also analytical. Going beyond PE's ire and Gerima's reticence, Spielberg's story of 53 Africans abducted into slavery, then fighting for autonomous recognition in an American court, awakens a deeper response to history and offers a clarified understanding that is so fresh it's breathtaking—and misunderstood.

Of the great movies disrespected in their time, *Amistad* is among the most entertaining and conscientious—and perhaps, in that combination, the most American. Yet that is the first block to its critical acceptance. Spielberg works in a lost, grand tradition that assumes the ability to address pop audiences seriously—a mandate some suspect due to the very factionalism and escapism this hopeful, rather than simply uplifting, movie seeks to repair. Yet it would seem that our great storyteller has chosen a story that end-of-century Americans refuse to understand.

Spielberg's virtuous technique and intellectual daring are not only unappreciated on this subject, they may be unwanted. Race screws up Americans. Since it is so fundamental to the way we live, bringing up the subject spoils the illusion—the party—of most Hollywood movies. Hence the reception of *Amistad* has differed markedly from the *Schindler's List* spectacle, where the entire apparatus of the American media— newspapers, magazine, TV shows, critics, politicians, editorial writers, educators—rose together in one horseshit hosanna. I choose a harsh term in response to those pompous reviewers who, in 1993, twisted their unrelenting disdain for Spielberg the boy-wonder into obeisance for his subject matter on that occasion. Because film aesthetics didn't enter into their consideration of *Schindler's List* (the praise was politically motivated), because they didn't really understand what made Spielberg an artist, supporters of that film's "humanism" and "historical consciousness" have no entry into *Amistad*, despite its exemplifying the most sophisticated Humanist expression in Hollywood history. If *Schindler's List* benefited from current concern about what the Germans knew and the Poles knew, here's a case of Americans knowing and not caring.

To clarify Spielberg's achievement in *Amistad*—and why he has grown to improve on *Schindler's List*—it's first important to note his daring. Artists of his caliber rarely attempt historical subjects. *Amistad*'s closest modern-day comparisons would include Roberto Rossellini's *Le prise de pouvoir de Louis XIV* (1966), Renoir's *La Marseillaise* (1938), and the Tavianis' *Allonsanfàn* (1974). Spielberg, like Altman with *Buffalo Bill and the Indians*, goes against the American grain by using his craft to redress American ignorance. He has thus provoked a cynical Nineties irritation—dismissed, in *The New York Times*' disingenuous terms, as a "civics lesson," and ridiculed by Ebert and Siskel as "talky."

In fact, the last time an American made a civic-minded movie as rich as *Amistad*, movies *were* silent. D.W. Griffith's historical pageants were poetic distillation of his contemporary concerns, romantic evocations of historical settings always aimed at affecting modern behavior and current circumstances. Each period tale in *Intolerance*—the decline of Babylon, the Christ story, the Huguenot massacre, all historically based— was not simply juxtaposed but fed congruently into the issues acted out in the fictional modern-day "The Mother and the Law" segment that made poverty, labor strikes, temperance leagues and urban rootlessness unforgettably vivid. This was 1916, before Hollywood institutionalized the idea of movies as nonserious entertainment, mere "product" made without the humanist and social passion that was key to Griffith's artistry. An intuition for historical continuity explains *Intolerance*'s majestic, time-shifting parallel edits just as in *Way Down East* the cut from Lillian Gish in danger to Richard Barthelmess' psychic alarm demonstrated Griffith's sense of humane continuity.

*Amistad*'s first radical transition is edited just as purposefully: from the eyes of an African child weeping behind bars in Massachusetts to the eyes of a doll reflected in silverware that, with a tilt, reflects the eyes of the child monarch Isabella II of Spain (Anna Paquin). That contrast carries a sense of the different fates in world history; its audacity begins to complicate the different points of view in the story being told. Spielberg's technique sometimes goes right past those viewers unprepared to recognize how amazingly he compresses complex information. When legal arguments are framed contesting the ownership of the Africans being held in an American prison, the source of the dispute has already been elegantly set forth. As the main characters' drama moves forward, so does historicity—an interpretation of events through adroit, telling images. Isabella II, age 12, isn't old enough to have initiated the slave trade, so it's shown that her comfortable position (like those distanced Nineties folk who claim no responsibility for the past) allows her the privilege of seeing to slavery's—and racism's—continuance.

Using such child-figures as a human essence (Isabella's bed romping is an Eisensteinian jape) remains a controversial part of Spielberg's filmmaking, especially for those who hold "youth" synonymous with "triviality." Children may be Spielberg's sympathetic fetishes, his personal mementos of innocent experience or experience misunderstood (as in the first third of *The Color Purple* where numerous children swarm the homestead, their innocence sought again by the adult sisters at the end of the film); yet his child figures, far from the saccharine typage of conventional movies, add depth. Critics often miss this. And a similar sentimentality cues a more unfortunate objection to Spielberg's presentation of the Other. Having characterized the Amistad Africans and singled out Cinque—they are among the figures he presents and so are part of the human experience he is interested in exploring—Spielberg makes questions about legitimate author-identification or condescension irrelevant. *Amistad* differs from films that presume a nonspecific American authority yet take a white point of view for granted. Spielberg refuses a claim on this particular historical moment by more subtly raising the issue of nationhood and individual sovereignty. From the circumlocutions regarding the African characters' identity, Spielberg discovers their background and origin, which for an American-bred cineaste means dramatizing their sense of alienation. This informed perspective was easier to take when trivialized in the sci-fi message movie *Alien Nation* (1988), but Spielberg and screenwriters David Franzoni and Steven Zaillian maintain a serious focus. In *Amistad*, the Other is no longer alien; we participate in the Other's feelings of dislocation, abuse and yearning. Given this, it is naive to ask for a more subjective presentation of the black African experience—Spielberg's passion is in connection, the transferal of empathy. In the quietly enthralling night scene of Black Africans gliding by white Americans in separate boats, *Amistad* shifts awareness between the different experiences. From African child to European queen, from American president Martin Van Buren (Nigel Hawthorne) to another, John Quincy Adams (Anthony Hopkins), then eventually interrelating community and national figures and the general feeling of fraternity.

But look sharp: *Amistad* is a movie of confrontations. It is not about "brotherhood," the convenient, often hypocritical bromide that makes *The Defiant Ones* (1958), *Cry Freedom* (1987), *Lethal Weapon* (1987) and *One Night Stand* (1997) incredible. That opening shipboard uprising powerfully announces a vigorous series of democratic clashes: Adams' wily congressional sparring; Cinque's baiting his counsel Roger Baldwin (Matthew McConaughey); John C. Calhoun (Arliss Howard) threatening Van Buren; between Black and white abolitionists (Morgan Freeman and Stellan Skarsgård), and between Cinque and Adams. These are fundamental showdowns, conciliations—but not, significantly, reconciliations—proving that a nation of immigrants must also be a nation of aliens. Divided by their own imperatives, these characters still are forced to face each other. Their safest recognition will be of a common fate such as moves the story from the sea to the courts. Yet *Amistad*, though largely acted out in courts, is not a courtroom drama.

Spielberg boldly elevates one of the more ingrained genre expectations: that a court story must be weighted with suspense. Defenders of *Titanic* insist that knowing the ending isn't important, but Spielberg, working more seriously, understands that the recorded outcome of the *Amistad* trials doesn't place an ending on his story. The court scenes open out the issues beyond 1839 into the moral context of human confrontation—Cinque's future and ours. So, while little tension is obtained about the courts' decisions, we attend to the politics behind them, absorbing the filmmakers' fascination with the interplay of language and phenomenon, motive and principle.

*Amistad* is played entirely with a sense of paradox—wonder alternating with certainty. Problems of the American past cast shadows on modern race matters through Spielberg's dual consciousness about what is to be done with this disputatious legacy. *Amistad* offers no solution to the race problem, but a stunningly sensible approach: the prodigious depiction of several cultures, languages and dialects intermixing in the New World. To help lawyer Baldwin communicate with Cinque, the team of abolitionists pace the port town searching for a translator by counting aloud in Minde. The fleet sequence is an enlightening tour of early American multiculturalism, ending with Theodore Joadson (Freeman) walking past a group of white sailors. Hollywood convention leads one to expect harassment—another director might seek a cheap show of tension—but from the midst of that quartet steps Kai Nyagua (Chiwetel Ejiofor), a Black sailor from the same African region as Cinque, who hears Freeman's stilted numerals as a voice from home. He has Anglicized his name to James Covey, but the look of reunion on Nyagua's face gives the film's first suggestion of rootedness, a mini-ballet of diaspora.

It is only on land that translation becomes an issue in *Amistad*. Louis Althusser could dress up the reason as based in colonialism's need of communication for trade and law, but the main thing is, it's dramatically potent. On the sea, on the slave ships, African languages are disenfranchised according to the western mode. Spielberg isn't repeating this prejudice—by first translating only Spanish, he actually exposes it. What his audience immediately knows, or can understand visually, is the African experience. Subtitles would be impertinent, an imperialist trope. Even without that false key, these first scenes are emotionally articulate, universal—as Griffith, a silent filmmaker, understood.

We have never seen African slaves characterized before (in Hollywood); it takes imagination. For the majority of Cinque's dialogue and narration, Spielberg trades the voice of Nyagua, making *Amistad* immanently about translated experience. That's what's so numbskullish about reviewers' complaints that the Africans are not dramatized but remain "savage" (*New York Daily News*) or "inhuman" (*Time Out).* In fact, all their behavior carries a sense of civilization and custom. One of the most startling scenes is a prison-yard argument over territory showing the Africans divided among themselves into tribal organizations. To persist thinking this is savagery shows film critics chained to the prejudiced insensitivities of Hollywood's past. It's far less perceptive than the Africans' first sight of dour white American missionaries singing "Amazing Grace," described as "entertainers" and "miserable looking." This sense of an African perspective is a major shift in Western storytelling. (African and European rituals are also linked in a funeral scene.) Spielberg forces critics, privileged customers of a narcissistic, racist film culture, to realize the details of alienation.

In the Civil Rights Era, well-meant movies like *To Kill a Mockingbird* (1962) used a simplistic emotional appeal borrowed from the high melodrama of the classic abolitionist narrative *Uncle Tom's Cabin.* But *Amistad* is probably the first American movie to take a truly intellectual approach to understanding the slave trade—not just slavery. Doing so through literacy and language—making lucid the misunderstanding of Africans, Spaniards, Americans, slaveholders, and legislators—is, for the most kinetically inclined of modern filmmakers, a peculiar approach to the peculiar institution. After the first trial verdict is held up and Baldwin apologizes for the law's intricacy, Nyagua explains, "There is no word for 'should,' You either do what you say or you don't." Nations betray themselves in their language, and lives languish in its traps. The same applies for cinema, though that may be a little highbrow for the cineplexes.

*Amistad* demands viewers focus their attention, their casual visual savvy, and finally recognize that blunt appeals to emotion (usually sorrow and pity) don't work. *Amistad* should not be confused with a guilt trip—Spielberg gives little time to the perfidy of the assault on Baldwin when leaving the courthouse, or the scene where he shows the death-threat mail he's received. The director cools out the fouled-up contemporary rhetoric on race through meticulous, redemptive imagery. Echoing Charles Burnett's *Nightjohn* (1996), Baldwin scrawls pictographs in the dirt to find out Cinque's origin—a brilliant display of communication, including the double utterance of dialogue, to signify their rapport. It's reminiscent of *E.T.*, when Cinque trudges away from Baldwin's crude map and walks a distance to proclaim, "This is how far I've come." The mists (myths) of history and ignorance stand between them. In these scenes Baldwin's and Cinque's need of each other importantly reworks the grotesque moment in *A Time to Kill* (1996) where a Black prisoner got off a hate speech separating himself from McConaughey—Grisham's? Schumacher's? misconception of Black dignity as something apart from human dignity. *Amistad* shames such misunderstanding by forcing our impoverished cinematic language to expand and explain history.

All efforts to clarify the personhood of the Africans lead to the soul struggle of each character. Their language, their testimony is key to telling their stories and revealing—discovering—their souls. With this knowledge, Spielberg divides *Amistad* into three trials. Only a gifted storyteller could accomplish such a strategy this smoothly. Instead of deteriorating into what Adams calls "an exercise in the vagaries of legal minutiae," the dandily precise screenplay and serene pacing keep attention peaked with a fastidious command of this least popular topic.

"Whoever tells the best story wins," as one character describes court procedure. The matter here is conflicting legal claims. Spielberg has chosen a series of historical events that distills the querulous subject to its essence. 1$^{st}$ court: sets out the Problem. 2$^{nd}$ court: transforms the circumstances into Story. 3$^{rd}$ court penetrates the narrative for a consideration of its Morality.

By exploring slavery as property-holding, an obscene diminishment of humanity, the argument is raised about ethical debate—the usual matter of Southern vs. Northern custom or agrarian vs. industrial methods. In the misbegotten *Rosewood*, John Singleton missed how property holds the imagination as the special prerogative of every ambitious individual or nation-state. Only our Westerns have approached this idea; *Amistad* demonstrates it as an American absolute—what, for some, is never to be questioned. Yet Spielberg exposes this capitalist faith. Even his introduction of former President John Quincy Adams asleep during a congressional session is situated around finance: James Smithson's effort to institute a national treasury. Despite lip service paid to being a country of men governed by laws, our national mythology offers little actual cinematic representation of the rules by which men live. *Amistad* is a rare American example of dialectical visual drama. Its precedents are all exotic: the Senegalese *Camp de Thiaroye* (1988) by Ousmane Sembene, the Italian *Le mani sulla città* (1963) by Francesco Rosi, where the politically engaged filmmakers conduct their humanist interest through political discussion—images of courtroom galleys bustling with citizenry or court participants entering an arena that focuses their dilemmas outside it.

Each of these films centers on a social catastrophe that throws individual conscience into relief; they hail from cultures that required each artist assess his position regarding history and contemporary politics—what to American filmmakers is extraneous. Sembene's characters invoke a history of colonial oppression and resistance; Rosi's are schematized into the oppositions of distinct political parties. Nothing wrong with that, but Spielberg chooses the former model. Sembene's Third World capacity to infuse discrete characterizations with social reality—a development away from the doctrinaire approach Italian leftists brought to neorealism—informs Spielberg's multicultural fiction. Making films about history (*Indiana Jones and the Last Crusade*), ethnicity (*Schindler's List*), and personal responsibility (*The Color Purple, Empire of the Sun*), Spielberg acquired sensitivity that sets his work apart from conventional Hollywood entertainment. Those films—but not only those—represent the moral demands integral to his artistic vision.

It's an insult to regard this new form of drama as a civics lesson (besides, what country could need it more?). Ethical imperatives, placing importance on court proceedings, make the legal action intense, more than minutiae. As presented— argued—these characters resist fixed dioramic positions. On the witness stand, Cinque is stymied when questioned about his own culture's slave customs. His inquisitor (Pete Postlethwaite) holds him to the same ethical examination as the European slave traders ("It all comes down to money, here or there"). This incisive probe doesn't mitigate Cinque's claim to freedom but condenses the entire slavery institution to hard economics in Postlethwaite's six hard syllables "Slave-Production-Money." (An echo of the powerful "Molasses to Rum to Slaves" song in the Declaration of Independence musical *1776*.) Drama and politics are made inseparable unless you reject one in order to disavow the other. But rather than refute *Amistad*'s scoffers, it's best to notice what they ignore: a cleaner form of drama.

Spielberg stages subsequent court sessions to build upon insights of the first. As much as Sembene and Rosi got their aesthetics from crucial social events (post-colonial liberation, post-WWII chaos), it is likely that *Amistad*'s legal emphasis derives from the impact of the O.J. Simpson trial on the American pop imagination and the country's racial psyche. (Proof of the importance of this modern-day Dreyfus affair is collected in *Birth of a Nation'hood*, an anthology edited by Toni Morrison in which this critic participated.) For reviewers to claim boredom at the prospect of race-on-trial denies the truth of the recent past (when people say they're bored with the Simpson trial—dismissing the case itself—it usually just means their capacity for dealing with the intricacies of law, crime, race, wealth is exhausted). *Amistad* brings back the shock of that case's issues through the succession of trials and two imprudent suggestions: "Juries can be dismissed," said when the first trial upsets President Van Buren's reelection prospects. And further panic: "Perhaps the judge will recuse himself," then "I think we should go further and dismiss the judge." Spielberg understands the significance of this judicial turnabout and satirizes it: The historic moment deciding a new judge's appointment is commemorated as a milestone of media manipulation—from a portrait photographer's p.o.v. it is seen as topsy-turvy.

These intrusions into legal process normally provoke pessimism, but Spielberg adduces them, then moves on—to spiritual expectation. His effort hinges on the most powerful courtroom moment, Cinque's cry "Give us, Us Free." This outburst releases Cinque's frustration and tension from the second trial's wearying, disorienting atmosphere. Pieced together from his rudimentary understanding of a new language (new law), the broken, desperate, exact words push human need forward to modernity. The word "Free" anticipates the concept of "freedom," that most poignant word of the Civil Rights movement. Not to lose this remarkable conflation, it is underscored with John Williams' direct musical cue— an inherent part of melodrama. Critics' fashionable distaste regards this sequence as manipulation, but it's something more ineffable—passion.

Panache describes the daring ideological montage of *Amistad*'s second trial. The Catholic judge (Jeremy Northam), appointed because he is thought to be cowed by religious prejudice, weighs his own principles against political patronage. At the same time, the African Yamba (Razaaq Adoti) discloses to Cinque a Bible he was given by one of those "entertainers," the abolitionist-missionaries. "This is just a story," Cinque says to Yamba, who sees it as more, and Spielberg elucidates those yearnings of liberation within the complexities of Christian ideology. Some mistake the film's tacit approval of religious teaching for proselytizing, despite the tough-mindedness proved when Baldwin first advances a claim-processor's position. His abolitionist-client (Skarsgård) insists on the moral a high ground, using Christ-among-the-Pharisees as a justification, but Baldwin coolly, smoothly prompts the analogy: "Christ lost."

It's not scripture Yamba shows Cinque, but the interleaved illustrations that visually reify its story; and Spielberg shows how these images parallel the Africans' liberation mission. "Their people have suffered more than ours… Then he was born… Everywhere he goes, he is followed by the sun… He could also walk across the sea… This is where we're going when they kill us." Each description accompanied by a condign image creates resonant parallels with the religious and social histories of persecution. This knowledge raises the intellectual level of the second trial's narrative. Not even the letters sequence in *The Color Purple* was as audacious. Contrasting politics and faith, it recalls the prayer montage from *Patton* (1970) ("Grant us fair weather for battle") that anticipated Coppola's baptism-slaughter montage in *The Godfather*. Spielberg's use of counterpoint is not sacrilegious but actually just more sophisticated (Griffith dared as much in *Intolerance*), reconfiguring notions of indoctrination, supplication, and reason. Yamba's personal interpretation of white theology—the source of liberation rhetoric in Negro spirituals—is joined to the Irish judge's personal practice as he goes to church, kneels and meditates on his decision. While other filmmakers don't think through such broad details, Spielberg goes all the way to their universal reach. In an uncanny juxtaposition, both men are seen making the sign of the cross—the judge over his heart, Yamba in the air. By this Spielberg suggests that a story equals a prayer; indeed, the judge is heard praying on soundtrack—an ideational flourish besting *The Godfather*'s baptism-slaughter finale. Extending the crucifix image into the sight of slave-and-trade-ship masts hovering over the roofs of the town mixes both salvation and dread with a pragmatism any historian should envy. Aversion to the magnitude of these courtroom sequences—like Ebert-and-Siskel's—seems a form of cinema illiteracy. It misses out on the emotional power of ideas, law, and history, wrapped in the beauty of spiritual aspiration.

Cinque's relating how he came to be in America—his tale of the Middle Passage—gives *Amistad* privileged identification (the sufferer's point of view) some missed in *Schindler's List*. It's placation, but with a difference—Djimon Hounsou is heroically beautiful. When *New York Magazine* groused that Hounsou is "monumentalized to a nearly intolerable degree," the adjective "intolerable" reveals what Spielberg is up against. He respects the actor's person—Hounsou is not a Riefenstahl Nubian but a living example of what was long denied by Hollywood glamour. After the first verdict is reneged, Hounsou fires Cinque's beauty into challenge, "What kind of place is this where you almost mean what you say!" At this moment, Joadson (Morgan Freeman) looks shocked to recognize Cinque's anger as his own. Stripped naked before the fire (next time, as James Baldwin would imagine), Hounsou's a more alarming figure than at the film's beginning. Both times Cinque's wrath is exceptional. Unlike the currently favored image of Black remorselessness, Samuel L. Jackson, we see life's force in Cinque's insurrection. (Silly complaints that Freeman isn't given enough to do shows an unwillingness to accept more than one commanding Black screen figure. Besides, the scene where Joadson goes below the Amistad deck and falls back into his chains reveals the psychic damage of slavery shattering a grown man's confidence. Freeman's cracked-voice call for "light!" more than makes up for his eating shit in *The Power of One* (1992) and toadying to Miss Daisy.) Tall, like Teddy Pendergrass, with strongly placed features, Cinque's sly looks to Joadson while directing his story to the entire room of listeners signals a warm, crafty intelligence. In him, Spielberg secures the emotional essence of history.

Watching Cinque's face as he recounts how he was kidnapped from Sierra Leone and listening to Nyagua's rapt voice is like falling off a cliff in a dream, slipping into history. Taking viewers into America's more horrific story—the one glossed over in most school textbooks—Spielberg transforms an individual tale into a shared experience. These images—an infant raised above the packed, tortured bodies in the ship's hold, the wet sound of blood flying off a whip, the chain of slaves pushed to their deaths in the sea, then sinking before our eyes into our memory—are deeply sorrowful, shocking and, when beautiful, awesome. That slave-drowning, replete with a music box's tinkling, countermands the white solipsism implicit in the underwater scene of Jane Campion's spoiled-feminist *The Piano* (1993)—a poetic revelation. Since slavery, unlike the Holocaust, is aggressively denied by conservative editorialists who think we should move beyond discussing it, Spielberg knows he must give the subject new potency and new images like that mysterious, from-the-bottom-of-the-sea perspective. We go beneath history's surface where terrible truth floats down to us—lost knowledge, history's secrets no longer forgotten.

In the third court where Adams makes his defense oration, *Amistad* is as pristine as John Ford's *The Sun Shines Bright* (1953); the trial is now mainly words and purest emotion through Hopkins' musical delivery. This performance, even cannier than his Richard Nixon, starts out irascible but grows gently into something rarely seen—humble wisdom. He has Schindlerian dignity, but it's not a matter of that reverse-fascist complaint—making a white man the hero. Adams achieves his stature only after measuring himself by the examples of other men—his father whose likeness he approaches in a row of busts, Joadson to whom he makes the plea, "What is their story?" but mainly Cinque. Adams' speech invokes the film's astonishing opening as a courageous feat and makes the undeniable revisionist assertion that if Cinque were white, he'd be festooned with medals. "Our children, because we would make sure of it, would know his name." In Adams' summary the film takes stock of patriotism. His red-rimmed eyes seem tired, as weary as the nation that has forgotten its promises and its potential. But by the end of his litany, when Cinque looks at Adams with clear eyes that widen in Arabian serifs, you can see Adams sparked, revived by humanism. Adams' acknowledgement "that our individuality, which we so, so revere, is not entirely our own. Who we are is who we were" is not homily, but central to the way *Amistad* looks into the soul of history. When Adams rejects the secessionist/slaveholder argument—ripping it in a theatrical demonstration of the Constitution's abuse—his declaration for "the last battle of the American Revolution" is justly heroic. Like Spielberg's post-Capra judicial procedurals, he preserves the idea of court, of ethical code. He's found the idea—the poetry— in law. The benedictory sequence that follows—a panoply of farewell confrontations—represents Spielberg's most vivacious portraiture. As Cinque presses his gratitude first to Adams, then to Joadson and Baldwin, his smile says what Alec Guinness sang as Prince Feisal in *Lawrence of Arabia* (1962), "You must be a general, I must be a king," and Rex Ingram as the Djinn in *The Thief of Bagdad:* "A slave is not grateful for his freedom!" The explanations and discussions, politics and politricks, that have gone before are made flesh—in the way the men look at each other—and then spirit, as each sees into the other's soul. Which is how a critic once described Griffith's close-ups of actors.

When the manacles are taken from Cinque's wrists, *Amistad*'s ending complements its opening—an appreciation of being unbound. This differs significantly from how Spike Lee opened and closed *Get on the Bus* (1996), just as *Amistad*'s careful moral reasoning is less wrathful than Chuck D's "Can't Truss It." Plainly a rift has erupted in the attitude of liberal consciousness (a New York journalist recently lamenting the death of liberalism also clocked its "significant other: guilt"), making pop cynicism seem proper. This may explain *Amistad*'s wide disapproval. Given the current fractiousness of social attitudes—so different from the Civil Rights Era when stories of Black-struggle were filmed with general consent—Spielberg's effort to channel righteous anger into understanding finds little agreement. Simply put: We expect less of movies now. Something's out of whack in the various disparagements of *Amistad*—whether Spike Lee's grousing of proprietorship of Black history or Simon Schama's belittling of pop culture. It disregards Spielberg's aim to make us see. Little explains this besides small minds missing the big picture.

As people watch *Titanic* or *Speed* or *L.A. Confidential* or *The Sweet Hereafter* or *Kundun* (1997), do they think they are not being manipulated? What is it, when it comes to Spielberg, that people resent being made to feel? If they hold their own emotions cheap and can give up tears thoughtlessly at a sinking luxury liner, then the real problem must be that they resent being made to think. This betrays Griffith's valiant ambition for the medium as a grand art giving form to large feelings. Spielberg specifically honors that in *Amistad*'s Griffithian coda. Without preaching, the shot of the Lokoto slave fortress being blown apart, pieces of the wall tumbling into the camera, delivers a primal need for hope, belief, and not cynicism. It's as necessary a flourish as *Intolerance*'s coda of children in white celebrating man's harmony. To resolve the music-box-and-torture Middle Passage scene, Spielberg shows president Van Buren tuning a harp rather than leading the assault on an oppressive institution, and yet there's insight here, too. Closing in on Van Buren's harp strings, Spielberg discovers one crucial black chord.

He makes audiences reassess their sense of history with movie-based spectatorial consciousness the same way Adams and Cinque relate to their pasts. Cutting from Cinque's Middle Passage memory to the court full of citizens and claims-stakers makes them all history's monitors, like the present-day audience—witnesses to what has just been vividly realized. One of *Amistad*'s least appreciated marvels is the careful visual strategies Spielberg and cinematographer Janusz Kamiński prepared. Working in color, they nearly desaturate it: A courier bringing Baldwin's letter to Adams rides on horseback past a flock of black, gray and white sheep that symbolizes the film's behavioral spectrum. This is one of the few films to capture the astonishing whiteness of Washington D.C.'s marble structures, but interior scenes, like the shipboard night sequences, are painterly dark—consideration given to the sensitive modeling of faces. Spielberg can't be accused of *Schindler's List*'s specious vérité, or of the prettiness that distracted some from *The Color Purple*. *Amistad* has a moral range of tones—not simply right or wrong but a presentation of mankind's ethical scope and genetic basis with shades of black in everything. Kamiński's photography resurrects the purpose of chiaroscuro: to discern dark and light in a realistic vision. There is more of Spielberg the personal artist here than in *Schindler's List*; that film was produced by Holocaust culture—the aggregate of his ethnic tutelage. This is more from the heart. Spielberg's response to art and injustice—an American tutelage, after all. ("I will call upon my ancestors and they will come, for at this moment I am the very reason they were ever alive at all." Apply that,

Cinque's oath, to fanciful film heritage, the source of his humane, near-flawless technique.) He doesn't heap symbolism on a single case that never asked for it, but expresses his vision of life through this incident—and through movies. The scene of Adams and Cinque admiring an African violet nods to the hothouse scene of *In the Heat of the Night* (1967), totemic of a more liberal political age. When Baldwin announces, "My client's journey began much, much further away," the *E.T.* reference is clear. When the Africans dress in white preparing for their release and journey home, it evokes *Close Encounters* as certainly as Adams' summation echoes *The Wizard of Oz*—and transcends it. None of this is frivolous; it amplifies serious history, sees the profundity in art, in ways most other filmmakers and pop artists only privately admit. What was the point of ever watching any of those movies if we didn't learn to see our responsibility to each other?

This revamped pop approach is exactly what our most popular and rewarded filmmaker owes the world. He knows without grace such erudition as his is worthless. (*Amistad* is as cumulative for Spielberg as *Casualties of War* (1989) was for De Palma.) So, the extratextual appearance of Supreme Court Justice Harry Blackmun reading the final Amistad decision moves this fiction into the realm of actuality. It's time to understand that Spielberg's filmmaking transcends feel-good entertainment. Escapism is no more his intention than it was Griffith's. We need to get back to the recognition of cinema as a medium capable of enlightenment through vision; filmmakers can help us to truly see. This recognition allows Spielberg to answer a question begged by *Schindler's List* and its enormous cultural impact: How does one deal with the world's unrelenting ethical crises? Spielberg has moved so poignantly and effectively toward moral questions at the center of our social and filmgoing lives that those who can't assent, who don't recognize the questions—or the problems—resist. *Amistad* is a better movie than the times deserve.

*Film Comment*
March-April 1998

# Playing the Favorite Atrocity Game

**W**HEN WILL *AMISTAD* get the respectful regard it deserves? Steven Spielberg's dramatic recreation of the 1839 insurrection by African hostages onboard the Spanish slave ship Amistad—the rebellion eventually settled in the U.S. Supreme Court as matter of international law as well as moral conscience—ranks with the most remarkable depictions of evil ever to grace the screen.

And yet the film has suffered a cool commercial and critical reception at odds with Spielberg's faith that the popular audience is ready to attend to the worst of American history. Maybe after *Schindler's List*, Spielberg has exhausted critics' store of humanism.

"There's a big difference between [Spielberg's treatment of slavery and the Holocaust]," argued *New York Newsday*:

> *Schindler's List* drew us into the concentration camp, made us feel through the Jewish characters the terror and indignity of living under a policy of genocide. *Amistad* touches on the fear and anger of the Africans, but only through the eye of the camera and the sympathetic observers.

Meanwhile, *The New York Times* lamented:

> What the estimable *Amistad* does not have is an Oskar Schindler. It has no three-dimensional

major character through whose flawed human nature an unimaginable atrocity can be understood. The *Amistad* slaves remain a mostly undifferentiated group except for Cinque.

These flimsy and specious claims mask something more fundamental. *Amistad*'s lack of appreciation—both by Jewish commentators and Black intellectuals—is a scandal of apathy and suspicion occasioned in part by the provocation of what is superficially perceived as Black history being depicted by a Jewish filmmaker. Both groups are uncomfortable because neither seems to believe any longer in the value of the integrationist principle that Spielberg has exemplified throughout his career. And so what should be the point of solidarity between Black folks and Jewish commentators is only ironically so—in their repudiation of *Amistad*'s affirmation of solidarity.

In this prickly social environment, Spielberg's humanist approach to filmmaking has been coarsely, inappropriately, politicized. Suspiciously, if temporarily, extolled by many Jewish commentators for *Schindler's List*—no doubt for its contribution to Holocaust studies—Spielberg has long found difficult acceptance among Black commentators who distrust white intervention in Black issues. Spielberg has always refused the easy ethnic identification people usually bring to movies and editorial pages. Which is why some consider *E.T.* for children, *Schindler's List* for Jews, and *Amistad* for Blacks, thereby failing to recognize that connecting all those movies is a distinctively spiritual view of human experience.

Spielberg's empathy has been evident in an aesthetic interest that ranges widely—across the philological revision of cultural imperialism in the Indiana Jones series, the romantic evocations of the Black feminist melodrama *The Color Purple*, the psychological dramatic epic *Empire of the Sun*, the fantasy *Close Encounters of the Third Kind* and even the "war" movies (including *Schindler's List*). All these efforts disclose the same utopian acceptance that appears in Spielberg's openness to Jewish, Christian and secular icons and ideas. Even the war films do not posit white heroes against non-white protagonists, as sectarians have argued, but invite audiences to a collective experience of shared tragedy and reciprocal hope.

*Amistad* simply continues this broader spiritual journey. Building upon *Schindler's List*, with its sensitivity to unknown history and human tragedy and connection, *Amistad* extends to Blacks the ethic behind the Holocaust museum. Spielberg's genuineness is proven throughout the movie, particularly in casting Supreme Court Justice Harry Blackmun to read the actual Amistad decision—a conflation of art and reality that connects centuries-old history to the present and provides an irrefutable witness to historical evil.

*Amistad's* signal achievement is to recognize the insurrection—and by implication, slavery—as an international story not just a Black story. The movie holds no truck with historical distortions that see Black appeals for justice as secondary or even chronologically later than others. It is Spielberg's belief in the significance of this history—as well as its relevance not just for Blacks but for the wider community—that raises the issue of Black and Jewish solidarity and commitment. Like another overlooked landmark, *The Crisis of the Negro Intellectual* (Harold Cruse's groundbreaking 1967 study of Black culture and politics), the film insists on recognizing the moral complements that link Blacks and Jews despite their obvious economic and political differences. Even when Blacks and Jews are not directly responsible for each other's history, it is unavoidable that we are still accountable for it—which means paying attention to it, taking part in its modern reception and acknowledgement.

The priceless instance of this leap across the chasm of race, religion and ethnicity in *Amistad* comes in the extraordinary sequence when Cinque (Djimon Hounsou) is shown a Biblical parallel to his own trial. As Spielberg melds the judge's Catholic devotion with the African's introduction to Christianity, the film contains the remarkable captioning of Scriptural illustrations with the line, "Their people suffered more than ours"—a reference to the children of Israel in Egypt and a clear connection between long-time world historical tragedies. By invoking the reference to underscore his transcendent vision, searching for an equivalence of Black and Israelite suffering, Spielberg refuses to play the insulting modernist Favorite Atrocity game.

Of course, not everybody is content with such refusals; they can't let go of the contests of suffering. When *4 Little Girls*, Spike Lee's documentary on the 1964 Birmingham church bombing, lost this year's Academy award to Rabbi Marvin Hier's Holocaust memorial *The Long Way Home* (1997), some enjoyed the repudiation of Lee's self-righteous manipulation of race history. That pleasure should have been fleeting. It could not mask a more alarming fact: the Academy's judgment of which tragedy was more worthy.

Compare the scant notice of *Amistad* with the celebration of *Schindler's List*. This disparity cannot be argued on aesthetic grounds—both films are serious films of quality. And so it seems at least plausible that an institutional dismissal was at work. Movies play a role in sanctifying particular historical events, through the unequal amounts of attention they give. Thus, if it was widely agreed that *Schindler's List* validated the Holocaust, the dismissal of *Amistad* clearly signifies an invalidation of the importance of slavery. The truth is that America's slave history is not a popular topic. The prevailing attitude is to ignore or deny it—similar to the way racists and fascists ignore the Holocaust.

Hollywood has tended to reflect this attitude. Until *Amistad*, the 1977 television miniseries *Roots* remained the only serious film to focus on the issue of the slave trade. Like Herbert Biberman's *Slaves* (1969), Haile Gerima's 1994 *Sankofa* was produced outside the mainstream system; John Berry's *Tamango* (1958) and Gillo Pontecorvo's *Burn!* (1970) were European productions. Even critics who had disparaged Spielberg's talent but praised the gesture represented by *Schindler's List* were less indulgent toward *Amistad*. Disdain for Black experience as significant world politics may have been the impulse or simply the urge to uphold the Holocaust as history's uncontestable atrocity. In either case, *Amistad*'s subject clearly weighed less on their own consciousness.

Spielberg's vision, though incongruous with desperate times, is partly the fulfillment of the difficult modern dream of universal community. And the insufficiency of the Black response makes clear that many Blacks no less than Jews are either frightened or put off by that utopian humanism.

Instead of greeting the first, pro-Black Hollywood film treatment of the slave trade with relief or gratitude, many Blacks in the media and among moviegoers shied away. Some would not associate themselves with Spielberg's compassion. Spike Lee even spoke out against *Amistad* publicly on *Nightline*, lumping it together with the pro-white historical distortions

*Mississippi Burning* and *Cry Freedom*. Although on that same show *Amistad*'s African-American producer Debbie Allen insisted, "I wasn't looking for a white or a Black director," *Washington Post* columnist Courtland Milloy said, "I don't think Steven Spielberg can embrace the pains, trials, tribulations and triumphs of any slave experience the way he was able to do with the Jewish experience." Strangely, not even Henry Louis Gates Jr., thanked in *Amistad*'s end credits, has spoken in favor of the film.

This rejection or suspicion of white benevolence isn't a new phenomenon. More than a decade ago, Spielberg's *The Color Purple* endured criticism from Blacks who distrusted a white director telling a Black story. Martin Ritt, the Jewish director of the exemplary dramas about Black life, *Sounder* (1972) and *Conrack* (1974), got into an argument with Black friends about the latter movie. "They felt I was doing a film about a white Jesus. They were into Black studies and such. And I've been into integration for fifty of my seventy years. I said to them, "Make your own picture, get off my back. This is what I believe in and I'm not violating anything I believe in…"

> I feel deeply about the dilemma of Black people, I always have. Certainly the Blacks in this country have been disenfranchised for most of their lives […] I'm aware of it and very sympathetic toward it and feel that it is one of the most grievous errors we have made in this country. I would like to make another movie about Black people but it would have to be a picture done at a price.

Spielberg is paying the price.

Jewish artists Ritt and Spielberg have demonstrated their conviction in the need to extend ethics, morals and politics beyond the small point of group think and tribal promotion. For their efforts, they were treated by some like traitors. But to whom? To what? Surely limiting artists to subjects experienced by their own social group will get us no closer to understanding art or each other.

Instead, *Amistad* affirms a humanistic vision that is imaginative and passionate enough to make history—and our own responsibility to it—clear. Its very presence epitomizes a Black-Jewish bond without ever sentimentalizing it. It appeals to common human experience, despite deep and superficial differences, and deserves to be recognized as a mighty contribution to American thought. It aims high because Spielberg knows: in suffering we have no solidarity.

*Common Quest*
Summer 1998

# SAVING PRIVATE RYAN (1998)

## Saving Private Ryan

"**R**EALISM" IS THE naive F/X. It's what unsophisticated children and literal-minded adults prize most at the movies—which is why the full metal attack of *Saving Private Ryan* has had stronger response than Spielberg's other, more wondrous films. His prodigious talent recreates World War II battle scenes with devastating impact, but "realism" insults the enormity of this achievement. Spielberg reclaims the profundity of death from the jokey nihilism of innumerable action flicks—and almost from the sanctimony of commemorative public-spirited war films.

Most war movies are implicitly pacifistic. *Saving Private Ryan* isn't merely so: Though it sees the inevitability of war as a separate moral endeavor, the fighting itself goes unhonored; these combat scenes—a slaughter—do the miraculous job of dividing viewers' usually passive sensibilities between the horror and necessity of killing. It's unnerving, and it's the right thing to do. Spielberg doesn't simply raise the stakes of movie violence, but had to leap right over the cheap regard of violence as a thrill. He gets to its spiritual devastation—the truth that his war movie benefactors Griffith, Ford, Welles, Renoir, Kurosawa, Fuller, Peckinpah and Huston were too dumbstruck by the effects of war to articulate as fully.

My experience is unable to confirm that *Saving Private Ryan* gets what war is really like, but no sane person seeing this movie will want to see another human being die onscreen again. Spielberg closes up the safe distance between art and emotion—that's why people have often confused the sheer marvel and elation of his comedies and adventure films with hackwork. They think it's easy. The historical contexts of his dramas allow people to seriously appreciate his suasion, but if they respond to *Saving Private Ryan* beyond the gut level, they won't live easily with its power.

Through his preeminent populist gifts, Spielberg expands and contracts the World War II narrative, telling both mini and macro stories: after Capt. Miller's (Tom Hanks) weary D-day campaign, his platoon gets a special, symbolic assignment to find innocent young Pvt. James Ryan (Matt Damon), the last alive of four brothers who enlisted in the war. Miller has been instructed to rescue Ryan from the European theater and return him home safely to his mother. The story balances poignancy and suspense and patriotism so efficiently it's difficult to comprehend the extent of Spielberg's breakthrough, or to trust its influence will last.

Precarious advances in moral sensibility (Altman's *M\*A\*S\*H*, Jacques Demy's *Lola* (1962)) often get assimilated and degraded in the pop onslaught. And war movies are just banal enough to be acclaimed (*Newsweek*'s puff-piece cover story announced "War is Hell!"). This has put Spielberg back in the good graces of people who don't understand his artistry. Only seven months ago, the brave, brilliant *Amistad* got him castigated for innovating an intellectual pop cinema and even daring to bring up racism and slavery. Now, without a single Black face onscreen—or an historical reinterpretation that might challenge the way people politick—Spielberg is receiving the best press of his career. But in gaining a moviemaker laureate, we lose an American original, an exuberant, big-league maverick.

I'm torn between awe and reservation because *Saving Private Ryan*'s reconstituted, all-white view of the world comes close to how Hollywood used to be before Spielberg's humor (*Jaws*), spiritual openness (*Close Encounters*) and kinetic dynamism (his entire oeuvre) turned American genre movies unexpectedly profound. The credit he gets for *Saving Private Ryan* amounts to the same dubious honor as *Schindler's List* being praised by Holocaust devotees in spite of his signature: It's all a reactionary distaste for Spielberg's mysterious private gestures, his transfiguring social instinct. Understand me: No way is *Saving Private Ryan* a bad movie. But it's in danger of being subsumed within cultural orthodoxy like a great piece of apple pie.

For the first time, Spielberg indulges vulgar Americana. Pvt. Ryan's calendar-art mom and Iowa home are viewed in polite measure, at moderate pace. Too elegant to be offensive, it skirts condescension; but previously, Spielberg would have trusted audiences to find goodness in a scrappy, tumultuous—maybe abject—urban or suburban American homestead. This emblematic sequence is Norman Rockwell-esque, but not an improvement on traditional sentimentality. It's touching rather than poetic: As War Office news of the dead Ryan brothers travels from East Coast bureaucracy to Midwest domesticity, the route seems predictable, which wasn't true of the missives sent through circuitous distances and a network of tangled motives to their fated destinations in *The Color Purple* and *Amistad*. Spielberg monitors fate dramatically— second only to

De Palma—but having defended his genius against detractors and other celebrants-after-the-fact, this hackneyed homespun sequence just doesn't feel like the moment to rejoice. It's bland even though it's likely to shake most Americans to their knees.

The (previous) best American war movies (*The Steel Helmet* (1951), *Glory, The Red Badge of Courage* (1951)) dared to question victory; it's usually done by tempering celebration or doubting the nationalist effort. *Saving Private Ryan* (like John Milius' *Rough Riders* (1997)) avoids doing either by relying on empathy and revulsion—that's not fecklessness, in fact it's a little too conscientious. I prefer Spielberg's radicalism (that's the right word); entertainment emboldened by emotion, technique and iconoclastic story. Every character in *Amistad* was original, every word, gesture, exquisitely tooled to signify. It announced a new American cinema that the '90s just aren't ready for. The trouble with *Saving Private Ryan* is that its officially sanctioned subject approximates a conscripted vision. Spielberg's amazing, career-long struggle to enrich public appetite or change consciousness in subtle, accomplished, vernacular ways is neither won over nor entirely resolved.

His current respectful reception (a hero's welcome) is too close to routinized hype. *Saving Private Ryan* will please people who don't normally like the intensely intimate view of goodness in Spielberg movies; they mistake his moral certainty for sentimental convention. The bitter realities of war fiction ("Every man I kill, the further away from home I feel." "Tell me I'm a good man.") will seem more serious to those unable to appreciate that one GI's disturbing childhood memory, and the conflation of an Abraham Lincoln letter and George Washington portrait, are comparable epiphanies. But it's the range of complexity that gives the war sentiments conviction.

As our great fiction-maker—a serious artist who also maintains youthful optimism and energetic technique—Spielberg's ability to communicate on pop terms puts him in an unusual bind: He's the filmmaker most apt to vivify and bring together facts of civics, war, culture and their results. This great talent risks trading profundity for easy perception, disturbing patriotic complacency as easily as giving into it. With violence and death viewed as facts of life, Spielberg and screenwriter Richard Rodat minimize the time-bound (Vietnam-fixated) concept of war and pacifism that flummoxed Oliver Stone's *Platoon*. (*Saving Private Ryan* takes a different, kinetic approach from, say, Iris DeMent in her Vietnam Memorial tune "There's a Wall in Washington," but the emotional richness is similar.) Spielberg's on high philosophical ground and fairer political territory by virtue of directly expressing human experience. But just as *Amistad* spoke a language too refined for '90s audiences, *Saving Private Ryan's* heightened terms of life may not be comprehended behind the three-dimensional sound and fury.

In this super-deluxe war movie, Spielberg uses his technique to sharpen effect and, most importantly, perception. Here's where he surpasses realism: His unique vision contrasts the Christian ideas American soldiers carried with them overseas and the violence they had to commit in battle—a paradox he views plainly, first aghast, then amazed. The film's few quiet moments are grief-riddled by the catastrophe war makes of religious principle (in the final battle the blown-apart foundations of a church signal a small town as no-man's land); while noise-filled moments, such as the opening landing at Omaha Beach (whizzing artillery, explosions, body thuds and blood splashes), feature warfare as seemingly interminable

**227**

agony. Spielberg begins and ends the war story in the eye of debacle, like Peckinpah's *The Wild Bunch*. The obliteration of troops is distilled to a similar, essential sorrow that no one will argue.

But will contemporary video-war audiences know what this bloodshed means beyond its documentary style? Or will they take it as shark bait? Since Spielberg's moments of transcendence ("I've tried to live my life the best I could") build off the savagery of the acclaimed battle scenes, the film's value lies in the implications that follow: Miller's ambivalent intelligence—the captain's commonness, which is his genius— apparent in Hanks' average-man, haunted eyes. Looking both soulful and thoughtful, Hanks' strange, frightened avidity keeps turning over the top-soil of this war tale: the personal into the political, trenchantly back-and-forth.

Spielberg didn't suddenly jump to this moral complexity; it was always part of his pop sensibility, surprisingly connecting him to the world outside the suburbs—as in the twist of "brotherhood" between Miller's American-boy troop and a German soldier. Set beneath the film's bluest sky, this episode will be mistaken for irony (the Nazi burbles up disarming trivia: "Steamboat Villy! Betty Boop! What a dish! Betty Grable! What gams! Fuck Hitler!") when its greatness comes from simple, shocking remorse at the men's opposition. Literal-minded viewers may prefer hard irony (like the "Is it Bach?" sequence in *Schindler's List*) but it's consistent with *Amistad* or *The Last Crusade*'s sincere insight into transcultural politics and emotions.

Spielberg never had to neglect fantasy for profundity, and he lowers his gifts when he employs them—though impeccably—on the pretext of literalness. People who love his films don't love them for realism, but for their poetic representation of serious emotions. The mundane long patrol and search is like every other war film only stirred by a raindrops/gunshots, leaves/water montage, or out-of-time respites when the GIs cross peaceful meadows (reminiscent of Miklós Jancsó's war ballets or Francesco Rosi's *The Truce* (1997)), touching on the ineffable.

But then there's the war—imagined on another, fantastic level that the *Titanic* generation (and Spielberg's detractors) must recognize is a critique of trivialized cinema as much as an historical recreation. Here Spielberg steps way beyond patriotism and politics to something harsh and elemental and undeniable: It cannot even be called tonic. Shattering will suffice. (So does Robert Warshow's phrase "the immediate experience.") These grim, bloody, unsparing deaths—each a moral étude and a moral question—go to redefine why movies are made: to force viewers to examine everything they thought they knew about life. During the invasion, Spielberg exposes the apparatus of the medium, showing mud- and blood-spattered lenses, plus shutter-blur that refers to newsreel cameras jamming or a meta-cinema effect of the projector shuddering in recoil. It's effective and damn highbrow, though its brutality may convince people who were indifferent when Spielberg used the same technique more sparingly in *Amistad*. (When the British colonel blew up the slave fortress and Spielberg recorded its crumbling with point-of-view, camera-shaking "authenticity" that was part of the film's transcendent dramatic context.) We no longer have a measurement for such aesthetic-kinetic power. Surely silent movies felt like this to early audiences. And these battle scenes obliterate all the feints and perversions of sophistication that people used to resist

*Amistad. Saving Private Ryan* is its emotional opposite, not a heart but a "Kino Fist" (pace Eisenstein).

Our most popular filmmaker is now the victim of ideological manipulation. Refuting the revisionism of *1941*, *Empire of the Sun*, *Indiana Jones and the Last Crusade*, *The Lost World: Jurassic Park* and *Amistad*—audacious, unlaureled filmmaking that actually argued the politics of great historical events—the media now uses *Saving Private Ryan* to deny politics by advancing the primacy of World War II. Spielberg's being celebrated for what he was always—falsely—accused of promoting: a conventional view of history.

Fact is, *Amistad* was too intelligent for this revanchist period in pop culture, and in *Saving Private Ryan* Spielberg proves once again that popular art can meet the personal emotional challenge of high art. But if all the current hoopla reduces Spielberg to the commemorative level the media understands, swamped in schmaltz, knee-jerked into piety, this existentially bold film will only be a Pyrrhic victory.

*New York Press*
July 1998

# Disturbing Behavior

**S**AVING *PRIVATE RYAN* changes everything. I see no reason to file another week of Hollywood catch-up, as if film culture were on the same course it was before. The way this film shakes everyone's presuppositions—just in time to repair the pop aberrations of *The Truman Show* (1998)—is a moment to savor. Spielberg's movie, a generally agreed ass-kicker, restores a sense of proportion—morality, intelligence and imagination— to how the public regards this art form. It isn't all high concept and promotion; its means can make people think and feel to a serious, humane purpose. That's something noisemakers Jerry Bruckheimer, Dean Devlin and Roland Emmerich, Peter Weir and Richard Donner know nothing about.

Now there exists a standard. *The Butcher Boy, Twilight, Bulworth, The Last Days of Disco, Live Flesh, Full Speed, The Farm: Angola USA, La vie de Jésus, The Gingerbread Man, The Truce, A Price Above Rubies* and *Out of Sight*—the next-best movies so far this year—all sustained the humanist tradition, but they weren't movies of mass appeal or large impact. *Saving Private Ryan* assumes the popular voice— making the mass perspective personal—and rejects thrill rides for evocative experience and moral challenge. It's not about war as excitement, or patriotism as a reflex, but man living in moment-to-moment choices—like '70s movies. Spielberg could have made it the great metaphor of our age—man in crisis—except that no one seems particularly exercised about or committed to the significance of public action. (It's all about the Benjamins, baby.)

**231**

That's what's brilliant in his DreamWorks production *Small Soldiers* (1998). Directed by Joe Dante in the same sardonic mode as *Gremlins 2: The New Batch*, *Small Soldiers* pierces the hypocrisy of privatization. It's about the frightening, laughable consequences of capitalist zeal. It's wrong to call *Small Soldiers* "a marketing concept in search of a movie." Nineties cinema cynicism overlooks the value of Spielberg productions that dare confront the marketing process (the toy shop here and in *Jurassic Park*). His films risk an appraisal of our current frenzy ("Don't call it 'violence,' call it 'action.' Kids love action!" says Denis Leary's greedy toy manufacturer). Similarly, in contemporary scenes that begin and end *Saving Private Ryan*, Spielberg consistently addresses America's current hellish retreat from principle and from history.

This isn't a war epic as it's been superficially described, but like *Amistad*, it's a soul epic revealing the innermost ideas behind historical events central to American character but never spoken of before: the trauma of battle and the complexes that undergird national efforts. Something new happens in these two Spielberg films: a spiritual reconsideration of American virtue. *Saving Private Ryan* is the first movie in a long time to transcend the conveyer-belt mentality that had taken over movie culture. Not just the latest piffle to come down the line, it's a mountain of circumspection in the middle of the capitalist speedway. As much a challenge as *Amistad* it's posed to the public in terms they can't ignore yet that are almost too much to comprehend on first viewing. It's the rare critic, like MSNBC's Gregory Solman, who understands it as "a film that does not mock patriotism but, like the translucent flag that opens and closes the film, sees through it as something of restless beauty."

Honesty forces me to admit that almost no first-impression review of *Saving Private Ryan* can be entirely trusted. Because *New York Press* was only granted late screenings, last week's notice was regrettably written under the gun, before the film's magnitude could sink in. (Publicist-favored media like *Time, Newsweek, Rolling Stone, The New York Times*, etc. were privileged with early sell-sell screenings, so their printed interpretations do reveal those media's inadequacies.) But I still feel embarrassment and sympathy for my high-profile colleagues when lowering themselves to lines like, "The Americans take that bridge" or "a framing device that could easily have been dropped." This reduces the film to America-first propaganda and crucially misinterprets Spielberg's concept. Without that framing device, this is just another combat film; it's there to extend the war into the present, making it part of the domestic experience of Americans who don't know their debt to the past or (as in *Amistad*) their responsibility to democratic ideas that others fought for and instituted, but that we merely profess. The bracketing "device" makes this war story richer. If it were only about acts of bravery and courage, Spielberg's moviemaking genius would be supererogatory, his emotional indulgence would be cant. But by being about the cost and responsibility of ideals, fighting, murder, death, the film is bigger than politics. Audiences, like critics, need time to assess *Saving Private Ryan*; it's indecent to pretend anything else. And though we get the movies—and politics—we deserve, we simply don't get movies this powerful every week, month, year.

WWII gets a reflexive response from filmgoers who view the violence and the infantry mission as a unanimous endeavor, but that's a coverup helped along by decades of insidious Hollywood boosterism. We've been taught to enjoy violence, rather than consider it. Spielberg's imaginative depiction of men in battle forces one into immediate kinetic philosophy. That's why the film's second movement is essential and not a slackening of Spielberg's technique. As in *Amistad*, he proceeds to extrapolate from the visceral exposition. He wants audiences to pay even closer attention. (A test most critics fail.) Against the '90s tendency to offer continuously heightened physical stimulation, Spielberg asks for reflection and inquiry.

At the last-minute screening I was invited to, there were WWII veterans who stood shaking and sobbing at film's end—and they weren't alone. It reminded me of grad school days, coordinating a weekend film program with Keith Gardner, now a TV professional. We showed *The Wild Bunch* one weekend and among the audience of Columbia students were two middle-aged Latin women from the Morningside Heights community. At the film's end, when William Holden, Ernest Borgnine, Jaime Sánchez and the bunch were killed along with the decimated Mexican army, those two grown women sat in their seats weeping. It was the first time I'd seen anyone respond that way to *The Wild Bunch* and I knew immediately that Peckinpah would approve; that theirs was the appropriate response.

Modern Hollywood only wants viewers to giggle, but Spielberg knows what Peckinpah knew and what audiences at *Saving Private Ryan* will be shocked to rediscover: The loss of human life exacts a toll. No matter how many WWII vets kept the misery to themselves (and lots of them retired to the Bowery, crime or institutions instead of expressing unpatriotic trauma to their kin), life means something to us as individuals; we have a spiritual connection to the things we fight for, which is where *Saving Private Ryan*'s fantastic, imaginative telling of an Army troop's fated mission becomes more than "the most realistic depiction of war ever filmed." Its delineation of human exhaustion and sacrifice takes on cosmic, epochal, scary significance. That's what Spielberg strives to convey following the sophisticated legal-moral philosophizing of *Amistad*; it's the great realization challenging pre-millennial culture. And any critic who claims to have instantaneously comprehended this is lying.

*The Village Voice*'s pathetic rote dismissal of the film would rather we watch movies of piddling ambition and simplistic craft (practically the entire independent movement of the past 20 years, ever since John Sayles dulled counterculturalism). This hipper-than-Spielberg attitude fails to penetrate our historical legacy (the work facing every living society); it also ignores the fascination of movies as a medium of rousing seriousness and cunning, thus underrating Spielberg's mastery of popular effect and his straight-faced fervor. *Saving Private Ryan* provides the perfect occasion for us to stop and consider: Do we want to continue thinking about films that don't mean jack, or reacquaint ourselves with movies that explore how people choose to live? Altman's *Short Cuts* (1993) was the last new movie to shake me to this degree, and the New York Film Festival's restoration last fall of Griffith's *Orphans of the Storm* was the last time a film overwhelmed my emotions and sensibility. *Saving Private Ryan* has made it impossible for me to think that movie culture has gone to hell completely. Depression over the commercial flop and critical rejection of *Bulworth* and *Amistad* is somewhat assuaged with *Saving Private Ryan*'s huge assault on—Spielberg's irresistible declaration against—'90s apathy. Think of the Nazi soldier's slow, intimate killing of the Jewish GI; Jeremy Davies' catatonic staircase scene, then his soul-destroying vengeance on a mound of rubble; Hanks' final futile gestures answered from above; or the bracketing cemetery homage to Richard Attenborough's *Oh! What a Lovely War* (1969) that poses essential questions to the audience. What's at stake in this movie isn't simply a well-told story or a weekend night's diversion, but the future of movies as more than commerce but part of human faith.

*New York Press*
July 1998

PART THREE

# A.I. ARTIFICIAL INTELLIGENCE (2001)

## A.I. Artificial Intelligence

B ACK TO THE womb in *A.I. Artificial Intelligence*, Steven Spielberg probes affections that get callused over with age, forgetfulness and cultural habit. It's the most profound treatment of a child's life since Terence Davies' *The Long Day Closes* (1993). More than Spielberg's other films, it dares viewers to remember and accept the part of themselves that is capable of feeling—a real risk these days. *A.I.* goes so openly and deeply into beneficent emotions it is bound to scare off pseudo-sophisticates—people who think it's progress to forget they were ever children. That's usually just a way of denying pure, uncomplicated emotion. *A.I.* proves it's small-minded to think that art should only be about conflicted feelings. It's equally foolish to assume Spielberg views childhood without complication.

David (Haley Joel Osment) is a mechanical child built to provide succor for a young couple, Monica and Henry (Frances O'Connor and Sam Robards), grieving over the impending death of their biological child. Exceeding its manufacturer's design, the robot starts to long for genuine feeling. The scientist (William Hurt) who wired him for the useful affectation of sentiment professed a personal stake in how children of the media-saturated era have had their instincts dulled, programmed, desensitized. This makes David an ideal representative of an over-mechanized age.

Though set in a plausibly projected future (after an ice-cap meltdown has submerged the coastal U.S. cities), David's story moves through scenes—adventures—that marvelously represent youth's stages of awakening. He experiences cultural confusion, seeks the solace of true feeling but is bemused by the mystery of private emotion—the very things coarsened and derided by today's pop culture, especially the movies. Advancing through ever-bewildering situations, David is abandoned to homelessness, joins other flailing, fugitive robots—including Gigolo Joe (Jude Law), a mechanical sex hustler—and suffers privation and abuse. Each narrative step is credibly dramatized, yet those scenes where David enters his adopted home are spectral, quintessential Spielberg. Rendered as pre-K fantasy, these sequences are primal—the paradise of family, of first education and instinctively formed attachments. The glowing, futuristic domicile somehow suggests one's own past distilled, and this is the core of *A.I.*'s miracle: Spielberg accepts and understands how human interaction, beginning in childhood, fetishized through toys and storybooks, is common to the middle-class American (if not universal) tradition of child-rearing and acculturation. He recalls that period so warmly it's startling; he reveals childhood's secret soul.

To describe *A.I.*'s reverie as nostalgic would be inaccurate. Spielberg modernizes childhood experience that's usually coddled—distanced—as fable. He investigates bedtime-story codes (even the ineffable affection toward teddy bears!) because these things first stir human perception. David's inquiry into parental love (the bond he forms with Monica) and adult trust (holding onto Gigolo Joe during a forest raid) perceives those connections freshly. ("I'm sorry I never told you about the world," Monica apologizes.) He's preternaturally aware of the significance of everything he goes through but incapable of controlling his fate. Like most of us, David's self-consciousness—his emotional intelligence—makes him poignant, a potentially tragic, restless figure. Even when he competes with his human sibling Martin (Jake Thomas) in a dinner table spinach-eating contest, the motivations for rivalry are no less unsettling for being absolutely clear.

I'm aware that *A.I.*, in a way, presents a story of privilege; and those with unhappy childhoods may not share Spielberg's agape. But don't reject the film on specious political grounds as either "too white" or "too bourgeois." In fact, I would not bet against folks from unfortunate, abused childhoods still identifying with David's quest for love and experiencing his longing just as powerfully. The blessing of childhood sweetness is what's reified in *A.I.* Before one can become suspicious of that phenomenon, Spielberg dares you to consider that it has nothing to do with class, and even transcends gender. It is, above all, personal. A spiritual view of human need, if you will. And that's *A.I.*'s claim to global relevance.

Pop entertainers are often demagogues, angling to make masses of people feel the same shallow thing. But a true pop artist is a rare and different matter: Spielberg works to make his deepest feelings understood. In David's only encounter with other children, he learns about the prospect of behavioral analogues—the difference between Mechas and Orgas (mechanical or organic entities) who demonstrate false or sincere conduct. These sci-fi suggestions of mysterious dread

(Is David malevolent? Are his designer or adopted parents selfish monsters?) are not the heart of the movie—despite one irresistible trope of Buñuel-mocking menace. Spielberg's art—moments of indescribable goodness—rejects the usual pessimistic sci-fi banality. He achieves Dreyerlike depth, Bressonian loftiness simply by contemplating irreducible Love. Don't short-change the toy-filled premise. Spielberg heightens human need into pure feeling, and that Mecha/Orga dichotomy keeps it rigorous.

Everyone's estimation of *A.I.* will depend on their interest in childhood mythology. Will they accept that Spielberg— from *The Sugarland Express* to *The Color Purple*, from *Hook* to *Amistad*—is the one filmmaker to sustain the link between fantasy and moral reckoning? Start with the film's audacious ad copy ("His love is real. But he is not"). It sets *A.I.* apart from Hollywood's mostly antipathetic films. Rather than indulging religiosity, as Spielberg's antireligious detractors charge, the movie phases into and through religious parallels toward a spiritual essence. Every image (whether a deceptive heavenly orb or Gigolo Joe's facial planes resembling David Bowie's *trompe l'oeil* makeup in the *Blue Jean* video) forces us to question the authenticity of things and feelings. Each part of David's journey through carnal and sexual universes into the final eschatological devastation becomes as profoundly philosophical and contemplative as anything by cinema's most thoughtful, speculative artists—Borzage, Ozu, Demy, Tarkovsky. So what if the project came via Kubrick? That's both a red herring and good fortune. Moments that Kubrick would have made cold and ugly are surpassed by Spielberg's richer truth—and that's as it should be. (Besides, *A.I.*'s not a Kubrick-only concept; Robin Williams' *Bicentennial Man* (1999) and

M. Night Shyamalan's odious *Unbreakable* fumbled strikingly similar ideas.) It's Spielberg's distinct sensibility that makes the difference. Rejecting the cynical trickery some people prefer in drama, his *A.I.* is equal to Kubrick's finest work.

Here's a more apt analogy: imagine D.W. Griffith (master of popular spectacle and emotional affect) remaking Neil Jordan's *The Company of Wolves* (1984) (a rare semiotic exercise that was also a mainstream reverie). Spielberg's uses of enchantment (pace Bruno Bettelheim) elucidate age-old affective responses to tales like "Pinocchio," "Hansel and Gretel," "The Snow Queen," *The Night of the Hunter* (1955). The story is as sophisticated as the erotic deconstruction in *The Company of Wolves* but, conveying Spielberg's personal expressiveness, it searches beyond academic rationale.

Think of *A.I.* as a way of reinterpreting—and transforming—"Pinocchio." The plot follows childhood's agitated state of grace (like Jim's in *Empire of the Sun*). But the "resilience" of children (as Truffaut specified it in *Small Change* (1976)) gets desentimentalized here. It's a state-of-being unrelated to age: innocence. As David flies through the red-light wonderland of Rouge City or is enslaved at the Flesh Fair (a public destruction orgy cruelly testing the Mecha/Orga opposition while surprisingly encapsulating the decadent pathology of Cronenberg's *Crash* (1996)), his tabula rasa consciousness survives all turmoil. He's Pinocchio as "Nature Boy" (his wish to be real essentially a desire to be loved), a state-of-being—and song—crudely misunderstood in *Angel Eyes* (2001) and *Moulin Rouge* (2001), recent movies that only pretended grownup sensitivity.

Through David, *A.I.* pursues the inner world of metaphor, intuition and dream. (Note David's symbiotic relation to

Teddy, his Jiminy Cricket companion. It's too mechanical to be "magic," yet too dear to be trite.) Spielberg reaches back to his own pop-mythological obsessions. Disney's "Once Upon a Dream" is heard in Martin's hospital; David wanders through an enchanted woods evoking Hawthorne, the Brothers Grimm, even *E.T.* (and an astonishing moonlight sequence rivals the imminence of *Close Encounters'* mothership). Few instances of humanist filmmaking have been so immersed in pop mythology, or conveyed dreaming so intensely.

Cinematographer Janusz Kamiński helps by suggesting the inexplicable twinkling of light into color, while John Williams' best score since *The Fury* modulates delicate emotional changes. And Haley Joel Osment provides exactly what is needed. Casting Osment (creepy in *The Sixth Sense* (1999) and unbearably precocious in *Pay It Forward* (2000)) was ingenious. He achieves amazing transparency in *A.I.* This looks like the most artless screen performance I have ever seen; David's naive conviction matches Tim Holt's pathos in *The Magnificent Ambersons* (1942). Contrived to detach us from sentimentality, Osment's performance does what the past two decades of teen movies could not—it cleanses our self-recognition of any immodesty.

There's been nothing in modern movies more grownup or sensitive than David's fascination with his sexy young mother. It's as if Spielberg took that key image from Bergman's *Persona* (1966) (of the small boy reaching up to the huge opaque image of Woman) and interpreted it from the inside out. Suspended in fascination, Spielberg introduces Monica applying her makeup—a vanity gesture shared with a female robot. Yet, where another filmmaker would stop at obvious irony, Spielberg dissolves/resolves ironies in love. This view nearly shuts out the father—Freud is both acknowledged and crushed by Spielberg's awe at that first relationship, the most powerful and baffling in everyone's life. *A.I.* analyzes how one loves by fathoming the need for love. "Are those happy tears?" David asks his distraught mother. In such moments, *A.I.*'s unprecedented combination of curiosity and intimacy is breathtaking.

*New York Press*
July 2001

# Intelligence Quotient

**"MIRACULOUS?"** SOMEONE ASKED me about last week's review of *A.I.* "Yes!" I insisted, because Spielberg has achieved a breakthrough—a breakthrough no one could have expected: raising fairytales to the level of great art. He also resurrects movie art, though you wouldn't know it from the clueless, defensive reviews. "Fascinating wreck," "It needs to be faster, lighter," critics complained—as if *A.I.* were ruinously flawed, as if art had to be "perfect," as if they'd know perfection when they saw it. Critics recoil from *A.I.* at precisely the moments they should reach toward and connect with it. Jean Renoir once said, "My films are incomplete. They need an audience." But most critics—Hollywood drones?—think good movies are the ones they don't have to think about. What they really want is a film that zips by without need for thought or reflection (*Memento* (2000), *Lara Croft* (2001), *The Fast and the Furious* (2001)); more of the junk they're employed to promote.

Reactions to *A.I.* reveal the aesthetic IQs of movie-lovers and critics. I'm not doubting individual intellects, but separating the hacks from the esthetes. It's a matter of taking pop mythology seriously. For all the jawing about genre and F/X and film savvy, it is Spielberg's intelligent use of technology that upsets critics. They'd prefer that his filmmaking have no ambition, thus appeasing the juvenile sensibility that favors cynicism over *A.I.*'s fascination with faith and the loving essence of humankind that the robot David represents.

Intelligence Quotient • A.I. ARTIFICIAL INTELLIGENCE (2001)

A major cause for the disrespect of Spielberg (and film art) is that people—Hollywood indoctrinated—want what they want. They want trash without high motives; no originality will be accepted, only derided. They want car chases and shootouts, explosions and killings—no meaning. Spielberg's problem is that he goes at devotion, faith, desire through pop. Kubrick took the easy route by claiming "art" from the beginning. There was no confusion of intent. Critics, now, won't let Spielberg be an Artist no matter how much artistry he displays. One journalist told me that Nabokov's was modernist art, yet Spielberg's was not. That's just fatuous. *A.I.* makes evident how pop myths (funhouse, videogames, tv, cinema) all come from the same source of needs and aspirations as religious mythology. Using the universal storehouse of pop culture and literary legends to address ubiquitous human needs is *A.I.*'s triumph of art over trash. Hitchcock, Lean, Cocteau, Kurosawa, Demy all knew it. How heroic that Spielberg took advantage of his skill, clout (and Kubrick bequest) to make something better than a kiddie or teen flick—to actually take the time, after *A.I.*'s first hour, to do a serious philosophical exploration.

If *A.I.* were "faster, lighter," it wouldn't be the great, cumulative, mythological assessment of our time, it'd be *Speed*. Reviewers betray resentment that Spielberg makes art rather than trash. This is surprising after *Pearl Harbor*'s (2001) critical drubbing; one deplored Michael Bay and Jerry Bruckheimer's choice, having the chance to address the world with untold resources at hand, yet offering nothing more than that pitiful post-adolescent love triangle. *A.I.* improves pop potential by adding what the 1940 *Pinocchio*—a movie for children— always lacked: a heartbreaking recognition of impossibility in a culture that has gone against the purest desires. That's why

**249**

it's emphatically a movie for adults. (At its deepest, one can feel adulthood asking childhood for forgiveness.)

Because this is the most remarkable achievement of my grownup moviegoing years ("It's the most amazing film I've ever seen!" slipped out of my mouth the other day) I can't muster much to say about *Pootie Tang* (2001). And why bother? *Pootie Tang*—like most other recent flicks—is best seen on bootleg video anyway.

Once again, Spielberg has raised the bar for movie culture. Instead of assenting, the dogs are yelping. Film culture has collapsed so disastrously that people no longer know how to read metaphor, allusion, analogy. They can't see the human condition in David's plight; insisting that he's a robot and therefore unpitiable. They don't recognize the coarsening of modern culture in the Flesh Fair, Rouge City or what Spielberg shows to be the ultimately untenable, Disneyfied place that is a world sunken in its own modern arrogance. A heart-stopping vision. Despite everything we live with—the dislocation between children and parents, the solipsism of narcissistic, unsatisfied adults and the truly appalling lack of craft and imagination in most Hollywood movies—critics insist on seeing *A.I.* as a failed *Star Wars* or *2001* (1968) comic. Worse, they presume themselves to be above the story's (Spielberg's) basic human emotions.

Worshiping at Kubrick's grave gives critics an excuse for not rationally considering the confluence of major filmmakers. They apply anti-*A.I.* criteria arbitrarily, not the way one made sense of Welles-Chaplin's *Monsieur Verdoux* (1947), Kurosawa-Konchalovsky's *Runaway Train* (1985), Fellini-Rossellini's *The Miracle* (1947), Truffaut-Godard's *Breathless* (1960) or even Spielberg-Scorsese's *Cape Fear* (1991). It's ridiculous to say one director has not fulfilled the intentions of the first; we sensibly expect the directing auteur to imprint his vision on the material—that's what determines how we read any film. Appreciating the magnitude of a Spielberg image such as the tear-like reflection of David's suicidal fall requires faith in the ability of film to encapsulate an experience imaginatively and then to find the image that simultaneously conveys the story's theme, the character's emotion and the viewer's awareness. Many people never approach a Spielberg movie that credibly.

But you can't go to *A.I.* to be hip. Hip is what has ruined film culture as critics—even middle-aged ones writing for the most stolid, antiquated, middle-class publications—claim hipness to be definitive modern expression. This fake intelligence is worse than blind, drunken stupidity because it fends off feeling, and prefers the comradeship of a cynical elite, priding itself on what it disdains rather than what they might open itself up to discover. (That would explain why some people prefer the shallow *Raiders of the Lost Ark* to the more politically complex *Indiana Jones and the Last Crusade*.) Hip critics who generally favor David Fincher, Harmony Korine, Darren Aronofsky, Quentin Tarantino, Lars von Trier—the past decade's prime scalawags—seek the cool, derisive pose of knowingness. *A.I.* offers something much better.

With the robot David's pilgrimage through future centuries of human existence searching for an ideal, *A.I.* puts viewers in touch with experiences—memories—they have forgotten but that remain lodged in their soul: the dream of ideal love. Rather than hipness, Spielberg recalls our common humanity, the most precious, least conscious part—David's desire for connection, his pure will to be accepted, to be loved. It's in the scenes when he attempts to become part of Monica and Henry's family, or searches the universe for his own origins (a resolution to which Spielberg's audaciously given us privilege). Contrary to detractors who think Spielberg's interest in childhood is trivial, *A.I.* refines what his past movie tropes (the aged sisters uniting by playing patty-cake at the end of *The Color Purple*; Jim finally closing his eyes in his mother's bosom in *Empire of the Sun*) showed to be essential longings. David's prayer to the Blue Fairy is more eloquent than *Pinocchio*'s simple theme song "When You Wish Upon a Star." Spielberg finds a delicate, adroit expression of longing that blows fairytale wishing sky high. This is spiritual aspiration—not mere hipness—and the final half-hour of *A.I.* achieves an erotic plateau that is also metaphysical. Whether you observe it as memory or theology, it's so beautiful it's shattering.

When *Saving Private Ryan* shook the summer of '98, it seemed like Spielberg would change the way filmmakers and filmgoers approached action cinema. Instead, soulless imitators from Ridley Scott to Spike Lee to Joel Schumacher tried upping the ante on vérité violence and fast-edits, completely refuting Spielberg's art and further degrading the medium. All the pomo hacks can do with *A.I.* is defy its large-scale, fully evolved concentration on human emotion. As in the days of Lang's *Metropolis* (1927), *Siegfried* (1924) and *Kriemhild's Revenge* (1924), Griffith's *Intolerance* and Murnau's *Faust* (1926), Spielberg expresses feeling undistracted by action, but more clearly expressed through exquisite, mythic detail (the Blue Fairy's resemblance to Virgin Mary statuary—and Kate Capshaw) and fantastic imagery (the neon miasmas of Flesh Fair and Rouge City and the modern world's destruction shown as a flooded Manhattan).

Hipper-than-thous always argue against Spielberg with cant—"manipulative," "sentimental." They're so used to technique meaning nothing—like the close-up exhalation of smoke by Tchéky Karyo in *Kiss of the Dragon* (2001) and shifting focus on lovers' faces in *Crazy/Beautiful* (2001)—that they can't appreciate when technique is used to say something. Audiences hooting and hollering at Jet Li putting chopsticks through a man's thorax tell you Spielberg's belief in human sympathy is out of fashion. It's dispiriting that *A.I.*'s heart, dedication, skill, imagination is wasted on audiences bred to want far less. Still, Spielberg restores cinema's essence: keeping one's eyes startled and mind open. It's inconceivable that people could look at David's quest to communicate—the most nuanced images of physical and emotional touching since *Jules and Jim* (1962)—and remain unmoved. It can only be because those scenes embarrass the modern effort to appear above need, to seem hip. Mentioning so many other films is my attempt to hint at *A.I.*'s significance as an achievement that reflects an entire cultural epoch. It recalls Henry James' assessment of a new, popular art work as "a state of vision, of feeling and of consciousness."

*A.I.* may be just a movie, but such filmmaking requires an intelligent audience that doesn't simply groove to F/X but is sensitive to what imagery means—that fairytale imagination many people have lost since childhood, just as film culture has lost appreciation for it since the silent years. The great hope of *A.I.* is that people will be reawakened to the magnificence of the film medium before it all crashes down into digital-video slovenliness, zero craft and impersonal storytelling.

*New York Press*
July 2001

# MINORITY REPORT (2002)

---

## *Spielberg Goes to Alphaville*

**S**OMEWHERE BETWEEN LEONARDO da Vinci's study of man (*Vitruvian Man*) and an orchestra conductor in rapt concentration, Tom Cruise, as Detective John Anderton, stands with his arms outstretched, his eyes, ears and mind fully engaged when performing *Minority Report*'s futuristic crime investigation. And it is a performance: in the Justice Dept.'s glass-paneled Pre-Crime Unit, Det. Anderton shifts and arranges media representations of crime—in mid-air— just as director Steven Spielberg surrounds the audience in the midst of imaginary events. Anderton conducts scenes from the future that have been downloaded to prevent crimes from happening. These horrific images cannot be watched or manipulated dispassionately. They require an ethical response from Anderton, his full, personal investment (both aesthetic and moral). It is, coincidentally, a metaphor for movie-watching as very few filmmakers these days demand it.

Set in the year 2054, *Minority Report* posits a future recognizably close to our contemporary social anxieties. The government believes it can eliminate crime by monitoring the premonitions of three psychics sequestered in a sensory deprivation tank. Mediating their brain impulses into two-dimensional images makes it possible to see crimes before they

happen, deduce the time, place, victim and perpetrator—
then intervene, preventing the occurrence of iniquity. The
resemblance between government and divine authority is
blatantly perverse. Anderton isn't a lawbringer, he's a soldier
used to enforce society's misguided will and Spielberg, essaying
his first cop hero since *Jaws*, understands the dilemmas of that
occupation. This time—unlike with most recent cop dramas—
the crisis is internal, exposing Anderton's flaws and society's.

*Minority Report* has nothing to do with racial "minorities."
Spielberg obviously doesn't buy into that conservative canard.
Instead, *Minority Report*'s arcane title is subtly critical; it refers
to a singular—possibly exculpating—crime report that's
been suppressed because it disrupts the standard, politically
convenient view. (Spielberg implies that corrupt, fallible police
procedure is an inevitable social threat.) Anderton's pursuit of
this typically ignored—misfiled—truth makes *Minority Report*
a socially significant, moral mystery—an extraordinary moral
inquiry—rather than a film noir in the classic sense. The movie
is way ahead of cliché cop dramas (and news reports) that
exploit urban chaos by reducing it to racial antagonisms. Class
tensions are still observable in the shocking difference shown
between the exurban lives of moneyed citizens and cramped
city-dwellers. But more than noir, this is poli-sci-fi—the first
movie since Godard's *Alphaville* (1965) to truly connect moral
fiction with political science.

And still Spielberg, working from a story by Philip K.
Dick, adds his transforming spiritual emphasis. Each pre-crime
that Anderton investigates has been prophesied by society's
scapegoats who are the damaged offspring of drug addicts
(spawn of cultural dystrophy and mankind's imperfection). This
psychic trinity, with the names Arthur, Dashiell, Agatha (after

Doyle, Hammett, Christie, the progenitors of mystery fiction, seers into human culpability), displays a wide-eyed, childlike sensitivity to suffering. They're generous, yielding creatures, even in the face of their government's exploitation. When Agatha (Samantha Morton) predicts Anderton's involvement in a future crime, he abducts her to clear his name and change his destiny. Wandering through the demoralized city—where everyone is watched, identified and their superficial desires hounded by advertisers and merchants—Agatha's pale, bald-headed languishing is a purified version of Anderton's strapping, aggrieved duty. In need of faith and deliverance, they're a pair of death-defying, spiritually questing moderns.

While the name Anderton suggests a declension of the traditional "Anderson" with "automaton," Anderton's mission also evokes the image of Freder, the industrialist's son in Fritz Lang's futuristic *Metropolis*, who at one point sacrifices himself by taking over the arms-out, cruciform drudgery of one of Metropolis' exhausted workers. That arms-wide, da Vinci stance perfectly symbolizes this film's ethical struggle—the difficult balancing of potential and necessity, life and death, cinema and reality. It's not a coincidence that Anderton's position recalls a music conductor, a film director or a film editor at his console; *Minority Report* explores the conscious manipulation and reception of images through Anderton's work with prophesy, dream and memory.

Spielberg engages cinema's history of visual investigation from Buñuel's *Un Chien Andalou* (1929), Hitchcock's *Rear Window* (1954) and Antonioni's *Blow-Up* (1966) all the way to Coppola's *The Conversation* and De Palma's *Blow Out* (1981). Anderton could be conducting his own movie, his own imagination—he's swept into moral conflict like John Travolta's character in *Blow Out*, a sound recorder who gets implicated in political conspiracy. These image-shifting/shuffling/conducting sequences dramatize the representation of crime—like a state-of-the-art, three-dimensional probe of the legendary *Blow-Up* photograph. We're put inside the scene of the crime. An extraordinary edit from the crime location interior to an exterior of Anderton rushing forward, and into it, kinetically measures the relationship of vision to humane obligation. (The scene does a De Palma on De Palma.) Not only does Spielberg repeat Buñuel's legendary surrealist assault on the eye in several shots (as a way of magnifying the issues surrounding perception), he also considers the consequences of vision that fascinated Hitchcock and Coppola's famous social treatises.

At this particular moment in pop history, Spielberg's existential forensics restore the moral excitement of images. Most contemporary filmmakers, rushing to embrace digital-graphics license, have shut their eyes to the aesthetics of action. *Minority Report*'s big set-pieces—Anderton chased by police, levitating through streets, alleys, tenements and an auto factory—offer dizzying, dynamic angles plus speed and humor. Spielberg shames the flashy techno-geeks James Cameron, David Fincher, Michael Bay, Ridley and Tony Scott, who are never concerned with what action means. His omniscient perspectives of crowded streets, shopping malls and housing blocks reveal the future's social structure (capitalism and totalitarianism in lockstep) while being dazzling. In *Windtalkers* (2002), John Woo's high body-count distracts from his appalling lack of craft (pixilated critics and audiences, caught up in adolescent shock, can't tell the difference); but Spielberg's action craft lets viewers grasp a violent or thrilling event and situate themselves philosophically.

With cinematographer Janusz Kamiński, Spielberg has devised a desaturated look real enough to avoid insult and abstract enough to avoid obscenity. Trumping the cgi fallacy of perfect imagery, Spielberg's simulated "vision" (the future in a glimpse) enhances how we see. In a garden and greenhouse where Anderton confronts Dr. Iris Hineman (Lois Smith), the scientist who pioneered the use of precognitive children as criminal prognosticators, only the brightness of one rare orchid-like plant contrasts the gray-drab miasma, the film's color scheme of distorted nature and society. Haze and flares make *Minority Report* Impressionist. Action kinetics perfected into art.

How Spielberg conducts Anderton to his greatest dread is bound to be controversial. In that climactic moment, Spielberg asks the toughest question that, perhaps, has ever been proposed in the popular cinema. He goes against the easy gratification of less serious, less conscientious films such as *The Pledge* (2001) and *In the Bedroom* (2001). It's consistent with Tom Cruise's best-ever performance (especially good when Anderton's anger is checked by his propriety) being mirrored in the principled zealotry of his government rival, Witwer (Colin Farrell), and his gravitas reawakening his mentor Burgess (Max von Sydow). These echoes reinforce the idea of individual moral choices over vacuous movie heroism.

Both Anderton and Agatha's urgent rebound from death (his son, her parents) deepens what otherwise would simply be another Philip K. Dick conceit. *Minority Report* challenges audiences unaccustomed to optimism in this usually dystopian genre. Spielberg's babes-in-the-woods postulants want morally satisfying lives and this is startlingly richer than what recent movies like *Fight Club* (1999), *The Matrix* (1999), *Memento, Training Day* (2001), *Black Hawk Down* (2001), *The Sum of All Fears* (2002) and *The Bourne Identity* (2002) have fed audiences. Numerous sci-fi/action antecedents get summarized then surpassed. (The fairytale verities in Anderton's meeting with Dr. Hineman are not to be discounted; *Minority Report's* humanist answer to sci-fi pessimism shows the influence of Gloria Foster's scene in *The Matrix*, although its payoff, Agatha's stirring recitation, is pure, beautiful Spielberg.) Spielberg's challenge stays consistent with the complex view of human behavior that started his career: Anderton's self-identification through his eyes—and his sight—evokes the story of greed and sacrifice in the 1969 *Night Gallery*. Spielberg's great skill has always exalted vision and he's always recognized its cost: responsibility.

Like da Vinci's study of the body, Spielberg graphs the body politic through Anderton's behavior—a reflection of morality, law and cinema aesthetics. It's a rare achievement because these days a moral movie is a minority report.

*New York Press*
July 2002

# CATCH ME IF YOU CAN (2002)

---

## Catch Spielberg If You Can

**A** COMMA BELONGS IN the title of *Catch Me If You Can*,
Steven Spielberg's defiant new movie that goes back to
the 1960s—the era conservative commentators point to as
starting America's decline—to show the complicated, forgotten
roots of our contemporary social frustration. Spielberg dashes
ahead of all this season's movies—*Antwone Fisher, Gangs of New
York, About Schmidt, 25th Hour, Far from Heaven, Auto Focus,
Confessions of a Dangerous Mind, The Hours*; even the best of
which barely articulate the connection between society and
family, politics and culture, history and the present. Telling the
true story of Frank W. Abagnale Jr., a con artist who switched
identities, posed as an airline copilot, doctor, lawyer and cashed
millions of dollars in bogus checks before he was 21 years old,
Spielberg locates the American myth of ceaseless ambition in
the neurosis of a boy attempting to emulate, please and avenge
his father.

Abagnale's criminal exploits (played as innocent eagerness
by Leonardo DiCaprio) spring from a desire to hold his broken
family together. His father (Christopher Walken) is a war vet, a
businessman and native huckster who married a French woman
(Nathalie Baye) during the Liberation but loses her when he
is hounded for tax evasion. That evasiveness is a trait the son

shares and Frank Jr.'s restlessness and imagination inspire Spielberg's bounding narrative. *Catch Me If You Can* moves like one of the Indiana Jones films—especially evoking *The Last Crusade*'s interplay of a son's impetuousness and a father's wisdom. Abagnale's nonstop adventures are, in part, a search for a more stable father figure and he finds it in Carl Hanratty (Tom Hanks), the FBI agent who stalks him. At every moment of Abagnale's filial panic, the story's flashback structure returns to the "present" where he is in Hanratty's custody—always a moment of self-reflection.

This way Spielberg defuses regular con-artist plot mechanisms; there's little suspense about Abagnale being caught or a trick going wrong as in *The Sting* (1973) yet *Catch Me If You Can* is so charming and watchable that some viewers will concentrate on Abagnale's gimmicks and ignore his desperation, the key to the movie's gravity. With every pulse of the film's forward movement, you're meant to think about the psychology underlying the young trickster's stunts. This constant repositioning of con-game delight signifies the film's moral advance (the cultural progress other filmmakers hereafter will have to catch up to). Spielberg returns the good name to "entertainment"—seriously damaged in the Michael Bay era—by offering more than entertainment.

*Catch Me If You Can* exudes immense cultural awareness. I can't recall another film that so reveled in pop experience while also scrutinizing its folly except for Jonathan Demme's 1986 *Something Wild*. This could be considered Spielberg's Demme movie for the felicitous way it braids together class and sex and genre but, in fact, these themes are always at the heart of Spielberg's most expansive fiction (*1941, The Color Purple, Empire of the Sun*). It is exciting to see an entire era recreated this way—not just surface detail (the opening scene of a *To Tell the Truth* TV broadcast) but also the spirit of the times. Spielberg's breathtaking evocation of the past only works because the period artifacts and settings are authentically expressive of the human experience he depicts.

Of the film's many extraordinary moments, one stands out for refusing disingenuous Hollywood convention: after Abagnale's sexual initiation, he resumes grifting with a new gleam in his eye, an increased appreciation for the women he sees and the avaricious potential that lies before him. Spielberg shoots this as a long pan across a row of female bank tellers, intercutting Abagnale's avid awareness. It helps to have a real movie star like DiCaprio put this across yet most moviemakers never get this rite-of-passage—and it's central to Spielberg's vivid demonstration of American ambition and Abagnale's preening innocence. Musical and visual cues are part of the rush: "The Girl from Ipanema," "The Look of Love," "Come Fly with Me," even a tonally consistent interpolation of the movie *Goldfinger*. Cinematographer Janusz Kamiński brackets the story in monochromes but the mid-'60s flashbacks have the stylized, ecstatic look of Sinatra album covers. John Williams' light-jazz score is like the experimental ones he used to write for Altman though it also suggests *The Pink Panther* (1963) theme shot through with intrigue.

Plaintiveness takes *Catch Me If You Can* beyond simple nostalgia; it captures the tangled essence of American desire. In Abagnale's fascination with flight (to escape the stifling working class), he fetishizes airline pilots—uniformed masculine figures of professionalism, prowess and progress. A dazzling airport ruse with Abagnale in the midst of smiling stewardesses reveals how these jobs brimmed with postwar promise. Although that's the opposite of the '60s hippie myth, Spielberg's vision is wide-eyed and wide-ranging; it includes the era's newly opened-up social landscape. A hospital sequence in Atlanta features a Black kid in an emergency room bearing a gruesome leg wound. Abagnale stares at it and asks the interns around him, "Do you concur?" Similarly the entire film asks what we assent to in our political legacy. It's the Trent Lott question posed by a socially aware pop artist, particularly as he examines a morally challenged kid like Abagnale.

That the story keeps coming back to the father's influence is crucial. Spielberg (and screenwriter Jeff Nathanson, who wrote *Rush Hour 2* (2001)) investigates Abagnale's personal motivation through symbols most filmmakers ignore. Wendell B. Harris' extraordinary con-man movie *Chameleon Street* (1991) (an obvious influence on this film) hinted at the significance of patriarchy then explored individual psychology. *Catch Me* roots its drama in the father-son dynamic to keep Abagnale from being viewed too romantically. DiCaprio and Walken match up superbly. When face-to-face, their gentle eyes contrast youth and age, optimism and pain. Walken has spent most of his late career playing hipster fantasy figures but this is the first time since Abel Ferrara's *The Funeral* (1996) that anyone's put Walken in a credible moral context. The way DiCaprio's delicate features verge into Walken's tormented face illustrates that sons who seek guidance sometimes look upon a void. ("Ask me to stop!" the boy insists.)

Yet, Abagnale's sense of family responsibility persists—even when misguided. His vaguely criminal tendencies are endemic and likened to the IRS' unfairness. ("It's illegal what they're doing to us!" Abagnale's mother says. "They ate the cake, now they want the crumbs," the father groans.) Spielberg knows we have as ambivalent a relationship to government as to our parents. That's where Hanks' Hanratty takes over. This responsible, dedicated G-man suffers his own broken home (he and Abagnale cross paths on lonely Christmas Eves), yet he provides a sense of conscience and understanding—a second father-figure. Their law-and-order dynamic suggests a Road Runner cartoon written by Mark Twain. The moral complexity they exhibit is funny and emotional: crafting his first phony check, Abagnale presses it inside a Gideon Bible. Hanratty takes a Boy Scout oath before Abagnale, but Spielberg conveys it as Trust and Admiration. Essential verities, now as then.

In the nauseatingly hip *Blow* (2001), a drug dealer chased the American dream hypocritically, narcissistically. It was impossible to enjoy or learn from that movie because of its dishonesty—pandering to the youth audience while pretending rebel, entrepreneurial cred. Abagnale's habit of collecting labels torn off product containers (Dad's Root Beer, Spam, Gallo, etc.) more credibly illustrates capitalism's effect on youth—the influence a consumer culture has on one's developing identity. In *Catch Me If You Can*, Abagnale's elusiveness derives from this product- and media-oriented lack of emotional connection. Like the Black protagonist in *Chameleon Street*, this white youth's alienation shows in the various guises he assumes. Encountering a former *Seventeen* magazine model, Abagnale and the girl (Jennifer Garner) are just kids acting out the culture's cynicism in which parent-child exchange frequently gets reduced to the level of bribes. Meeting cute, these lost kids—a baby whore and a baby thief—barter the cost of things, then themselves. (Their high-fashion shoes meet first.)

The depth and bold social critique in scenes like that are typically ignored by Spielberg-haters who make the unoriginal complaint that he merely promotes the Hollywood system. They're also the sort of dull-witted moviegoers who miss that a lingering shot of Abagnale's hotel room number isn't just a close-up of a door but narrative proof of the room number he gave to Hanratty. What's more, it's a visual representation that confides and confesses a character's feelings. This is the epitome of complex, masterful filmmaking. *Catch Me If You Can* has a grave, dark undercurrent despite its surface pastels— the pinks, blues, greens, yellows, sunshine. This vision of the life Americans once idealized also measures the distance we've gotten away from it. Lazy film-watching and dishonest filmmaking won't do. Catch Spielberg, if you can.

*New York Press*
December 2002

# THE TERMINAL (2004)

---

## *Now Playing: The Terminal*

*T*HE *TERMINAL* IS the movie of the moment—especially this moment when the mainstream media trumpets *Fahrenheit 9/11* (2004), buying into the dollars and nonsense surrounding Michael Moore's pseudo-documentary. Steven Spielberg's social comedy treats a wide range of issues that have most preoccupied Americans since 9/11.

Critic John Demetry cites how it restores "the unifying potential of symbols, the validity of signs, the faith in gestures." And he asks Michael Moore and his idolaters: "How can we achieve and practice, organize and institutionalize compassion without imagination?" Accusing Moore of (mis)using facts to put up a "wall in the cultural process," he notes that "Spielberg and *The Terminal* know no boundaries."

The media's failure to recognize *The Terminal*'s significance inspires these pieces by Eric Greene and Gregory Solman, necessary salvos in *First of the Month*'s counter-programming. Think outside the blockbuster.

*First of the Month*
June 2004

When co-editing *First of the Month*, I had the opportunity to get three of the best film critics I know to comment on Spielberg's film—his first new production since the watershed of 9/11 and the beginning of what could be considered his 9/11 trilogy: *The Terminal* was followed by *War of the Worlds* and *Munich*, each film offering perspective on the new world order, the changed consciousness about citizenship, foreignness, humanity, safety.

I had not reviewed the film but Demetry, Greene and Solman's insights aided my reflections on it and its place in Spielberg's filmography. His previous contemporary-set films had all been fantasies, now he was embarking on modern-day realism. But this project is actually a projection of present-day concerns.

*The Terminal* appeared in the same year as the Michael Moore film *Fahrenheit 9/11* and is the exact opposite of that politicized alarum. Spielberg's initial official response to 9/11 is a romantic fable about Viktor Navorski (Tom Hanks) who lands in the U.S. at the moment when a revolution in his Balkan home voids his papers, leaving him stateless. He is in the circumstances that post-9/11 Americans feel spiritually— uncertain about where he belongs and unsure whether his status is secure.

This Homeland Security story reflects Spielberg's ease with American convention illustrated by the lavish, impressive yet common airport set (the most spectacular part of the film's $60 million budget) which in its theme-park normalcy serves as a tribute to the capitalist miracle of America itself. Viktor must make himself at home in this spanking clean site of free enterprise, now entering a phase of HLS crackdown.

Spielberg avoids post-9/11 xenophobia for a tale about Viktor's ad hoc survival—he's a stranger in strategized territory. *The Terminal,* titled as both a port of entry and civilization's end-point, plays out the *e pluribus unum* myth of the American melting pot. This is consistent with the internationalism of the Indiana Jones series and shares a similar openness about emotional and political exchanges between characters. From Viktor's idealized romance with the erratic flight attendant Amelia Warren (Catherine Zeta-Jones); janitor Enrique Cruz's (Diego Luna) love pursuit of customs agent Dolores Torres (Zoe Saldana) to the contrasting senses of duty demonstrated by airport security officer Frank Dixon (Stanley Tucci) and the blue collar baggage-handler (Chi McBride) and custodian Gupta (Kumar Pallana), the panoply of multicultural characters is kept in narrative holding patterns; each person involved in a story of love or labor as a defining essence of U.S. life.

*The Terminal* (based on the actual story of Mehran Karimi Nasseri who landed at Paris' Orly airport in 1978 just after the Iranian revolution) looks past the seriousness of an international incident. There's beneficence in the amusing riff that Gupta does on the one-man Tiananmen Square revolt. That bold stand-off took place not so long ago as part of the recent political reality that Spielberg repeats as when translating the horror that 9/11 forces us to associate with air travel and global interchange into crowd-upliftment. The rest of post-9/11 Hollywood is shaken, unable to rebound.

Spielberg also transforms destruction into art. Viktor hand-crafts an airport rest area via intricately assembled mosaic pieces—a collage of refuse, inspiration and aspiration—to impress Amelia. Expressing his ardor and his creativity is both contribution and tribute. The richness of this gesture makes for one of the many instances when yearning and effort, desire and risk, well-up into a full experience; the mosaic symbolizes the purpose of Viktor's sojourn to America. (His resourcefulness recalls young Jim's versatility and survival skills throughout *Empire of the Sun*.) It is revealed that he comes here out of family duty and is drawn toward the spiritual beacon of jazz, the musical form created as the highest practice of communication originated by people of the country's socially oppressed. As Greene said, Viktor "sees America the way we would like to be seen, the way we feel we used to be seen by the world." The most present-day film of Spielberg's career sees that fractured, splintered America has a future. Spielberg rebukes millennial cynicism with art.

# WAR OF THE WORLDS (2005)

## *La Guerra de Todos Mundos*

**W**ITHOUT DOUBT, THE most anticipated summer release will be *La Guerra del Todos Mundos* by Estaban Digamont. No one expects American filmmakers to be capable of making genre movies that also deal with urgent political topics. It's customary to accept political themes from foreign filmmakers whom we don't associate with big-budget studio extravaganzas. If you've seen the trailers for *La Guerra del Todos Mundos* in theaters (or on tv), you know that its power will only be denied by the blind or the willfully mean-spirited. Catch the terrifying image of contemporary destruction intercut with Common Man (and Everychild) awe. It's a B-movie trope, but it reimagines the world-unifying moment of this millennium as a haunting pop myth. This summer, expect Digamont to confirm the power of genre movies.

*New York Press*
May 2005

# Refugees and Searchers to the Movies

## ONE

"**A**RE WE STILL alive?" That's the line incarnating the unexpectedly avant-garde challenge in Steven Spielberg's *War of the Worlds*. It's when the film steps beyond the simple conventions of genre filmmaking—of being a movie about an invasion from Mars—and expresses our very contemporary concern with survival. Yes, this line speaks to post-9/11 consciousness. It gets said when dockworker Ray Farrier (Tom Cruise) and his two children have retreated to a basement bunker in a suburban home to escape an unseen, explosive cataclysm that comes deafeningly closer. But more than that, it's when Spielberg sublates our sophistication about filmmaking—and film watching—to address the worries that people have in their heads, even as they tell themselves they're merely seeking "entertainment."

In that avant-garde challenge, Spielberg lets the screen go black for about five seconds. The communal experience of film-going then becomes a shared nightmare. With the screen unlit, the emergency lights in the theater are the only source of illumination. If you jump (as I did), you fear for a moment that the movie has stopped—the reel fallen off its plate, the fantasy interrupted by unfunny, drop-dead reality. "Are we still alive?" whispered by Farrier's daughter Rachel (Dakota Fanning) is an inquiry that invokes our own doubts about our safety, our capacity to dream, our possible awakening to dire reality. It recalls how many people felt after 9/11. Are we dreaming? Are we still alive? Bringing everyday experience and existential contemplation together so forcefully, Spielberg joins the ranks of the most audacious avant-garde filmmakers: He turns the popcorn movie experience into a consideration of the abyss.

*War of the Worlds* is the most powerful movie of the new century thus far. It's no surprise that many critics have been skeptical about its meaning and its effect, because it overturns every assumption that is casually held about the purpose of movies. *War of the Worlds* challenges how we reconcile our need for entertainment with our awareness of political reality after 9/11.

Let's immediately dispose of the naive assumption that this is an entertainment about aliens—*E. T.* angrily remade by *Bad Santa* (2003). It's something far different—not snarky but alarmed. Spielberg's previous film, *The Terminal*, confronted convivial, in fact benign, issues about America as an international symbol of freedom and welcome. It was a response to 9/11 that asked Why? Dramatizing Spielberg's (and our) bewilderment, it jumped off from the notion of America as a world help-mate—a capitalist Arcadia no one would object to but might, possibly, have underappreciated. Tom Hanks' misplaced immigrant Viktor is stuck at JFK airport while his home country undergoes a plausible eastern European revolution—thus leaving him stateless. But the naïf Viktor, doesn't simply buy into mainline America's preferred version of that utopian myth. The Statue of Liberty idea ("Give me your tired, poor and restless, yearning to be free") was passed on to him by his ancestors—through his father's reality-based affection for American jazz music; the articulation of a downtrodden people who magically found a means of

**273**

expressing their dreams in a land that formerly enslaved them. *The Terminal* examined Hope. *War of the Worlds* is the equally valid post-9/11 examination of Fear. Instead of Why? it asks: What do we do now?

Working within the innocuous context of the science-fiction/fantasy genre, Spielberg has made a movie that, surprisingly, gets real about the need to prepare for war. (Just as *Close Encounters* contained images of awesome agape, *War of the Worlds* is filled with awesome shock.) That Pirandellian moment that wakes up viewers by blacking them out and leaving them in a felt state of emergency through the imbrication of theater houselights forces our consciousness about the cinematic and cinema-going process into moral awareness. We're not just here to be entertained but to connect our imaginative faculties to what is most important in our lives.

Spielberg is aware American popular culture cannot, conscientiously, be made the same way after 9/11. And, despite conventional critical wisdom, he's the one pop artist most alive to the profundity of the way we live now. He has remade *War of the Worlds* not simply as an homage to Orson Welles' 1938 radio spectacular or Byron Haskin's Technicolor 1953 dazzlement. Rather, Spielberg re-conceives this make-believe—internalizing the psychic trauma of 9/11—but with the faith, like Viktor's, that American art-making is a serious endeavor. Movies like *The Color Purple, Schindler's List, Amistad* and *Saving Private Ryan* were not Oscar bait but efforts of a Hollywood practitioner to contemplate the world and history more earnestly—though he proved it in the dark like a deceptively playful jazz artist.

# TWO

Tom Cruise's father figure at War first becomes memorable during a moment when he is stunned, rendered helpless. After seeing the attack of the aliens first hand, his face covered in the ash of vaporized innocent citizens, Ray Farrier becomes a lightning rod for his children's awareness of the terrible state of things. How his daughter Rachel and his son Robbie (Justin Chatwin) react to the dire phenomena shows Speilberg's real-life sensitivity. Ray isn't sure what to do; yet he and his children have notions beyond the survival instinct. "Is it the terrorists?" Rachel wonders aloud. "Is it the Europeans?" Robbie asks, dredging up the recent hostility the European community has shown towards the American government.

Critics have been unwilling to see how the film plays out Spielberg's not-namby-pamby, not conventionally "liberal" response to 9/11. His concern is with the younger generation's clear-eyed identification with the cause of humanity; their natural feelings and political instincts as embodied in the son's insistence that he be allowed to "enlist" or at least personally observe the battle. ("You have to let me do this!" he insists to his understandably protective father. Those who think Spielberg follows the standard Hollywood-liberal line might be taken aback when they realize that Spielberg is not mocking youthful bellicosity and patriotic fervor, a young man's willingness to "sign-up.")

*War of the Worlds* is about fear and action. While liberal critics enthused over the nonsensical references to George W. Bush in *Star Wars: Episode III – Revenge of the Sith* (2005) ("This is how liberty dies, to thunderous applause." And "Only

**275**

a Sith believes in absolutes"), they conveniently disregard how Spielberg dramatizes war experiences: Rachel's trepidation, Robbie's eagerness to join-up and fight. This young generation's idealism takes the movie beyond their father's desperation and caution (which evokes the trepidation of the older generation and the cluelessness of the doctrinaire Left). Spielberg digs into grass roots intuition—the aggression that legendarily spurs us on. That's why the movie ends in Boston, with a shot of a Minuteman statue that illustrates the historic American struggle for freedom and independence. This piece of statuary is a startling reminder of what freedom looks like; for alert viewers it may even serve as a deliberate contrast to those famous 2003 images of Saddam Hussein's statue coming down (again and again) in that Baghdad square.

It is a sign of Spielberg's uniqueness as a pop artist that he uses avant-garde, high-tech filmmaking means to articulate what some would call a conservative patriotic message. Leftist critics insist this is proof of his non-progressive thinking (his "lack [of] self-knowledge" according to *The Nation*). But *War of the Worlds*, so kinetically adept and visually astonishing, is certainly the work of a film artist fully in-tune with his emotional responses. What left pundits don't realize is that he is also instinctively in touch with how audiences take in cinematic stimuli, aware of their subconscious response. Snob critics, satisfied with their sense of superiority, constantly relegate Spielberg to realms of non-seriousness and trivial manipulation. But it is an observable fact that audiences at *War of the Worlds* do not hoop and holler as they did at *Independence Day*, enjoying the violence, savoring the nifty death routines. That silly film (and its recent doomsday equivalent, Roland Emmerich's *The Day After Tomorrow* (2004)) wasn't concerned with "Are We Still Alive?" It was demonstrably non-political. *War of the Worlds* should be appreciated for its political sophistication and subtle power.

# THREE

The "Are We Still Alive?" moment evokes the scene in Hitchcock's *The Birds* (1963) where a family under siege waits in their home, anticipating the worst. Spielberg recreates that ominous quiet but then extends the action-movie formula for excitation in taut, anxiety-inducing increments. After 9/11 he won't play with dread. The poetic anguish of *The Birds* is revived here but re-imagined—ready for a world in which 9/11 has stirred long-suppressed fears among Americans who had previously imagined war as something that happened elsewhere—not in one's backyard. Among the extraordinary images in *War of the Worlds* is the scene that follows that "Are We Still Alive?" blackout. As if awakening at some terrible dawn, we see an American home with its front blasted away, a downed jet-engine turbine where a dining table used to be. The juxtaposition is surreal. Farrier carefully instructs his daughter not to look, to keep her eyes on him no matter what. He doesn't want her to see the destruction, the upheaval and devastation of domesticity.

Spielberg takes audiences through precisely what parents, after 9/11, are unable to shield their children against. He treats comfortable American audiences like war-torn refugees, not sci-fi geeks. The opposite of this noble impulse can be found in Sam Mendes' *Jarhead* (2005). Instead of addressing Operation Iraqi Freedom, Mendes goes back to the 1991 Desert Shield-into-Desert Storm. He rewrites David O. Russell's good *Three Kings* (1999)—a surprisingly thoughtful and wide-ranging observation of American power and innocence—then slickly invokes Vietnam-era skepticism that was featured in *Full Metal Jacket* (1987), *Platoon* and *Apocalypse Now*. Mendes, a British citizen who has never made a movie about his home turf, is committed to the easy, supercilious tactic of satirizing the follies of the world's largest superpower. As slick as Mike Nichols, he knows this plays well among the left media. In *Jarhead* he casts a quick, lame glance at American foreign policy without risking the dissension caused by Spielberg's native understanding. Mendes commits an insulting revision of pop art and pop politics when he implicitly encourages his '05 audience to adopt a kind of unearned version of the cynicism once expressed by those who underwent the Vietnam experience. (His GI grunt tale never evokes Oliver Stone's *Born on the Fourth of July* (1989) perhaps because Mendes' shallow social consciousness was born no earlier than March 2003.)

*War of the Worlds* pushes its avant-garde political art toward a new understanding of American history—lessons derived from the most complicated, not most fashionable, cinema. Spielberg has finally made his version of that movie brat staple *The Searchers*, John Ford's 1956 western reverie of the Indian Wars that was also a revelation of the conservative and liberal split in America's consciousness. Spielberg is fully cognizant of Ford's political ambivalence; recent history has caused him to share it. Ray Farrier isn't a racist pioneer like John Wayne's Ethan Edwards but he does venture into new territory—the post-9/11 American trepidation that is not racist, nor xenophobic like Ethan Edwards', but healthily skeptical, practical and defensive. *The Searchers* doesn't have a moment as stressful as Ray's conflict with Harlan Ogilvy (Tim Robbins). Probably many lefties were disturbed by Robbins' casting as a half-crazed survivalist; they expected him to personify the usual lefty positions of his own propaganda films *Bob Roberts* (1992) and *Cradle Will Rock* (1999). But Robbins applies his full artistry to portraying a complicated, modern type—the scared American unable to rationalize his defenses. When he and Ray clash (a harrowing tête-à-tête that is also a power struggle), the shifts between heroism and cowardice, intelligence and desperation are actively visualized.

Spielberg realizes he's portraying the reality of uncertainty—the doubts about American might and right and the difficulty of determining which character ultimately represents which. But the logic of his narrative implicitly endorses Ray's will. Ray must take action he cannot fully justify to his daughter and, again, commands her not to look. The pop-wise audience is momentarily spared the sight of murder, but Spielberg subtly admits it in an ensuing moment of vicious pantomime: an alien, image-ed as a glaring eye—a nightmarish depiction of self-consciousness—is literally beheaded. The instant of Ray's inhumanity, when he submits to his own murderous impulse, is also the moment when he kills his own sleep. He is neither condoned nor condemned. By the end of the movie, Spielberg clarifies the personal consequences of the ugly act that Ray was forced to commit, acknowledging what all the movie brats from Scorsese and George Lucas to Paul Schrader and John Milius have been reluctant to admit about Ethan Edwards in *The Searchers*. Although they celebrate intransigence, they don't face up to the discomfiting reality of John Wayne's hard man. Spielberg exposes their obliviousness in the controversial final moment of *War of the Worlds*, which fools mistake for sentimentality.

In this scene Ray Farrier is excluded from his family's reunion. He is kept outside the miraculously preserved homestead in an image constructed just like the closing scene of *The Searchers*. After all he has gone through and what he has seen and done, he cannot sit easily at the American family hearth. And despite gossip column pariah Tom Cruise playing the part, the suffering of his character Ray Farrier is noble. It should not be disdained, nor his wartime suffering ignored as happened with Vietnam vets. He must stand outside the American home—a civilian-soldier whose humanity and psychic well-being have been sacrificed. This is not standard self-reflexive, postmodern iconography but a prescient movie image built on Spielberg's familiarity with the cost of life during wartime—from pop zeitgeist (*1941*) to contemporary remembrance (*Saving Private Ryan*). The image of Ray removed from domestic idylls poetically defines the situation of citizens in crisis from the Twin Towers to Hurricane Katrina, from refugees to searchers.

Ray's forlorn figure standing in solitary on an autumnal suburban street reveals that weight felt by every post-9/11 American desperately holding on for something to believe in, wondering "Are We Still Alive?" For some, the answer to this moral question may well be unimaginable, as if the screen of our collective consciousness has gone blank. Spielberg's final scene fills in our doubt, suggestively. It anticipates every family reunion that occurs as a result of Operation Iraqi Freedom— that is, the lucky ones.

*First of the Month*
December 2005

# MUNICH (2005)

---

## *Spielberg Climbs Another Mountain*

**H**OW DO YOU show the effect murder has on the cosmos? Steven Spielberg essays that question in an awesomely expressive moment of his new film *Munich*. A scene depicting the massacre of Israel's athletic team by the Palestinian Liberation Organization's "Black September" terrorists at the 1972 Olympics in Munich, Germany, contains a shocking, matter-of-fact portrayal of slaughter. During the mayhem, a young man is riddled by bullets and blood spurts out of his body, spraying the wall behind him. Spielberg dissolves from those pink and red gore patterns to the fiery sunlit tint on clouds being viewed through an airplane window by Avner (Eric Bana), who's employed by Mossad, Israel's foreign intelligence. Avner's what Saul Bellow would call a dangling man: suspended—airborne—on a mission to track down and kill the engineers of the Munich slaying.

Avner's imagining of the Munich horror suggests a flashback, yet it isn't; it's both historical recall and spiritual recoil. When that bloodshed blurs into the heavens, it creates a stunned realization unlike any other aftermath of violence seen in the movies. Battle scenes may typically break up, soak and despoil the earth, but this transition abstracts mortal combat. By showing the celestial imprint of murder, Spielberg suggests that it disrupts one's consciousness. So Avner's nightmare wakes him—not at sunset as a banal filmmaker might literalize the shift from red-to-red, sadness to depression, but at dawn. That's Spielberg's singular, personal vision in one image. He isn't interested in the cynical politics of doom but the poetry of humanism which *Munich* portrays through Avner's struggle to keep living—and live sanely—despite the world's horror and the countdown to his own deadly task.

Striving to sustain moral continuity with the virtues taught in Judaism, Avner feels obligated to act on behalf of the state. His relation to the cosmos gives *Munich* depth that viewers of espionage thrillers are unaccustomed to exploring. Assessing Avner's scruples is Spielberg's way of elevating the assassin genre so that it contains the moral inquiry of the highest forms of drama. You have to compare it to Greek tragedy because Hollywood has inured most viewers to the intricacies of consciousness, of violence-with-consequence, of moral certitude. In both aesthetic and political terms, Spielberg has taken the high road.

But that doesn't mean *Munich* peddles lofty bromides. The sun doesn't rise over a happily united Holy Land. Actually, *Munich* may be the most down-and-dirty espionage movie ever made—more moving and exacting than any film produced during the Cold War. Call Spielberg "The artist who came in from the cold," bringing humane standards to a medium that regularly earns profit by the cool exploitation of man's inhumanity to man. Scenes of killing, and the moments of cunning that lead up to death, are done here with absolute, graphic realism. (Nothing is cheaply ironic like blood splashing on a portrait of Jesus in *Capote's* (2005) massacre scene.) Spielberg's almost casual, reportorial observation of murder is intimate, shocking and reverberates long after the movie is over. Watching the savagery in the Israeli athlete's dormitory feels so much like an existential trap that it has dull, dreadful terror. That refusal to "wow" proves Spielberg's respect for history; it is shown through his exquisitely subtle technique that calls on our imagination and thus moves one to utter sorrow.

Unfortunately, some people consider themselves beyond such feeling. Their objections to Spielberg's sensitivity (suspicious that it is manipulative and opportunistic), shows nothing more than their emotional detachment from human experience. Accessing compassion used to be the basis of moviegoing. *Munich*'s power comes from Spielberg's insistence that audiences once again feel a basic repulsion about killing; that they be willing to rethink the political and artistic conventions that offer bloodlust as an acceptable solution for moviegoers, terrorists or avengers.

Virtually reversing the axiom spoken in *Schindler's List* ("To save one life is to save the whole world entire"), Spielberg uses Avner's story, inspired by the Mossad's actual—rarely admitted—mission of taking lives in revenge, to mourn the degradation of mankind entire. His focus on Avner and the stealth team of killers who help carry out his gruesome errands invites contemplation of our civilization-wide depravity.

Each man in Avner's murder squad has individual feelings about responding to the Black September group's Munich atrocity: Steve (Daniel Craig), a blue-eyed embodiment of Sabra spirit, is driven by vengeance; Robert (Mathieu Kassovitz), a young bomb-maker, shares a sense of mission, even though it takes him outside his expertise; Carl (Ciarán Hinds) is older and resigned to the duty but is ethically split;

while Hans' (Hanns Zischler) quiet maturity masks lethal resolve. Their dedication to Israel, combined with expressed hostility or ambivalence about their targets, makes the movie suspenseful in a more meaningful way than an ordinary action film. Spielberg doesn't create superficial excitation; every action (Avner casing a Mediterranean honeymoon hotel as a potential bomb site), every violent set-piece (a botched mission that turns into a nighttime street shootout), tests what each of these counter-assassins believes in.

*Munich* is a reminder of the morality that mere politics would have us forget. It applies principled discipline to acts that have been sanctioned by personal passion in the political world and by slack ethics in Hollywood. Spielberg and screenwriters Tony Kushner and Eric Roth refuse any form of vicious delectation. Their globe-trotting storyline, as Avner's death team hunts down Black September across Europe, coincidentally takes in an itinerary of Western subterfuge. Something tragically fated emanates from each locale (Italy, France, Greece, England, Holland, Brooklyn), as if the legacy of Western history with its stories of conquest, domination, subjugation and warfare (the pogroms of Russia, the horrors of WWII and the partitioning of Palestine), had led ineluctably to Mossad's secretive brutality.

There hasn't been a historical screenplay with such fleet action—ideological discussions paced by momentous events—since *Amistad*. Spielberg has developed a special sophistication. Note the extraordinary moment when Avner receives his calling from inside the Israeli government's inner sanctum and meets Prime Minister Golda Meir (Lynn Cohen, combining soft guile and iron will—an uncanny performance). The presence of recognizable real-life figures evokes those scenes of *Angels in America* where historical personages intersect the modern plane of the living protagonists. Meir tells Avner, "Every civilization finds it necessary to renegotiate compromise with its own values." Politics, the past and prophecy converge on Avner's head through Golda, their sly agent. He is immediately launched into future history—which becomes the forward movement of the film we watch.

How do you convey what murdering does to a person's soul? That transformation, that damnation, is what Avner's personal agony reveals. Before receiving his assignment, news of the Munich massacre is broadcast to the world through a montage of intercutting TV news images of the dead Jewish athletes with dossier photos of the dead Palestinians—a two-sided media eulogy, a double-edged tragedy. Avner takes on this bifurcated awareness; being both a Sabra and a young husband with a pregnant wife, Daphna (Ayelet Zurer). This son of Israel experiences the average man's overwhelming confrontation with political obligation. His youth, sexual avidity and casual assumptions are all put in doubt. Bana has a good face for this—boyish yet virile. His simple, dark eyes seem to get darker the more he kills (he acts with his irises)—the face of a man who's seen too much. Through the enormity of Avner's pain, *Munich* addresses that of the conscientious world. It even enfolds the young Palestinian men's similar crisis in *Paradise Now* (2005). And when Avner holds his newborn baby in his arms, fortunate filmgoers may recall the scene in Marco Bellocchio's *Good Morning, Night* (2005) when a politically-conflicted young radical cradled an infant: both images suggest the personal caretaking of a country's future (Israel's, Italy's), but they also depict a young soldier's confusion about his innocent self.

Spielberg gets so deep into the psychic tortures of his conflicted protagonist (Avner warns Carl, "Stop chasing the mice in your head") that the simultaneously meditative and pell-mell narrative of Avner's journey in hell may confound viewers who want a routine action-thriller—a James Bond movie, a *Dirty Dozen* (1967) update, a *Usual Suspects* (1995) correction, probably even *The Delta Force* (1986). But *Munich* makes no attempt to satisfy such juvenile taste. It is the film's soulfulness, not simply its narrative efficiency, that makes it compelling. While showing the forces that cost Avner his peace, Spielberg undertakes to revise the genres that have distorted or trivialized our understanding of politics and morality.

Most action films never require us to think beyond the gears clicking in a killer's head; *Munich* achieves multileveled postmodern analysis by paralleling Avner's killing mission to the recent cinematic history of political distrust. Elaborate sequences, such as the plan to install a bomb in the Parisian apartment where a Palestinian lives with his wife and daughter, hold us in a moral, negotiating vice—like those daring, suspended-time sequences in Sam Peckinpah's *The Killer Elite* (1975) and Jonathan Demme's *The Manchurian Candidate* (2004). Avner's deliberation becomes our own—that is, if we don't simply hunger for bloodshed. It's as if Avner becomes our moral surrogate when he and his men feel unaccountably besieged. They're suspicious of the boat they rent for a journey; Avram dismantles a bed (looking for a bomb) when fear prevents him from sleeping. He—and we—enter the paranoid world of *The Conversation* where the not-innocent are overwhelmed by their own guilt.

How brave that Spielberg calls the U.S.A.'s alliance with Israel to such moral account—but does so through the familiar codes of film-watching (and more rigorously than the trifling *Syriana* (2005)). *Munich*'s amazing subplot of Avner's collusion with a family of French mercenaries (Michael Lonsdale as Papa and Mathieu Amalric as the son, Louis, who supply weapons plus the names and locations of PLO agents) rewrites Francis Ford Coppola's political oeuvre (from *The Godfather* to the French colonists' dinner sequence in *Apocalypse Now Redux* (2001)). Coppola's deluxe panoply of American family- and social-consciousness informs this concise story of political and familial corruption. The baroque intrigue of hideously complacent bourgeois operatives and the tension of father-son competitiveness taunts the severe lack that fatherless Avner feels in his own life. Engaging such a well-defined Oedipal myth reflects Avner's tribal guilt. We're brought inside the terrible unofficial network of international politics without overlooking the way personal inclinations affect political activity.

Next, Spielberg and Kushner boldly shift from Papa and Louis' demoralizing seduction to Avner being praised by his mother (Gila Almagor). "A place on earth," she intones. "We have a place on earth at last." Her land-poor satisfaction recalls the avarice and selfishness the bourgeois French family exhibited. The tenets of homeland venality contrast Avner's visionary insight of blood in the clouds—the intuition that man is part of everything, as is God. By this point, Avner's disgust with the worldly aims of war allows us to see through his mother's exultation—to see it as morally pathetic. This moment reflects back on the Meir scene of the mother as politician and, again, Avner is pressured by his love for everything this woman represents. Nothing in even Jean Renoir's great oeuvre matches this ambivalence. Avner is stretched between devotion and uncertainty. When Louis tells him, "We don't like any governments. We're ideologically promiscuous," his bad example only facilitates Avner's sins.

Today's movie culture has so thoroughly written off the concept of sin that any movie ridiculing it (from *Hellboy* (2004) and *My Summer of Love* (2004) to *The Squid and the Whale* (2005)) is guaranteed to be widely praised. This fondness for transgression might explain the trouble Spielberg has run into with *Munich*. He explicates a grievous sense of wrong-doing that communicates best to those who are open to an ecumenical view of life (or if that term scares you, Judeo-Christian). *Munich's* vision is truly Judeo-Christian in that it doesn't confuse morality with politics. It uses one to test the other.

Surely it is the concept of sin that angers Spielberg's current detractors. They don't want any selfish or transgressive actions to be judged. The fact that *Munich* won't settle for memorializing Israel's revenge offends some propagandists' self-justifying nihilism as surely as it also spoils (but enlightens) the action-movie party. Blood-seekers simply can't get off on *Munich's* complexity. *Munich* doesn't arouse vengeance; it isn't about "fairness" or even-handed allocation of blame. It's about how retribution (eye-for-an-eye politics) unbalances the universe, how Avner unquiets his soul. Throughout his killings, Avner carries a consciousness of heritage and the weight of history; plus, a sense of justice challenged by a sense of responsibility—burdens. Miraculously, this story of mankind's moral burden becomes the perfect summary for Spielberg's 9/11 trilogy—the most significant event of 2005 cinema.

*The New York Press*
December 2005

# INDIANA JONES AND THE KINGDOM OF THE CRYSTAL SKULL (2008)

## *Another Indy Classic*

I NDIANA JONES FIRST appears in *Indiana Jones and the Kingdom of the Crystal Skull* being thrown onto the ground. He's in the midst of some ongoing escapade with new-to-us foreign-accented villains and a treasure-hunting mercenary— familiar stuff, although it doesn't quite give us our bearings. Yet this is true to form for the most problematic movie series in Hollywood history; it was less about Indy in peril than the filmmakers working through disoriented feelings about Americanism and the world.

The 1980s Indiana Jones trilogy was notable for starting out fresh every time. Unique for a Hollywood entertainment enterprise, it was made during the era when pop filmmakers could experiment in philology—as in the self-reflexive overture sequence of *The Last Crusade*: It made Indy's backstory both a biological jest and a catalog of chase-movie conventions. The clichés of the serial adventure form had become the staple of television, but Steven Spielberg elevated them with cinematic wit.

As the most versatile Hollywood film artist since D.W. Griffith, Spielberg can't help showing off his mastery, doing so in a challenging, though eager-to-please, way. During a marathon *Kingdom of the Crystal Skull* chase scene—one of those non-stop, gear-shifting, three-ring-circuses-on-wheels that you expect from the series—a brief interval shows a character bounced from a hurtling jeep and then moving bodily through trees as if in an aerial ballet. The details of this swinging, rapturous jetée must be seen to be believed (and its humor instantaneously interpreted). Spielberg turns a jokey, lowbrow movie reference into a distillation of character and an anthropological theorem—without ever slowing the moment's pace, or lessening its significance as a plot point. Film craft at this level is wondrous indeed, not only surpassing expectations for the Indiana Jones formula (action, action, action) but enhancing it with a bonus of suggestive lyricism.

But most impressively, *Crystal Skull* carries the burden of making popular entertainment that must also be taken seriously. Spielberg assumed that mandate through the conceit of planning the Indiana Jones films in the mass-art style of afternoon movie serials but with a modern sensibility that could galvanize the revanchist Reagan-era culture. It worked almost too well. The 1981 *Raiders of the Lost Ark* was a hyper-smart action-movie pastiche—produced by super-square George Lucas before Tarantino made such things hip. Lucas and Philip Kaufman's story idea was written by Lawrence Kasdan in the revisionist spirit of '70s American Renaissance movies, yet remained essentially juvenile like Lucas' *Star Wars*. When the impudent, postmodern imperialism of *Raiders* was followed by the comic essay on the morality of speed in 1984's *Temple of Doom*, both needed some crucial political correction— eventually provided by *The Last Crusade*'s overview of Western political and religious heritage.

Between those films, Spielberg had made the radical-humanist *The Color Purple* whose cultural-racial insight helped him alter Indy's jingoism, compressing a psychological arc—from national arrogance to enlightenment with honesty that the slickly nationalistic James Bond series never dared. In the stout-hearted person of Harrison Ford, Indy was a new generation's Ethan Edwards—a young John Wayne-bwana dispatched to curate the Third World. Not an identity-cloaked sci-fi superhero but a bullwhip-toting, fedora-wearing, two-fisted sophisticate who respected the Bible and saved the children of India—a superb hero yet an intrinsically nostalgic figure.

Spielberg turned claptrap into a reconsideration of what tickled America's sense of international sovereignty; non-thinking adolescent viewers (of all ages) could thrill to the can-do effrontery. Now, in *Kingdom of the Crystal Skull*, archeologist-adventurer Indy confronts fascists and mercenaries on native soil. It's 1957 Nevada, yet it feels startlingly close to home. Action then moves to South America where Indy attempts to rescue Oxley (John Hurt), a professor devoted to finding the Crystal Skull of Akator. Indy outraces Irina Spalko (Cate Blanchett), a Soviet agent with Nazi ties who seeks to use the occult, extraterrestrial powers of the skull as a paranormal military weapon.

So it's back to claptrap but phenomenally executed—as in that wondrous, airborne divertissement. And that's what sticks. Think back on those relentless battle scenes in *The Lord of the Rings* trilogy, the unintelligible carousing in the *Pirates of the Caribbean* movies or that stupendously stupid dinosaur chase in Peter Jackson's *King Kong* (2005). They all reduced movie kinetics to CGI excess. Since the last Indiana Jones film (1989's *The Last Crusade*), we've seen the standard for crowd-pleasing action lowered year by year—reason enough to justify Spielberg's decision to resurrect his and Lucas' series, to go at their Americanism project once again.

The pressing challenge of *Kingdom of the Crystal Skull* is for Spielberg to address the generation that grew up with Indiana Jones and may now feel they have outgrown him. But to avoid that fickle self-loathing (the sort that made the *Star Wars* generation turn against Lucas' *Star Wars* prequels), Spielberg has to raise their appreciation of action-movie tropes. Not an easy task when the lusterless, pandering *Iron Man* (2008) is lavished with praise due to its bland political postures. *Crystal Skull*'s chase and fight set pieces and its scenes of natural and anthropological spectacle (such as a waterfall sequence that compares to *Way Down East*) feature comically laid-out cause-and-effect routines (like that land-and-trees car chase), plus untricked-up action-clarity (keeping track of each hard-charging character; balancing strategy, fluke and danger). Virtuosity as, apparently, only Spielberg and editor Michael Kahn know how to do.

First, Spielberg has to compete for his stolen, degraded audience (kidnapped by Peter Jackson and Gore Verbinski; simplified by *National Treasure* (2004), *Godzilla* (1998), *The Mummy* (1999)). Then, he needs to work through the geo-political quandary of post-9/11 pop. This is what makes the series of cliffhangers more than rote; their flamboyance becomes trenchant. *Last Crusade* taught Indy his place in global politics; but when that lesson was applied in Brett Eisner's *Sahara* (2005), the example of political engagement went unappreciated. Going back to the "naiveté" and isolationism of *Raiders* would be unconscionable, so Spielberg and screenwriter David Koepp patch together an intermediate solution: These action scenes are reminders of courageous effort, the impetus that has seeped out of American pop culture except when practiced by characters who are gangsters or drug dealers. (Courage is anathema in today's mainstream depictions of soldiers at war.) *Crystal Skull* may lack the contemporary political relevance of *Sahara*, but it sublimates post-9/11 paranoia into a version of Spielberg's cosmology while also depicting past political lessons about which we are no longer naive.

*Crystal Skull* puts Indy into the Cold War '50s—of Elvis Presley's "Hound Dog," the homegrown Red Scare, incredible suburban sprawl, Soviet espionage and fear of The Bomb. These slightly updated stakes are not a retreat; Spielberg can only hope his franchise will appeal to a matured sense of history that the original three films gradually established. It should enable audiences to take in an expanded historical view. *Crystal Skull*'s self-referential concept is also philology but complicated by an emotional disturbance that any pop adept (who isn't thinking like a *Variety* tout) should realize parallels our deeply troubled national-domestic confidence. This is a remedial *Raiders*. Koepp's plot closes a circle for the series, providing Indy a young '50s juvenile delinquent sidekick named Mutt (Shia LaBeouf) and re-establishing Indy's relationship with *Raiders'* Marion Ravenwood (Karen Allen).

To view *Crystal Skull* as commercial gimcrack is superficial; it blithely ignores the ethical and aesthetic project that always troubled the series. Far from perfectly conceived, it slaps together a family reunion and an ancient celestial visitation almost desperately. Karen Allen pops up with wide-eyed pluckiness, but she can't resolve the 1981 problem that she and Ford have no rapport; their bonding feels conviction-less. LaBeouf works better as the smug Mutt (a perfect name for Boomer-era privilege and a kid who combs his ducktail as a narcissistic

tic). When Mutt discovers that Indy is more than a teacher, he looks genuinely impressed—and filial. Mutt's entrance in leather jacket and jeans on a motorcycle intentionally evokes Brando in *The Wild One* (1953) as a shortcut cultural marker. Its glibness is excusable only because it quickly folds into a *Back to the Future* (1985) 1950s spoof: Indy prompts Mutt to start a fist-fight in a diner to distract a pair of Soviet goons and the melee (a preppie shouts "Get that greaser!") ironically reminds us there was class conflict in the context of the Cold War. Through these scenes *Crystal Skull* looks at American history Indy-wise—as a pursuit of cultural knowledge.

The low point comes (unsurprisingly) from bad luck Blanchett's Spalko; this off/on, Soviet/Nazi, rapier-wielding, kung-fu fighting, dominatrix/sorceress belongs to no specific era. Spalko's pursuit of the Crystal Skull and trifling with the otherworldly suggests *Mad* magazine (without the jokes). Her treachery is best revealed in the subtle crosscut from Indy inside the Crystal Skull temple to an exterior where the sound of gunshots from Spalko's troops introduces a pan over the bodies of dead jungle natives—genocide memorialized in a glyph. Unfortunately, these travestied Third Worlders retrojects *Crystal Skull* past *Sahara*, back to the shallowness of *Raiders*. Koepp could have created a South American archeologist to personalize the threat of global fascism. Indy's quote of Robert Oppenheimer quoting from a Hindu bible ("Now I am become death—a destroyer of worlds") lacks urgency; avoiding that kind of chauvinism is what makes *The Last Crusade* the peak Indy film.

Like Griffith, Spielberg uses pop idioms without corrupting their cultural significance. Genre-manipulating directors like David Cronenberg and Todd Haynes cannot claim such pop articulation. Our familiarity with Indy (Harrison

Ford's principled, clean-cut, robust, determinism) makes his exploits relatable. This older Indy runs by shifting his body weight for stability. It's an unavoidable adjustment, like the cinematography that shows Janusz Kamiński's one limitation: He can't match Douglas Slocombe's polish, that sharp gloss that was itself a comment on the Hollywood imperium. But when *Crystal Skull* works best, the battle of good guy/bad guy motives comes down to observable action—logistics match dialectics and we knowingly behold contemporary myth.

That's the significance naysayers deny about Spielberg's imagery. Note the extraordinary elegance of the film's first car chase, a camera-and-vehicle maneuver that puts the one-note, overemphasized torsion of Tarantino's *Grindhouse* (2007) car chase to shame. Because it also plays out Indy's anti-fascist effort, it has rare expediency. Another instantly classic sequence—a poetic etude like that airborne ballet—shows Indy stumbling upon an American suburb where he hears a '50s TV jingle echoing throughout a neighborhood that's as eerily uninhabited as that housing tract in *L'Avventura* (1961). This scene discloses a time warp of domestic paranoia, utterly true to the '50s but that traps Indy—and us—in a state of moral suspension that uncannily evokes post-9/11 trauma. This is Spielberg at his most pop and most amazing: turning the shiny American quotidian into an authentically numinous and strange experience. The astonishing image of Indy rising from post-WWII rubble to observe a nuclear mushroom cloud has the effect of situating historical catastrophe in modern terms. (Something Richard Kelly bungled in *Southland Tales* (2006) and that the Wachowski Brothers' goofy astrophysics never came close to in *Speed Racer* (2008).) It simultaneously updates the *Raiders* series' original, mid-century setting while implicating the modern audience as conscious, wide-eyed witnesses to the phenomena of modernity. Playfulness at this level gives way to shock and awe.

In *Crystal Skull* Spielberg moves beyond the WWII topics that the media has lately glued to him; a deeper move into the efficacy of fiction. This storytelling gift is what's most widely acknowledged about Spielberg. Yet, paradoxically, it's also what's least understood about his art: He displays aplomb conscientiously. At the Kennedy Center Honors two years ago, too much emphasis was placed on Spielberg's "serious" war dramas, dismissing the personal essence of his other films. Having transcended genre—especially recently in *A.I.*, *War of the Worlds* and *Munich*—Spielberg returns to his Indy genre for the very reason Godard outlined in *Histoire(s) du cinema*: "Form tells us what is at the bottom of things."

*New York Press*
May 2008

# The Whip and the Fedora

THE RECENTLY ISSUED *Indiana Jones: The Complete Adventures* on Paramount Blu-Ray comes at the right moment—that is, with enough passage of time—that now a reasonable assessment can be made of the entire series. Despite the historic impact that *Raiders of the Lost Ark* made in 1981, each succeeding sequel has surpassed it. The original now looks rather stodgy (even with the vivid Blu-Ray transfer—no matter how many people pledge nostalgic preference for it) because Spielberg's aesthetic momentum improved—astonishingly—with each sequel.

Now it can be said: *Raiders* is the least of the quartet, despite its early '80s novelty, coming at the tail-end of the '70s American Renaissance when filmmakers brought modernist revisionism to Hollywood genre. *Raiders* is preferred by those who refuse to take Spielberg (and pop culture) seriously. It's actually less elegant than the widely disliked *Kingdom of the Crystal Skull* which is, in fact, far richer (although the amazing cinematographer Janusz Kamiński failed to light it with Douglas Slocombe's smooth, gorgeous ultra-Hollywood sparkle that distinguished the first three films). *Kingdom* builds on *Raiders*' ideas and complicates them. Arriving two decades later, it is the series' true sequel—refined and elegant.

The other Indy films stand alone: *Temple of Doom* is a rambunctious comedy with some of the greatest action-directing (that rollercoaster ride through the mines) that one can ever see. And *The Last Crusade* is the series' pinnacle—a masterpiece. Harrison Ford's Indy finds his best ally in his dad

**297**

(Sean Connery, evoking the crowd-pleasing ingenuity of the James Bond series that was the forerunner to this action-cycle) and then the All-American adventurer bumps into his perfect foil (Adolf Hitler signing his autograph—on the book that represents Indy's family legacy).

In *The Last Crusade*'s overture sequence, detailing Indy's boyhood (played by the late River Phoenix), we get a perfect example of relay-race ingenuity as well as a condensed history of cinema kinetics. As teenage Indy goes from horse to train (a semiotic condensation of John Ford's *The Iron Horse* and Buster Keaton's *The General* (1926) in the guise of Barnum and Bailey circus transport: *mise en abyme*), Spielberg achieved one of the most cinematically resonant sequences in modern movies (until Joseph Kahn paid homage to it in the train/motorcycle/run race of *Torque*).

It is in *The Last Crusade* that Spielberg comes to grips with Imperialism and the politics and ethics behind Indy's (the West's) anthropological urge. Manifest colonialism meets its spiritual destiny. Destiny resonates when one revisits the now-disappointing *Raiders of the Lost Ark*. It simply doesn't move fast enough—either rhythmically or intellectually. It now just looks like a slow exploration of genre possibilities; in the end a childish folly; a rehash of serial movie triviality. This exercise was fascinating in 1981 (starting with the signature visual puns on the Paramount logo that always begin the caprice—signaling the viewer to appreciate movie history) because no one had thought about Serials as a genre for decades until the lame *Star Wars* revived the concept in 1977. *Raiders* was livelier and more human than *Star Wars* (and seemed fresher than *The Empire Strikes Back*, the best film in that woebegone series) yet over the years *Raiders* has not aged particularly well. (Indy running ahead of the onslaught of a rolling boulder has been so overexposed that the modernist joke is lost. Now *Journey to the Center of the Earth* (1959), from which Spielberg stole the joke, proves to have more dramatic context.)

Consider *Raiders'* confrontation with a black-garbed Arab swinging a scimitar and Indy's very American response (reversing the axiom about "bringing a knife to a gun fight"). In '81 it felt cool—shocking and very American—but three decades later, especially now in the era of international trepidation and foreign policy appeasement, Indy's gunplay feels embarrassingly overdrawn. *Raiders'* concept of American fun and might went around the globe, entertaining audiences everywhere, but al-Qaeda's payback on 9/11 haunts it now.

Indy's moment of retaliation has come to seem futile or ill-considered—far different from the American awakening from isolationism depicted in *Casablanca* (1942). That gun violates the symbolism of Indy's whip and fedora (his prowess and his mind). It also connects to what's problematic in the series—*Temple of Doom*'s insensitive, tacit racism that turned the Otherness of Indian cults into bloodthirsty villainy. *Raiders'* climactic shift into Judeo-Christian sanctity (using the power of the lost Ark of the Covenant as both a moral force and a final reference to the cultural touchstone of *Citizen Kane*—a cinephile's covenant) was clever but only temporarily satisfying. Spielberg needed both the process of making *The Color Purple* which fully empathized with the experience of the Other and the pre-*Schindler's List* wit of *The Last Crusade* to finally face up to and fully explicate the series' Western perspective. *The Last Crusade* is the film in the series that holds up best after our loss of innocence post-9/11. When revisiting the project in *The Crystal Skull*, Spielberg broadened that perspective—

historically (the magnificent mushroom cloud nuclear bomb recreation), astronomically and metaphysically.

Given the mess of contemporary cultural expression—the West and the Mid-East's unresolved feelings about history and destiny now exploding all about us—the Indiana Jones series may be America's last example of global adventure filmmaking. How do we imaginatively utilize Indy's bullwhip and fedora in the midst of Arab Spring and Arab Winter?

*CityArts*
September 2012

# DREAMWORKS SKG

## The Big Picture: The Men Who Would Be King

I N *THE MEN Who Would Be King*, Nicole LaPorte chronicles how Steven Spielberg and his generational peers David Geffen and Jeffrey Katzenberg—all showbiz veterans—banded together during the Clinton era to form DreamWorks SKG, their own custom-designed production studio and the first new Hollywood studio in 60 years. But instead of celebrating the three men's effort, LaPorte's counternarrative constantly sneers at it.

That's because artistic aspiration has evaporated from contemporary Hollywood. LaPorte, a former reporter for *Variety*, nearly pinpoints a hidden skepticism when she writes: "Jealousy wasn't the only emotion Spielberg generated in those close to him. He also aroused feelings of protectiveness." Her book is as much about the envious, ambivalent feelings with which insiders greet everything Spielberg does as it is about the Musketeer-like unity that Spielberg, Geffen and Katzenberg displayed throughout the fraught years of their historic venture.

LaPorte records their individual roles in the DreamWorks organization. Each contributed $33 million to get the studio started, and they divided responsibilities based on their expertise: Katzenberg, who had recently been booted from

Disney, where he oversaw *The Lion King*, managed DreamWorks' animated features; Geffen, the record magnate, took charge of the company's music label; its feature-film slate was left to the supervision of the man who made *Jaws, Close Encounters of the Third Kind, Raiders of the Lost Ark, Jurassic Park* and *Schindler's List*. LaPorte's story always comes back to Spielberg, or takes place within his aura. The DreamWorks endeavor was expressly defined by Spielberg's vision. He referred to the prospective studio as "our identity" and "our own homeland." This reminder of Jewish belonging and self-governing makes DreamWorks a quintessentially American story of ethnic pride and professional success, which LaPorte deflates when she delivers her conceit: "It was time to claim what was rightfully his—the position of Hollywood's acknowledged ruler."

By invoking the notion of sovereignty in an account of recent American movie history, LaPorte combines tabloid celebrity worship with an older oddity: the incongruous fact that a free market also produces resentment, especially when a competitor like Spielberg demonstrates leadership, superior achievement and undeniable success. He's one of the few filmmakers still committed to exploring the human condition—and in popular terms. This is what sets him apart and makes him admired, envied and even inscrutable to those who think only in craven terms of business and royalty.

LaPorte produces not so much as a single quotation from any of the principals in which they ever expressed a desire to wear the Hollywood crown (all three turned down her interview requests). She also ignores their attempt to do what regular studios would not: create distinctive works (as in the case of DreamWorks' first animated film, *The Prince of Egypt* (1998)) rather than formulaic ones. Katzenberg, Geffen and

Spielberg were all known for creating distinctive works, not formulaic ones, yet LaPorte oversimplifies their ambition by imputing domineering, if not dictatorial, motives to them. In her portrayals, Geffen is a shady, hot-tempered Godfather type ("superagent and resident fix-it guy"); Katzenberg furiously battles against changes in the digital-animation revolution while waging a breach-of-contract suit against Disney; and Spielberg, stretched thin, balances his own commitments but also presides over the work of other filmmakers.

This narrative is meandering and diffuse, an overawed yet cynical response to Spielberg's pre-eminence. In LaPorte's telling, he is reduced to a blockbuster adept and tycoon. Had she used mere chess metaphors to clarify Hollywood gamesmanship, the DreamWorks initiative would seem no different from the precedent-setting efforts of D. W. Griffith, Charles Chaplin, Douglas Fairbanks and Mary Pickford in 1919, when they created United Artists. The author looks at Hollywood not as an enthusiast or a critic, but as someone who sees things strictly in terms of box-office success and industry accolades.

LaPorte's gossipy perspective is inimical to true artists, yet feels submissive to boastful, flamboyant big shots. She emphasizes Spielberg's business inadequacies and concentrates on corporate intrigues, thereby making his remarkable success and singular personality seem common. LaPorte says that "the studio's creative promise rested with Spielberg," but she plays up the studio's noncreative mix-ups and combustible characters. Katzenberg is described as "the kind of always-on achievement junkie that Hollywood considered its own breed." Geffen, who left DreamWorks in 2008, is called "a cunning *macher* who lived to maneuver all the players on the board according to whatever scenarios he was advancing." Spielberg, however, remains confounding throughout.

Employing tabloid terms and the slanguage mindset of trade papers like *Variety* produces a terrible conflict between the pop-art intricacy of the films themselves and the documented crassness of mass production: big paydays, Hollywood luxe and arrogance. LaPorte glamorizes the bad behavior of moguls, underlings and power players; for example, she fawns over Spielberg's production executives, the husband-and-wife team of Walter Parkes and Laurie MacDonald (Parkes has "the kind of overpowering self-confidence that is indigenous to Hollywood"), and the publicity executive Terry Press, who browbeats a colleague for describing something as ironic: "Do you even know what irony is?"

"As for Spielberg, what he actually stood for, personally, beyond virtuoso filmmaking and commercial success, was hard to articulate," LaPorte states. She demonstrates her own critical insufficiency by slagging off *Amistad*, DreamWorks' first ambitious release. She bungles the plot; the slaves are on trial not for murder, but to determine their status as humans or property. She quotes sources who castigate the film as a "vanity project," an "after-school special," and writes gloatingly: "The marketing department was already calling *Amistad* 'the spinach movie.' As in: good for you, but not exactly mouthwatering fare." Spielberg told a reporter who visited the set: "Comparisons between Black slavery and the Holocaust are essential. You can't look at history selfishly." Yet LaPorte shows nothing but disrespect for DreamWorks' highest objectives.

LaPorte seems to measure excellence the same way Hollywood does. She notes, for instance, that "in the end, *Gladiator* [2000] triumphed." Her appreciation is guided by profit and hindsight, not art. She indulges industry-think when praising the slickly cynical *American Beauty* (1999) (because it won Oscars) and giving short shrift to the profoundly frightening *War of the Worlds* (Spielberg's daring 9/11 allegory). Her most embarrassing passages recount the premiere of *Shrek* (2001) at Cannes (she doesn't seem to mind the movie's crass opening scene) and the domestic box-office take (more than $100 million) of the forgettable *Dreamgirls* (2006)—all the while virtually ignoring the ambitious and aesthetically adventurous film *The Terminal* and slighting the powerful *Munich* (dumbly referred to as "a kind of *Schindler's List II*").

LaPorte, who more than once repeats the old saw about Spielberg's immaturity ("Everyone knew Spielberg had a short attention span"), winds up with a summary that is superficial toastmaster stuff:

> DreamWorks was a failure of expectation, one that resulted from all of the relentless hype [...] Spielberg had so long been considered infallible that he seemed to believe it himself. Geffen and Katzenberg had so carefully maintained and buffed their public images that they, too, seemed to have forgotten that they were, well: *human.*

So it's a tabloid book. We can only hope it doesn't become the historical record. LaPorte undermines her research with a headachy repetition of anonymous informants ("one insider," "one former executive," "one source"). She concludes that "inherent in all of it was hubris." But a story this significant, about world-changing movies, doesn't need homilies. It needs a detailed, impassioned and insightful telling, one that would help us better appreciate a frequently misunderstood, underinterpreted pop artist whose work connects with the public, defines the complexities of human experience and dwarfs most of contemporary Hollywood's output. DreamWorks calls for a sensitive sociologist—a Tom Wolfe or a Norman Mailer or a Pauline Kael—who can discern the deep, divided heart of Hollywood.

*The New York Times*
June 2010

# THE ADVENTURES OF TINTIN (2011) AND WAR HORSE (2011)

## *Game Changers*

**M**OVIE-WATCHING CAN NEVER be same after the double header of Steven Spielberg's *The Adventures of Tintin*, his first animated film, and his live-action *War Horse*. Each film upgrades the way our imaginations construct the world, the way we see ourselves in the digital age. All art devotees should recognize the history being made.

Tintin, the intrepid boy reporter from Belgian author Hergé's cartoon storybooks, and Joey, the young stallion traversing WWI-era Europe as in the hit Broadway stage play, both emerge from the childhood reveries that often start Spielberg's fictions. These imaginary protagonists go through large-scale comic and dramatic escapades that not only span the breadth of human experience but apotheosize it.

In the language of pop immediacy, Tintin and Joey's stories are immersive—a term for the right-now gratification encouraged by both digital media and the exhausted cultural legacy recently eulogized in Godard's *Film Socialisme* (2010). Tintin's childhood curiosity and resourcefulness, Joey's natural grace and endurance are captivating on so many levels that the usual terms of film appreciation hardly apply. This may be key to why many critics under-appreciate Spielberg, they react conventionally to these unconventional films and are bewildered by Spielberg's refinement, precision, piquancy and vision.

Perhaps the best way to understand the achievement of these two revolutionary films is to realize that they do nothing "new." Their revolution is in Spielberg's technique—very familiar after almost 40 years of popular and profound entertainment—but now with a new impetus and subtler depth. As a modernist filmmaker he turns *Tintin* into a commentary on traditional genre expectation—and pushes beyond it toward the personal feelings about history and legend that are stirred by fantastic exploits and imaginative catharsis. In *War Horse*, Joey is at the center of historical events that define what came to be known as modernity—eternal class struggles intensified by war that level all our ambitions and vulnerabilities whether English, German, French—or, American. (It purifies global human values, as Denis Villeneuve's *Incendies* (2011) also showed.)

Embarking on digital, anime methods, Spielberg has answered the need to reconceive the pleasure to be had from the adventure genre and war movie—*The Adventures of Tintin* is state of the art, *War Horse* is commemoration. Both are prophecy.

For Spielberg entertainment equals enlightenment. Not realizing that, critics take *Tintin*'s on-screen miracles for granted. There's too much for ordinary critics to look at, starting with the opening scene of Tintin having his portrait made at a street fair: "I think I have captured something of your likeness," he's told by a painter. When we see it, it is, of course, the Hergé drawing—now a caricature of a cartoon.

From that image onward, Spielberg toys with ways of seeing. Lenses, binoculars, window reflections, magnifying glasses and mirrors pop up everywhere (clever self-consciousness in the script by Edgar Wright, Joe Cornish and Steven Moffat). A less thoughtful filmmaker like co-producer Peter Jackson would settle for telling Tintin's story (maybe even making it as convoluted as the awful *Lord of the Rings* trilogy which set back the intellectual development of digital fantasy). But Spielberg continues the modernist ethic of heightening viewer awareness. Intrepid Tintin becomes our digital-age surrogate, reenacting chase movie traditions like River Phoenix in *The Last Crusade* (basis of the credit sequence's silhouette overture) but at water-slide velocity. This is far beyond the hackneyed talk of "dreams" in Scorsese's banal film-school lecture *Hugo* (2011). Spielberg believes in cinema as kinetics, prioritizing movement—not antiquated "cinephilia."

As ultimate cinema, *The Adventures of Tintin* features the bliss of camera movement. A sequence in Tintin's apartment where the model ship he purchased at that opening street fair becomes the object of an action-ballet burglary, has ingenious slapstick speed. It was Hitchcock who famously exclaimed, "Spielberg doesn't think in terms of a proscenium;" *Tintin*'s p.o.v. is positively gyroscopic. The images are always vertiginous as when sailors slip-slide in their bunks, or pet shop canaries circle a man's head after he falls. This wittily stylized activity evokes how we dream. As we watch, we live the history of cinema and animation just as spectacularly as Andre Bazin theorized our recognition of nature and experience in photographic realism.

*Tintin* advances the motion-capture technology that Robert Zemeckis fumbled with for years (hideous faces in *The Polar Express* (2004) but Halloween expressiveness in *Monster House* (2006)). The improvement allows animation to affect cinematic realism unlike Scorsese's out-of-scale CGI but as aestheticized dream play. Spielberg's narrative escalates when Tintin, seeking the secret of the Unicorn model ship, encounters drunken Capt. Haddock and learns the ship's history. In Haddock's meta-narrative, legend segues into visions, then flashbacks and vice versa. These endlessly inventive transitions (a ship in a desert mirage morphs onto roiling seas) salute David Lean's *Lawrence of Arabia* as well as Roman Polanski's *Pirates* (1986) (the latter particularly in Haddock's Walter Matthau-countenance and -bluster).

Yet Spielberg's sensibility controls the fable's crescendo—the friendly confidences Haddock, Tintin and his white terrier Snowy share recall the emotional connections to history and family in *Catch Me If You Can* and *The Last Crusade*. Haddock chronicles a legendary competition between his ancestor Sir Francis Haddock and pirate Red Rackham that ties the Unicorn to three lost scrolls and leads to even more awesome spectacle. Spielberg shows lyrical inspiration: an amazing sea battle where one pirate vessel swings on the mast of another ship, leaping from churning waters to aerial sparing. Nothing in *Pirates of the Caribbean* compares. Mere fancifulness is heightened in favor of centrifugal force. These vectors are repeated in a later joust between gigantic cranes that surpasses the dynamism of Michael Bay's *Transformers: Dark of the Moon* (2011).

Chief among *Tintin*'s climaxes is an extended chase sequence that may be the greatest in movie history; it juggles characters, narrative strands, those scrolls, plus Snowy and a mischievous falcon—and stretches across the screen. This ribbon of hurtling delight recalls *Temple of Doom* but with clearer, brighter imagery. Spielberg uses 3D width, not just background-foreground depth, which is more than practitioner James Cameron ever conceived and closer to Paul W.S. Anderson's panoramas in *Resident Evil: Afterlife* (2010) and *The Three Musketeers* (2011).

Scorsese's sad, dull use of 3D in *Hugo* just seems part of contemporary Hollywood's techno hoodwink to sucker family audiences and intimidate cineastes. But Spielberg utilizes the gimmick as an occasion for reexamining cinematic imagery. Confronting Hergé's *Tintin* rendering with his own green-screen *Tintin* startlingly brings together 20th and 21st century modes. Ready or not, the double image of cartoon and 3D Tintin propels us forward.

If 3D was ever to be an acceptable narrative technology, it would have to unlock viewers' imaginations (as in Zack Snyder's *Legend of the Guardians: The Owls of Ga'hoole* (2010)) and not blatantly repeat the primitive "realism" of early movie hucksters, which Scorsese unhelpfully romanticizes. Neither Wim Wenders' *Pina* (2011) nor Werner Herzog's *Cave of Forgotten Dreams* (2010), recent exercises in 3D documentary realism, were as good as their fictional predecessors, Altman's *The Company* (2003) or the 1959 *Journey to the Center of the Earth*. *Tintin*'s cartoon mode defies Wenders-Herzog's banal gimmickry (which is why it will also work as 2D, offering as much carnival delight as *Temple of Doom* and *1941*).

*Tintin's* 21st century artistry redeems our corrupted taste for narrative and spectacle—it's the best kind of restoration. This re-discovery inspired the aesthetic behind Spielberg's follow-up project: *War Horse* looks like a cinematic version of an illuminated manuscript. Its cavalcade of human longing and suffering during the First World War has an uncanny spiritual tow thanks to how cinematographer Janusz Kamiński's glowing frames combine storybook and Hollywood epic grandeur.

Joey, the horse bought at auction by a struggling farmer, becomes a surrogate for young Albert (Jeremy Irvine) whose attachment and faithfulness are tested when Joey's taken into service by the British army and on the Continent becomes part of the lives of two German brothers, a young French girl (Celine Buckens) and her grandfather (Niels Arestrup) and anonymous soldiers on the battlefield. Anyone who takes for granted the emotions elicited in *War Horse* fools themselves to think they're slogging through clichés. The human emotion reflected through Joey's sojourn are purified to a spiritual essence. There is an uncorrupted, pre-sexual belief in human potential in this series of tales. The critic Dennis Delrogh insightfully caught Joey's resemblance to the African slave's travails in the criminally neglected *Amistad*. Indeed, *War Horse* views Western "civilization" from an indentured soul's distance (same as *The Color Purple*) that is almost prelapsarian—not just anti-war but wartime seen with honest, not idyllic, moral complexity.

The first battle scene brilliantly confronts us with the horror of undefended Germans attacked by brutal Brits; the unexpected shock is matched by the poetic startlement of riderless horses seen leaping over machine guns—this image is as haunting as Griffith's seminal "War's Peace" in *The Birth of a Nation*, capturing the irony in ritualized killing. Spielberg uses Joey's story to achieve the equivalent of an outsider's unbiased detachment, fair to the tragedy and beauty of worldly experience. This richness derives from concentrating narrative skill with popular perceptual needs. It shames the shallow view of war (and Germans and violence and love) that Tarantino disgraced in *Inglourious Basterds* (2009). QT's nihilistic revisionism negated the humane values previously held in wartime narratives. Spielberg challenges such cynicism while encouraging viewers to recover their basic emotional responses. QT wants audiences to enjoy killing and vengeance—the folly of the post-Vietnam unengaged, anti-military sensibility; Spielberg steps back from that and resurrects the profundity of war service. What he learned from the research for and reactions to *Saving Private Ryan* causes him to practice the same scrupulousness as earlier generations of war vet artists from John Ford to Kurosawa. The result produces either catharsis or the confusion felt by those who have grown comfortable with cynicism and are inured to the beauty that comes through Kamiński's supernal images.

Spielberg's flaming sunsets are more referential than QT's film geek echoes; they evoke *Gone With the Wind* romanticism but with the same modernist sentiments as Coppola's *The Outsiders* (1983) and Techine's *French Provincial* (1975), films that used the movie past to articulate a contemporary longing. It's the height of sophistication, achieving complex expression with phenomenal simplicity. Spielberg has arrived at David Lean-John Ford's visual grandiloquence and emotional clarity—greatness at his fingertips but it's also the result of artistic integrity. Every sequence in *War Horse* may seem summary, because each episode—whether Albert and his family, or various civilians and soldiers including Tom Hiddleston as the figure of sacrificial British rectitude—suggests a parable on anguished human aspiration and arrives at its point with elegant simplicity.

This is especially true of Joey's wild attempt at escape, enmeshing himself in trench wire. An extended metaphor for the terror and absurdity of No Man's Land, it eschews warfare but symbolizes tormented flesh and anxious spirit—Joey as one of God's noble creature. It is a sequence of sustained agape, the stark animal = soul image suggests the full range of torture, enslavement, cruelty and finally—breathtakingly—hope through mankind's humility. War movies inherently memorialize but Spielberg uses his gift for action to capture frenzy plus its moral implications. The scene goes beyond mere genre filmmaking but it also brings us back to reflect on genre and what styles and methods of storytelling mean to modern consciousness.

*War Horse* has a different kind of resonance than *The Adventures of Tintin* but it isn't necessarily better. Each is an experiment that could only be possible after the distillation practiced in *The Adventures of Tintin*. Spielberg's reconsideration of cinema aesthetics allows him to refine the cinematic image, to create, as critic Robert Storr said of Gerhard Richter:

> works of art that attempt—and I believe succeed—in fundamentally repositioning the viewer in relation to [...] the 20th century's running narrative of utopianism and despair.

*Tintin* and *War Horse* range between utopianism and despair through comedy and drama but it's important to note how their nearly abstract visual styles address our changing perception of the moving image narrative. Only dullards would misunderstand these visions as either trivial or clichéd. By altering the imagery of his Indiana Jones cycle and stylizing Hollywood's pictographic classicism, Spielberg uses cinema "in a way which is both extremely personal, even idiosyncratic, and extremely pointed, even polemical [...] verging on the abstract"—to quote Peter Wollen, also writing about Richter's paintings-based-on-photographs.

In the digital era, our basic assumptions about movies have changed along with the methods of their exhibition and consumption. Movies won't be the same, we know that from the way critics settled for the shoddy look of the *Iron Man* and *Harry Potter* flicks, *The Artist* (2011), *Hugo*, *The Descendants* (2011), *Midnight in Paris* (2011)and others that have no visual quality to speak of. Movies as we knew them are over; today's increasing artifice concedes to digital but Spielberg finds the perfect expression of new imagining.

*CityArts*
January 2012

PART FOUR

# OBAMA

# LINCOLN (2012)

―――――――――

## *On the Immediate Future of the Arts*

I N THE ARTS, Fall isn't a season of rebirth but the season of double-down. It's when producers and publicists join hands to promote their latest wares. In New York, Fall arts take on the illusion of rebirth because of the break in summer humidity (and those who are privileged with summer homes come back to the city, after a brief breezy respite, ready to resume their grind). Working Joes are placated with manufactured "new seasons"— primarily in television but also theater, museums and movies.

Fall sees film culture change the most—especially in the past decade, since Hollywood has foreshortened its normal release patterns and geared foot soldiers and audiences alike toward awards fever. The canard that Fall is the time for "serious" movies covers up the fact that Fall is when moviemakers seek bonuses (gold-plated flattery) to go with their inflated paychecks. It's really the premature start of Awards Season. Even the festival circuit plays this game: The Toronto Film Festival has been taken over by Oscar touts who turn that Canadian city (an outpost where cinema-starved citizens challenge the movie-love of hype-besotted New Yorkers) into a new Sundance—that is, Beverly Hills Way North.

Hype for "Oscar-worthy" movies overwhelms genuine interest for the films themselves. In the insightful documentary

*The American Ruling Class* (2005), Hollywood producer Mike Medavoy warned, "There are no more movies, just content. Content for various delivery systems." As an example, take the trailer for Steven Spielberg's upcoming *Lincoln*. Even after the follies of the Toronto Film Festival, and the insanities of the Venice Film Festival (which annually awards pretentious epics, this time, *The Master* (2012)), most film folk are buzzing about the trailer for *Lincoln* released on the web last week, timed for the fig leaves to fall from Hollywood's naked ambition.

A movie trailer is a perfect form for Fall "content": It's short; its nature is essentially anticipatory rather than participatory since the narrative is abbreviated to such a point that no cognitive involvement is possible. This may explain why Spielberg, Hollywood's most envied (as opposed to respected) popular filmmaker, commands the Fall arts moment. Not even his movie-brat colleague Brian De Palma's return to the scene with *Passion* (2012), his first movie in five years premiering at the upcoming New York Film Festival, has sparked interest comparable to the *Lincoln* ad.

Brief glimpses at Spielberg's classically lighted historical images should tickle anyone who remembers his widely panned *Amistad*—the film that the *Lincoln* trailer most resembles. This new "content" cannot possibly excite those who were unmoved by *Amistad*. Hollow anticipation is all. This is evident even in Paramount's new Blu-Ray release of the *Indiana Jones* series, an event that allows reassessment of one of the late 20th century's cultural touchstones. Like every maturing artist, Spielberg has lost touch with the popular audience—especially the audience accustomed to hollow content.

Indy vs. Lincoln in a competition between what once was genuinely popular film culture and film that no longer unites the audience—except in shared consumerism. This connects the Fall's *Lincoln* trailer (the film itself won't premiere until year's end, closer to the Oscars) to the upcoming presidential election. It's another distraction from issues the candidates will not discuss—including the legacy of slavery which will never be mentioned but can be part of how some voters project their hopes onto a candidate's hollow platitudes.

In the Fall arts, content must be challenged by meaning. That's the opportunity that artists and audiences ought to hope for. Upcoming work by Kanye West, Iris DeMent, Paul W.S. Anderson and the Taviani brothers, whose *Caesar Must Die* (2012) premieres at the New York Film Festival, could show work that goes beyond seasonal hype. They could bring fresh thinking—and real feeling—back to culture. This *CityArts* section on the fall season covers the season from the impact of our digital cinema future to celebrations of dance, theater even Streisand's Brooklyn homecoming.

*CityArts*
September 2012

# The Pageantry of Rhetoric

"**Y**OU BEGIN YOUR second term with semi-divine status," the 16th President of the United States is told in Steven Spielberg's film *Lincoln*. The evidence of that status is in the film's mythifying visual style that presents Abraham Lincoln as an icon—silhouetted, spectral, sculptural. The people around him, such as white and Negro Union soldiers relating their Civil War experiences of the 1865 Jenkins Ferry massacre during the film's introduction, are also made into myth. (These weary men have already committed the Gettysburg Address to memory—a presentiment of the schoolboy's homework in *Minority Report*.) Spielberg's intention to line up with "the right side of history" turns the film into cult-of-personality deification. It's on the side of power—which makes it one of the weirdest pieces of supposedly democratic Americana ever to come out of Hollywood.

The story in *Lincoln* dramatizes the President's efforts to install a 13th Amendment to the Constitution that abolishes slavery. His struggle is more than politically correct; it is presumed inarguably correct which takes the movie outside of history; outside of dramatic immediacy. Watching *Lincoln* is very much like observing a flesh-and-blood diorama. Everything is soon to be settled (within 2½ hours); there's no emotional suspense.

The trick Spielberg needed to pull off was to make the characters' moral choices dramatically compelling; analyzing ethics in politics (those pragmatic procedures that deemed the Emancipation Proclamation "a military exigent"). Yet that's where the film becomes dodgy—open to accusations of merely being a civics lesson, or worse: Spielberg's equivalent to Richard Attenborough's still-born hagiography *Gandhi*, rather than a companion-piece to his thrilling, brilliantly analytical masterpiece *Amistad*.

In *Amistad* Spielberg cannily transformed the issue of Slavery into the intricacy of Law; human endeavor and spiritual struggle were historically modified into argument and principle. The *Amistad* characters Cinque the African (Djimon Hounsou) and John Adams the political forebear (Anthony Hopkins) grappled with the fact of Slavery. This time Slavery is anthropomorphized. The introduction's two docile and truculent black soldiers patronizingly prophesize modern attitudes; Lincoln himself (played by Daniel Day-Lewis) describes Slavery as a "disease" which distances it into abstraction. *Lincoln* attempts to dramatize mere rhetoric. Despite high-flown language, it turns the experience of human lives into platitudes, homilies and predetermined theorems.

For a lesser filmmaker, the prevarications in *Lincoln* would be disastrous. But Spielberg's innate filmmaking resources consistently provide rhythmed imagery: Conventional—as when Lincoln's aides race to get his disingenuous communiqué. Daring—as when Lincoln dreams his forthcoming struggle as an eerie ship voyage. The film is always something to look at. Congressional arguments are composed to show the vitality of faces and individuals—the elite body politic—like period versions of Francesco Rosi's courtroom scenes in *Hands Over the City* (1963) and *Salvatore Giuliano* (1962) yet without Rosi's worry about literal political corruption. Spielberg's vibrant style just barely offsets the mundanity of parliamentary debate. The fact that *Lincoln*'s drama comes from predictable dialectic, rather than an in-the-moment philosophical conundrum like *Amistad*, reveals its insufficiency. *Lincoln* tilts toward magniloquence, using important sounding words and an exaggeratedly solemn and dignified style.

Spielberg shrewdly chose the histrionic Day-Lewis to impersonate Lincoln with twinkling eyes and a wily, high-pitched voice that humanize the icon. Day-Lewis' long face is given built-in hollows and shadows that match the Lincoln Memorial and postage stamp figures while also suggesting mysterious depths. His every close-up suggests historical reverence. But this immortality contrasts the fascinating mortal portrayals by Sally Fields as Mary Todd Lincoln, Tommy Lee Jones as Thaddeus Stevens and James Spader as W.N. Bilbo who act through their flesh, courtesy of Janusz Kamiński's portraitist lighting that suggests the grain of historical painting animated by fluid camerawork. At one point ("It's too hard"), Fields' transition from agony to aggrieved diplomacy is as much the director's triumph as the actress'. Spader's grungy agitator feels lived-in while Jones enlivens a cliché Congressional hack—his toupeed-role reaches back to a key idiosyncratic characterization in D.W. Griffith's *The Birth of a Nation*.

With *Lincoln*, Spielberg assumes his place in the descent of American cinematic mythmakers following Griffith and John Ford—a fact already evident—and earned—in *Amistad*. Here it's done self-consciously. Not because it's impossible to portray Abraham Lincoln any way other than worshipfully but because Spielberg and screenwriter Tony Kushner (adapting a book by historian Doris Kearns Goodwin) manipulate Lincoln into a contemporary political paradigm.

Without clarifying the intricacy of the 19th century Republican party and the different principles of early Democrats, Spielberg and Kushner claim Lincoln as their model autocrat—

always the smartest man in the room—which becomes a form of adoration. Thaddeus Stevens even refers to Lincoln as "the purest man in America." Distinct from the cultural myth in Ford's *Young Mr. Lincoln* (1939) that was widely shared in less jaded times, *Lincoln* presents a new-style giant (a storyteller of superhuman probity and only fleeting moments of the most admirable self-doubt) probably influenced by the current hunger for a great leader whose outstanding talents must be either prefabricated or whose failings go ignored in order to answer a desperate contemporary need for power.

Here's how *Lincoln* prevaricates: Scenes where Black characters show flawless nobility and strength (whether as a silent, pious gospel chorus entering the Senate chambers or unimpeachably dignified servants). Scenes where white politicians focus on issues with little motivation beyond hectoring opposition. These convenient and very modern political defects prevent *Lincoln* from achieving the historical reach of *Amistad* or the miraculous suasion that made *Mr. Smith Goes to Washington*'s (1939) change-of-heart scene so moving.

When Lincoln proclaims, "We're stepped out upon the world's stage now, the fate of human dignity is in our hands. Blood's been spent to afford us this moment. Now! Now! Now!" the stage metaphor exposes playwright Kushner's smugness. *Lincoln* is rife with Kushner's pedantic tendency. Speechifying characters (especially Lincoln) display conceited literacy, over-stating their differences (their career positions) but never embodying the passions that made Michael Apted's Wilberforce biography *Amazing Grace* (2007) such a remarkable drama of moral inspiration. Kushner's self-congratulatory approach to the 13th Amendment doesn't enliven our sense of personal conviction and political maneuvering. Even the powerful "Molasses to Rum to Slaves" trading song in *1776*, the Declaration of Independence musical, more clearly outlined America's practical and political functioning. Both *Amazing Grace* and *1776* worked as ideational histories; *Lincoln* merely, well, fantasizes.

Justifying political manipulation and the idolizing of a single politician forces Spielberg and Kushner into the weird position of displacing the moral rigor that distinguished their collaboration on *Munich*. When Lincoln bases his notion of equality on Euclidian principle, referencing a 2000-year-old secular book as his foundation then praising "a great invisible strength in a people's union," Kushner's vagrant communist-sympathy comes into play. The platitude is barely disguised by Lincoln's out of nowhere wish to visit the Holy Land "where David and Solomon walked."

As with *Angels in America*, Kushner is partial to formula, prescription, disquisition—the pageantry of rhetoric. But Spielberg thrives on movement and imagery and there isn't enough to keep *Lincoln* from bogging down in verbiage. It frequently resembles the self-pleasing sophistry favored by this era of punditry and hero-worship.

But cinema's most memorable political histories have always been films like *Young Mr. Lincoln, Amistad* and *Amazing Grace* that attain the ineffable by honestly clarifying history and daring that Capraesque link between dramatized conscience and delineated principle; that's what stirs one's soul in Albert Finney's conversion scene of *Amazing Grace* which found the perfect symbols and actions to express the passion of ideas. *Lincoln* weakens from the current political era's disingenuous pageantry of rhetoric.

In the popular fashion, Spielberg and Kushner fall back on the "great man" theory of history. Their iconography is vague, a fantasy where equality is learned through logic—not experience or faith because in this film's view no human beings can be taken on faith (as when Lincoln says he doesn't know any Black people; the film's one-dimensional, anachronistic Black characters indicate Spielberg and Kushner's progressive elitism; they never absorbed the richness of Jonathan Demme's Slavery-era *Beloved* (1998)). This dream of Lincoln, fitted to the solipsistic subjectivity of the political moment lacks *Amistad*'s beauty and historical clarity to favor a "semi-divine" (that is, non-spiritual) view of political heroism. The fantasy might well be re-titled *Dreams From My Father.*

*CityArts*
November 2012

# After the Debate: Fact-Checking Hollywood's Propaganda

**W**HEN FILM CRITIC Hillary Clinton, in the October 9 Presidential debate, raved about having seen "the wonderful Steven Spielberg movie called *Lincoln*," saying it was "a master class watching President Lincoln get the congress to approve the 13th amendment," she confirmed a suspicion I've long had. Spielberg's film always struck me as less than "wonderful." Rather, it was a murky, visually dark glorification of political chicanery, deviously designed to be a celebration of Barack Obama as a political and cultural icon who is already placed on a pedestal (with just as much alacrity as he was awarded the Nobel Peace Prize) alongside Abraham Lincoln.

For *National Review Online* readers, here's how I sussed out the first move by Spielberg (a big Hillary Clinton donor and fundraiser) into political propaganda (originally published in *CityArts*, November 13, 2012).

*National Review*
October 2016

# STEVEN SPIELBERG'S OBAMA (2013)

---

## Spielberg's Obama

T HE WORST STEVEN Spielberg production ever is, without doubt, his Obama homage, *Steven Spielberg's Obama*.

Unlike his disingenuous Obama-in-disguise campaign feature film, *Lincoln*, this two-minute satirical short looks artless and slapdash; it was made for last weekend's White House Correspondents' Dinner—an annual event for fatcats that contradicts the United States' supposed allegiance to democracy by gathering the nation's most empowered people (media celebrities) to gently lambaste but mostly celebrate their empowered peer, the President, as the most casual, supercilious, inviolable and narcissistic cat of them all.

Newscasters have disgraced their profession and politics by making movie cameos with apparently no qualms about the implication that news is just another form of celebritized fiction. There's an unholy alliance between the news industry and Hollywood. No matter the deprivations Americans across the country still suffer from Hurricane Sandy, Sandy Hook and West, Texas and the economy, the Correspondents' dinner is a ritual for the privileged, the ruling class that Americans like to think doesn't exist. That's one reason they go to the movies (the most shameful reason) and Spielberg made this short to further that ends of mystification, misguidance and manipulation.

The mockumentary's unfunny jokes start with Spielberg asking "I mean who is Obama, really? We don't know. We never got his transcripts." This would only be amusing if it weren't true. There's obscenity in joking about the media's protection of Obama's image and its implicit lack of decorum which began (negatively) with the media's assault on George W. Bush's presidency. But Nevermind. (That might have been a cleverer title for the short—what, was Tony Kushner too busy reading *Entertainment Weekly*?).

*Steven Spielberg's Obama* was made redundantly, to disguise the euphemistic Beltway metaphors of *Lincoln* (such as that despicable moment when Lincoln, arms outstretched, mendaciously emulates the scales of justice—but politicking with his right hand and prevaricating with his Left). Yet, those who care about the honor of Spielberg's best work have to pay mind to this short's dishonesty. It gainsays the fact of Obama's media-based mythification by joking about it.

Spielberg pretends in the short to be thinking about doing a first film about Obama and smirks, "Picking the right actor to play Obama that was the challenge. So I needed someone who could dive in and really become Barack Obama. And as it turns out the answer was right in front of me all along: Daniel Day-Lewis." This plays the moviegoing public cheap, as if they weren't smart enough to catch that Obama was already the subtext of *Lincoln*. Spielberg knew this, he let screenwriter Tony Kushner go forward with the rhetorical ruse which *The New York Times* only cottoned to after the film's release.

In an analysis titled "Confronting the Fact of Fiction and the Fiction of Fact," two thumbs-up reviewers chimed "*Lincoln* isn't just about how President Lincoln navigated the passage of the 13th Amendment; it is also about President Obama whose presidency could not be imagined without that amendment." So goes the limits of *Times* critics' imaginations. They finally admitted that Spielberg and Kushner's fabrications were rooted in the dark heart of millennial White Liberal fantasy, not historical fact or African-American dreaming.

Because Obama has become the fulfillment of White Liberal dreaming, his mythification in *Lincoln* and throughout the mainstream media is accepted without vetting—so much so that even Spielberg can contribute to the mythification, attempting to sway an election and then kid about it. His short's suggestion that the Obama myth required an actor of Day-Lewis' stature is inadvertently revealed. Spielberg boasts about Day-Lewis' method of "becom[ing] his character: Hawkeye from *The Last Of The Mohicans* (1992), Bill the Butcher in *Gangs of New York* (2002) and Abraham Lincoln from *Lincoln*. And you know what, he nailed it." Nailing it is the correct, crucifying term for the Washington Correspondents' Dinner's deprecation of American history.

Spielberg's litany accidentally links Obama's presidency to questionable representations of American history: James Fennimore Cooper's White fantasy that Leslie Fiedler once explicated (in *Love and Death in the American Novel*) as the embodiment of Eurocentric fears and the basis of America's racial delusions (a critical thesis now forgotten in the Ebert age); Scorsese's post-Vietnam imagining of America's hostile social legacy and immigrant brutality. Spielberg ties all that to Lincoln, not to absolve it but to unconsciously root it to the racial and political confusion about slavery and identity that the unvetted Obama represents.

But, wait! It gets worse! Obama himself takes part in Spielberg's charade. After once claiming, "I have a lot on my plate," Obama generously took the time to complete Spielberg's fantasy by showing how he prepares for public performance: Looking into a mirror, Obama preps "Hello, Ohio! Hello, Ohio!" "I love you back." "Look, look, let me be clear about this." The only thing that's clear is that the gathered media aristocracy (including the low-down yet highly-placed of Hollywood and Manhattan) approves this disingenuousness. It's all right with them. They want a President as lacking in dignity as they are, so they reduce him to their level—morally, professionally, politically.

This short is Spielberg's most Brechtian comedy: he gets the President of the United States to ridicule the supposedly sincere reasons his constituents support him, undermining the prestige of the Office that even his opponents are obliged to respect. (One could argue that the media's out-of-control disrespect for the presidency began with George W. Bush or maybe our lapdog media was born during the Clinton administration.) For Spielberg, Obama willingly portrays a performer in the act of deceiving the public. (Only Bill and Hillary Clinton taking on the roles of the mafia gangsters The Sopranos was as offensive.)

It is not funny when Obama-as-Day-Lewis confuses things, saying "The hardest part? Trying to understand his [my] motivations. Why did he [I] pursue 'health care' first? What makes him [me] tick? Why doesn't he [I] get mad? If I was him I'd be mad all the time. But I'm not him, I'm Daniel Day-Lewis." It's as bad as a *Saturday Night Live* skit. Or a Jon

Stewart *Daily Show* skit. Or a *Real Time with Bill Maher* skit. (Or a *Morning Joe*, *Rachel Maddow* skit, I mean, "newscast.") That's how low the producer of the terrific early Zemeckis-Gale comedies has sunk.

For the past seven months I've personally been fielding questions about why I didn't like the movie *Lincoln*. Going through the unpleasant effort of explaining the film's basic inaccuracy and unfairness to people who were prepared to love and defend it simply because it was customized to their political sentiments, made my explanation all the more frustrating. (When die-hard Spielberg scoffers praised *Lincoln*, I knew their commendations had nothing to do with aesthetics or history, only with the film's slanted politics and strenuously forced contemporary parallel to Obama's lame-duck presidency.) Now, after the disappointment of the Kushner-Spielberg *Lincoln*, we get its unfortunate sequel—actually a coda. A coda ought to reinforce a work's preceding revelations but it's become apparent that after his previous great films showed the humane aspect of the human experience, Spielberg has taken up the partisan view. Now that Spielberg shows us what *Lincoln* actually meant, one can really, rightfully rue it.

*CityArts*
May 2013

# BRIDGE OF SPIES (2015)

## The Dark Days of Spielberg

THE DARK, CREEPY murk of Steven Spielberg's 2012 *Lincoln* also seeps into his new film, *Bridge of Spies*, an account of the 1957 exchange between the U.S. and the Soviet Union of captured espionage agents, the Russian Colonel Rudolph Abel and the American pilot Gary Francis Powers. This gloom can be attributed to Spielberg's suggestion, in both films, of American political anxiety. After the ebullient history of *Amistad*, he has gone to the shadowy partisan chicanery behind *Lincoln*'s 13th Amendment to the Constitution and now to this consideration of the United States' lack of innocence in global matters. Scenes of Abel's and Powers' secretive missions, and eventual imprisonment, juxtapose how our government and military matched Russia's unprincipled subterfuge.

In *Lincoln* the weird darkness passed for cynical realism, but in *Bridge of Spies* it conveys disillusionment. When attorney James B. Donovan (Tom Hanks) defends Abel before the Supreme Court, the imagery is overcast, somber; when Powers is detained by a Russian court, sunlight shines through the casements. Seem anti-American? In visual terms, *Bridge of Spies* is an ACLU movie. Through Donovan's difficult maneuvers (against public disapproval and family discouragement),

Spielberg pursues the sanctity of civil-liberties issues. Donovan, an insurance lawyer who served at the Nuremberg trials, must fight Cold War paranoia—presented as an eternal threat to American democracy.

Good guy Donovan (his stern face features Hanks' twinkling eyes) represents a common man nobly acting against judicial and CIA expediencies; he defends the principles within the Constitution, referred to as "the Rule Book." Robert De Niro's overlooked *The Good Shepherd* (2007) was a more complex history of the social ideas at stake in CIA operations, but *Bridge of Spies* shows simplistic sentimentality when Donovan exclaims, "American justice is on trial! We're in a battle for civilization!" Those are Tony Kushnerisms, hangovers from his over-rhetorical *Lincoln* script, which encouraged an unfortunate sanctimony in Spielberg's newly politicized vision. After Kushner, the lights have dimmed in Spielberg's worldview, making *Bridge of Spies* a glum experience.

This script, co-written by Matt Charman and Joel and Ethan Coen, is surprisingly free of the Coen brothers' usual sarcasm, but Spielberg's emphasis on heavily shaded imagery is but another form of derision. He wasn't a *noir* director until he entered this current phase of visual mourning. *Bridge of Spies* gives reproach to America's former sense of exceptionalism. By showing the difficulty Donovan faced in recognizing the humanity shared with a Soviet spy, and then insisting on diplomacy over conflict (saving Powers' life as well as that of an American student trapped in partitioned Berlin), Spielberg continues the contemporary allegory that made *Lincoln* so unappealing. (Some have praised that film and this new one for Spielberg's consistency with Washington's current political powers and their machinations.)

The opening sequence, in a New York City subway, uses a profusion of fedoras and Cavanagh hats in a pantomime of mistaken identity that teases the cliché of post-World War II conformity (movie brat Spielberg turns Bresson's *Pickpocket* (1959) into a game of hide-and-seek). Despite this culturally specific period gag, two contemporary pet phrases get repeated throughout *Bridge of Spies*: "Show these men who we are" derives from President Obama's catch-all admonishment "That's not who we are." And there's Donovan's characteristic actuarial insistence when he negotiates with the Germans and Russians to release two Americans: "That kid matters. Every person matters." *Bridge of Spies* is not one of Spielberg's race movies, yet these expressions purposely echo/exploit contemporary racial politics, more ACLU cant. The problem with this is Spielberg's aiming toward approval through partisanship—something I would never have accused him of in years past. It has dulled his artistry.

Spielberg has lost the native all-American exuberance that made the atomic-bomb/refrigerator exploit in *Kingdom of the Crystal Skull* so wondrous. Here, he mocks "duck-and-cover" Cold War training films, the public-school Pledge of Allegiance, and even Donovan's "Big American breakfast" as part of obsolete cultural foolishness that deserves *noir* cynicism. This is pop art at its most disingenuous.

Everything in *Bridge of Spies* happens in the shadow of the Rosenbergs, as if Spielberg—tied to leftist self-pity—cannot forgive American political anxiety even while giving into it. Donovan's singular intransigence contradicts Spielberg's artistry. Hanks and Mark Rylance (who plays Abel) are equally, amusingly understated, but the Powers character, agent of the American military, gets short shrift. Yet this stick-figure All-

American hunk (Austin Stowell) occasions one of the film's most impressive shots: Through his open parachute, Powers watches his jet plane explode—the only real energy in a film that, like *Lincoln*, moves rather mournfully. The other good image is a slow panorama of Donovan's son putting his finger through a bullet hole in a window while his father contends with community threats, the feds, and a jingoistic cop.

Spielberg seeks to correct such modern democratic mayhem rather than fully display American ambivalence. ("Don't go bleeding heart over an Ivy League kid who decided to study Soviet economics," warns a bad-guy operative.) Unable to find a common dynamic between the era's political disagreements, Spielberg makes Donovan's exhausting struggle too sanctimonious. He means this to be a tale of patriarchal integrity, like that of Joel McCrea in *Stars in My Crown* (1950) and of Gregory Peck in the lesser, more famous *To Kill a Mockingbird*. It is Donovan himself, not just the daunting Glienicker Brücke, who is the bridge between spies, balancing all options, healing international suspicions.

Still, Donovan's Americanness feels like a rhetorical trope, not exactly reactionary but moralistic. His fatigue exposes Spielberg's own—although a briefly glimpsed moment of children's backyard play provides a charming, disturbing, genuine metaphor for freedom. Swayed by today's pop politics, Spielberg blurs the difference between humanist filmmaking and humanitarian grandstanding.

*National Review*
October 2015

# THE BFG (2016)

--------------

## *The Notorious BFG*

**S**OME SPIELBERG WATCHERS, of whom I am one, have had cause for concern: Can the great populist filmmaker ever regain his popular touch? Ignore box-office receipts and consider what's become of his once-unifying, art-advancing cultural expression. Spielberg's collaboration with didactic playwright Tony Kushner proved exemplary in the Mossad drama *Munich* (2005), a moral examination that divided critics according to their stance on Israel's self-defense. (It remains among the most captivating of all 9/11-inspired movies, second only to Spielberg's awesome *War of the Worlds*.) Yet, the Spielberg-Kushner team's *Lincoln* (2012) lost all dramatic interest. *Lincoln* was something new in Spielberg's cosmology; its period story expounded political partisanship, which prevented the film from attaining populist assent. Working under the influence of changing political winds, Spielberg and Kushner turned a biography of the 16th president of the United States into a myth infatuated by the 44th president, whose administrative difficulties they strove to explain and defend through historical allusion. Not only was this effort unpopular, it felt anti-democratic, lacking transparency as much as any secretive Cabinet meeting, but with the worse result that Spielberg seemed to have lost the unerring grasp of universal emotion that had distinguished his previous filmmaking. *Lincoln* was the first Spielberg film that felt glum; the second was the Cold War apologia *Bridge of Spies*.

All this is *de rigueur* in an era that no longer takes movies seriously. But for an era that takes its politics so very personally, Spielberg's artistic shift reflects a definitive change in social temper. Political intent cannot be overlooked despite the escapist surface of his new film, *The BFG*.

*The BFG* is based on a Roald Dahl story in which an English orphan girl, Sophie (Ruby Barnhill), befriends Big Friendly Giant (Mark Rylance), a benevolent leviathan who, being derived from the legacy of British childhood fantasy, stalks the streets of London inducing dreams into the unconscious of sleeping children. On first sight, BFG is ominous, as scary as *Jaws*, as unknowable as the flying saucers in *Close Encounters*, as threatening as King Kong when he reached his lascivious hand into a woman's bedchamber. That's how BFG kidnaps Sophie and takes her to his kingdom of giants, where he, a fellow misfit, stocks subconscious dreams while placating other, malevolent giants: Fleshlumpeater, Bloodbottler, Bonecruncher, Childchewer, Gizzardgulper, Meatdripper. (*The BFG*'s verbal descriptions evoke a miscellany from *A Midsummer Night's Dream* and *A Clockwork Orange*.)

The giant's fantasyland recalls Spielberg's 1991 *Hook* (British make-believe based on James M. Barrie's *Peter Pan*) more than it evokes the archaeological history of his Indiana Jones series, but, really, *The BFG* combines both. Spielberg appears to justify his own identification with Otherness as part of a developed spiritual and political faith. *The BFG* evokes historical legend while also exploring innocence and maturation. Sophie's loneliness is relieved by her empathy with the benevolent alien. Her adventure in the giant kingdom eventually leads to a climactic feat of social activism: Sophie and BFG enlist the Queen of England, becoming allies in a moral battle similar to what Spielberg depicted in *Saving Private Ryan*.

If you think I've spoiled the plot, you're ignoring what's more fascinating than plot. This has to do with the complex of Spielberg's creativity meeting his politics and his ultra-humanism. Yes, *The BFG* is being sold as a children's movie, but it's much more than that.

In Molly Haskell's upcoming book, *Steven Spielberg: A Life in Films* (part of Yale University Press' Jewish Lives series), she quotes Spielberg as saying, "Everything about me is in my films." That explains why the hero in *The BFG*, who is both an outsider and a towering figure of social benevolence, has a physical resemblance to Spielberg. This half-human, half-digital BFG recalls writer Bruce Handy's unbeatable *Vanity Fair* description of Spielberg as "both elfin and rabbinical." But there's an additional celebrity resemblance, a spiritually and politically inflected likeness that gives the film a different, unsettling meaning.

We could expect Haskell to delve into Sophie as a feminist figure. The little girl boldly dons a dead boy's red uniform jacket, then turns it inside out (to queer gender identity as well as detach her from the little girl in the red coat in *Schindler's List*). But most critics—and most people who don't take movies seriously—might be content to ignore the significance of Sophie's infatuation with BFG. Yet all one need do is look at what's on the screen.

BFG is almost a shape-shifter. He eludes adult detection by stealth. His large, heavy head hangs on his skinny neck like a street lantern as he stalks the nighttime city. (The film's first images of London's Tower Bridge at night have the clarity and wonder of images in a View-Master stereopticon.) Sometimes hooded, BFG holds onto his dream-blowing trumpet/staff like an Old Testament prophet. He has Spielberg's smile, but, when he's excited, his large ears flap like fish gills. Those ears also suggest Spielberg's cinematic idol David Lean (just as the *Close Encounters* alien suggested Jean Renoir), but BFG mostly resembles our current president, the phantom figure behind Spielberg-Kushner's *Lincoln*. BFG's Big Daddy Obama ears hear all. He's a figure of liberal dreams who provides citizens their own dreams. *The BFG* is the most extravagant send-off Hollywood has ever given an American president.

Explore the metaphor: A transition from a sleeping boy imbibing dreams from BFG's trumpet to an English landscape shaped like the boy's body is a political transfiguration. Spielberg's Obama idolatry becomes mythic symbology. This deification goes beyond anything in *Lincoln*. It even surpasses Darryl F. Zanuck's effort to idolize Woodrow Wilson in the 1944 *Wilson* (a movie as forgotten as Spielberg's *Lincoln* is already forgotten).

Timed to celebrate Obama's last year in office, *The BFG* hides its hagiography behind the filmmaker's personal self-delusion—and behind his skill. *The BFG* flaunts what Spielberg learned from making his 2011 two-fer *War Horse* and *The Adventures of Tintin*. Their gyroscopic elegance is extended in these vertiginous, dream-like images. The mash-up of political history and fantasy is not coincidental—it's multilateral. Just as Spielberg rationalizes Obama's mythos, he honors Britain's imperial legacy. When Sophie and BFG visit Windsor Castle (for a comic, exaggerated high tea), they convince the Queen to save England's children from beastie threats.

In a housekeeping scene, dust gets wiped off a Queen Victoria portrait (Spielberg's traditionalist sympathies confound his notorious liberalism), thus updating modern political allegiance. The Queen (Penelope Wilton) issues a command to her commanding officers to "put some army in it!" for the fight against the malicious giants. Spielberg disrupts the childhood whimsy with helicopters, paratroopers, and the machinery of modern warfare. Then—damn him—he includes an image that goes back further than The Good War: Sophie dangerously walks through Giant Land meadows like David among a field of sleeping Goliaths. Whatever Spielberg's politics on the question of open borders, this metaphor for the threat from ISIS and al-Qaeda is indelible.

Without ever questioning BFG's motives, Spielberg assigns him almighty benevolence, imagining him as an alien figure who is an idealized answer to liberal dreams. (A bonus: BFG's lair, where dreams are stored in glass jars, evokes the multi-colored lobotomies in Steve Martin's *The Man With Two Brains*.)

*The BFG* isn't a remake of *E.T.* or *A.I.* but its own peculiar, alien-worshipping epic. It's an involuted fairy tale, leaning both Left and Right, expressing the quiddities of utopian imagination. Spielberg's childlike optimism brings quixotic ideas to life. (Imagine if Scorsese's insipid *Hugo* had visionary lyricism.) Through its witching-hour presentation of potential moral and political alliance, *The BFG* teaches the movie-loving electorate to simply dream. It should be a lesson to politicized Spielberg watchers.

*National Review*
July 2016

# THE POST (2017)

---

## *Spielberg Rides Politics' Slippery Slope*

"**S**TOP WATCHING THE news" is the savvy advice Morrissey sings on his politically oriented, recently released album *Low in High School* (2017). He then explains: "Because the news contrives to frighten you / To make you feel small and alone / To make you feel that your mind isn't your own." This provocative assessment of contemporary journalism felt positively restorative after watching the deceitful glorification of "the news" in Steven Spielberg's *The Post*.

Morrissey's complaint cuts through to the truth about modern journalism—as Spielberg does not—by exposing how what we consider "the news" has become the illusory practice of a primarily Left-centered, conspiratorial institution that operates to manipulate a susceptible public. In other words, Morrissey knows that journalism has become corrupt, whereas Spielberg's movie normalizes that corruption. *The Post* is a fawning account of *Washington Post* publisher Katharine "Kay" Graham (Meryl Streep) and editor Ben Bradlee (Tom Hanks) crying "Me, too" when the *New York Times* scoops them with the precedent-setting publication of the Pentagon Papers in 1971.

Spielberg looks to that turning-point event because the past is the source from which today's leftist sanctimony—and particularly the media's maddening "resistance" posture—claims its validity. All of today's social-justice movements—Black Lives Matter, fourth-wave feminism, the transgender-equality brigades—derive their sentimental impetus from the memories of halcyon protest and counterculture dissent that transformed America.

*The Post* is a snootily white-collar movie faking common-man virtues. Spielberg directs it as an addendum to *All the President's Men* (1976), the most narcissistic of all newspaper films. Not only did it alter popular consciousness about the media—fabricating a holy war, between journalism and government, that ceased only for deference toward the Obama administration—but it had an overall destructive effect on American civic ambition. That film's false modesty (enacted by former culture heroes Robert Redford and Dustin Hoffman) romanticized the hubris, of taking down a presidency, that infected subsequent generations of communications students and ambitious reporters. Through that film's convoluted, pretend-mystery plot, journalism wannabes regarded their own political partisanship as qualifications for the job; white-knight vanity replaced the self-effacing detective work of the old-time crime beat. Ever since that tedious movie, the news media have magnified their own mythology and sense of power.

Now, using his own dark-tinted "realism" (as in *Lincoln* and *Bridge of Spies*), Spielberg counters the lavishness—of the dichotomy between justice and corruption, and of the contrast between the glowing and the chiaroscuro—that cinematographer Gordon Willis gave to *All the President's Men*. Black-and-white photography might have implied documentary investigation, but media mogul Spielberg wants dramatic *persuasion*; he, too, has fallen for the media's sanctimony and so makes a 21st-century version of John Ford's maxim on history: "When the legend becomes fact, print the legend." Yet, *The Post* is irony-free.

The legend offered here is motivated by the resolve of the national media industry to countermand the 2016 election, first by going back to establish the *Washington Post*'s bona fides when it followed the *New York Times*' publication of the Pentagon Papers. This is where Spielberg and screenwriters Liz Hannah and Josh Singer automatically accept that publishing the Defense Department's classified government documents was a journalistic prerogative. To question that decision is now considered anathema. *The Post* validates the slippery slope that brought us to today's shameless media partisanship.

Daniel Ellsberg, the Rand Corporation wonk who appropriated the documents and released them to the *Times*, is portrayed (by Matthew Rhys) as a minor character whose trendy anti-establishment crime (47 classified volumes sneaked out over two months) is merely the film's pretext. Ellsberg's backstory, like Spielberg's cleverest gambit (a blue-shaded montage of presidential prevaricating on Vietnam through four administrations), leads up to the film's real subject: the gallantry of the media class.

Kay Graham and Ben Bradlee are aristos. They spend little screen time discussing the ethics of "whistle-blowing" or connecting it to their own homes or corporation (where disloyalty would hardly be tolerated). But they do compete and collude with the *Times*, and, being media lords, their opposition to the Vietnam war is not just journalism but noblesse oblige. Because the purloined documents proved that the government had lost confidence about the war, publishing them, against pressure from Nixon's White House, becomes justification for any unethical, self-serving action. ("What will happen to the reputation of this paper if we sit on this?")

The way Spielberg films Hanks and Streep in heroic profiles, their faces full of virtuous strain—tough-guy pride and rich-lady timorousness—isn't really about freedom of the press; it's a Mount Rushmore of Hollywood and Beltway liberal alliance. (Film-history note: The clash between Streep and Tom Cruise as Iraq War-era journalist and politician in *Lions for Lambs* (2007) offered deeper philosophical debate than anything here.) No underlings contradict Graham and Bradlee; the film depicts a media class united with D.C. social elites, powerbrokers who all think alike (thereby implying that the public should think as media instruct them).

These white-collar folk are shocked at what the Papers reveal ("This has never happened before! Not in the history of the Republic!"). But their shock never leads to self-reflection about their duty as citizens. The turn from being professionals to being activists relieves them of patriotic responsibility. Compare them to the characters in Mel Gibson's *Hacksaw Ridge* (2016), living out the difficult moral quandaries facing conscientious objectors. *The Post*'s mash-up of conscience and egotism simply idolizes Graham and Bradlee as they incorporate sedition into the function of journalism. It's possible to think that the profession, and American optimism, died at that moment.

Alert viewers should see through Spielberg's admiring perspective and recognize it for what it is: a class crisis. He unwittingly shows the haughtiness of bourgeois journalists who feel superior to their readership and to the subjects they cover. Spielberg valorizes this arrogance but without examining the privilege so apparent in the recent move toward editorializing commentary in news stories that should be strictly factual.

*The Post* presents journalists as our saviors whose authority is guaranteed solely by their social position: Kay Graham's money and Ben Bradlee's editorial fiat. Neither icon's judgment is challenged. Spielberg simply looks back in awe. (Interestingly, they have the same spiritual lack as Spielberg's Lincoln does.) Their naive disillusionment about dishonest politicos (Bruce Greenwood plays a contrite Robert McNamara) is Spielberg's ruse, attempting to domesticate D.C.'s elite—Bradlee's daughter's lemonade stand and his speechifying wife's (Sarah Paulson) turkey sandwiches nourish the journos as they work overtime. This casual class snobbery is the film's worst defect—an object lesson in the ever-widening divide between the ideological dictates of mainstream media (which Morrissey sings as "mean-stream") and the actual lives and best interests of the popular audience. Spielberg, once our great suburban auteur, squanders the potential of such a narrative. Have his private dinners with Obama corrupted his vision?

Here is some of the most dishonest filmmaking of Spielberg's career: There are strategically placed blacks and women in nearly every scene (though not on the *Post*'s editorial board—shades of *Spotlight*). The storyline seems slapdash, TV-movieish but without the urgency of a revelation that needed to be rushed to the screen in order to capture an important political moment. Spielberg never had Larry Cohen's B-movie, tabloid genius, and he's lost the feel for the zeitgeist that Morrissey has rediscovered. Instead, the film swings into feminist groveling.

Streep is at her most obnoxiously "unassuming" when the Supreme Court sanctions the *Post*'s defiance of President Nixon's effort to obstruct the paper's publication. It's cringe-inducing to watch Streep maneuver down the steps of the Supreme Court into radiant sunlight while throngs of women beam at her as if she were Hillary Clinton incarnate.

The *Post* then shifts from hagiographic mode to pandering. A *Post* reporter reads Justice Hugo Black's own fawning opinion on the Court's decision: "The Founding Fathers gave the free press the protection it must have to fulfill its essential role in our democracy. The press was to serve the governed, not the governors." Black's hoary, big-little binary has occasioned Spielberg's least credible fantasy, which brings us back to Morrissey's great warning: This film's salute to the foundations of "mean-stream" journalism is designed to make you worship Hollywood, the Beltway, and media elites; to make you think they care about YOU. Spielberg ignores that journalism works in a totally opposite way now in its constant, brazen, unscrupulous efforts to govern people's thoughts and votes.

Spielberg's wishful craft can't disguise this hoax. Ending the movie with trite suspense, modeled after a Marvel Comics post-credit sequence cliffhanger, he fixates on a leftist fantasy that the Watergate scandal—and the self-righteous vigilantism it unleashed—symbolizes America's political destiny. The *Post*'s cynicism is unworthy—and worthless.

*National Review*
December 2017

# READY PLAYER ONE (2018)

*Spielberg's Crowd-Pleasing Escapism*

*R*EADY *PLAYER ONE* starts with dystopia: a Columbus, Ohio, housing ghetto in 2045, known as "The Stacks" for its resemblance to piled-up recreational vehicles, that is home to the film's hero. Then the movie shifts gears from depressing hyperrealism to escapist fantasy.

But this escapism is so self-aware that it remains unconvincing. Wade Watts (Tye Sheridan), the film's 18-year-old hero, seems younger. He's become accustomed to nearly autistic diversion; he evades the misery of poverty, joblessness, isolation, and orphanhood (he lives with his aunt in a makeshift broken home oppressed by an abusive adult male). Secluding himself behind a visor and a pair of hand switches, Wade enters the OASIS, a virtual-reality-simulator game that provides his only release. His avatar is "Parzival," an unexplained misspelling of a character from Arthurian mythology, who acts out his desperate venture in digital battles. Haptic technology gives him virtual contact (both visible and tactile) with anonymous but politically diverse playmates. They are Wade's OASIS tribe, even including an adolescent love interest.

The above description should concern you because it's full of cultural politics. Cultural politics enter *Ready Player One* when it becomes clear that Wade and the gamers all uncritically worshiped the digital manufacturer of OASIS, the late James Halliday (Mark Rylance acting absent-minded). As a way out of their dystopian despair, they pursue Halliday's posthumous challenge to find three special keys to his bequest, a kingdom of corporate riches and earthly dominance. Unthinking viewers will see Wade's venture as mere entertainment. But thinking viewers should see this tale as director Steven Spielberg's parallel for the modern condition and a justification for escapism—another disappointing, though confessional, version of *The Greatest Showman* (2017).

Look at how Halliday clearly represents techno mogul Steve Jobs, hybridized with an earlier generation's Walt Disney. Spielberg plays sorcerer's apprentice to both, causing competition between the techno and visionary sides of his genius: insidious commercialism clashes with quasi spirituality, the mogul vs. the artist. The Halliday scenes evoke *Citizen Kane* yet are almost as hallowed as those in *Lincoln*.

Spielberg submits himself to playing out scenes of ultimate fanboy fantasy, but his nimble storytelling can't hide depths of unacknowledged political despair. The social conflict implicit in Wade's race for Halliday's prize (hidden within digital "Easter eggs") works against the adolescent thrall with pop culture that inspired Ernest Cline's 2011 source novel. (Cline also wrote the script for the charmingly innocent, unjustly overlooked 2009 film *Fanboys*.) Now Spielberg uses that thrall to inveigle his audience; this film's title blatantly invites viewers to enjoy a cascade of pop trivia.

Paul W. S. Anderson's game-based movies, especially his stirring remake of *Death Race* (2008), and Edgar Wright's exhilarating *Scott Pilgrim vs. the World* (2010) have definitively presented gamer fantasy as an allegory for real life. But

Spielberg never gets to the irony of virtual reality's vicarious experience—which Luc Besson already spoofed throughout *Valerian and the City of a Thousand Planets* (2017). None of this story's dramatic tensions—Wade's rivalry with the corporate boss Sorrento (Ben Mendelsohn) and a longed-for romance with Art3mis/Samantha (Olivia Cooke)—ever amount to real-world awakening. Spielberg's imagery makes one's head spin without provoking thought. The finale is as trite as Bong Joon-ho's in *Okja* (2017). The desire to celebrate video games and pop junk is such an unrewarding idea that it makes *The Lego Movie*'s (2014) satire seem transcendent.

Spielberg's insistence on this juvenilia after four demoralizing political films suggests a creative crisis. While *The Post* looked and felt tossed-off, Spielberg is clearly applying himself here, as shown in the immediacy of the lead performances. Wade's anxiety is conveyed through Sheridan's awkward-age pubescence, and he's ideally paired with Cooke, who evokes the womanly promise of Deborah Van Valkenburgh and Carla Gugino (the film's true movie-geek Easter egg). Though Spielberg's genius has been missing of late, it shows up in the film's one great, dramatically adroit image, when Wade confronts Sorrento. The face of the villainous adult is reflected in Wade's visor—right between the boy's eyes—perhaps a prophetic image of Wade's unconscious self. That one shot surpasses all of *The Last Jedi* (2017).

Marvel fanboys who are unaccustomed to action-movie panache will probably be wowed by Spielberg's ten-minute gaming race, an extended tour de force. Parzival and other virtual-reality gladiators speed past one another, crashing through explosions and obstructions that could be a condensed history of our collective pop-culture detritus—

from *King Kong* to *Jurassic Park*. This sequence, patterned after Spielberg's dazzlement in *The Adventures of Tintin*, is so advanced that it seems post-cinematic. Laughter is cut short by awe. Super-video-game images hurtle by, beyond dream logic, into a realm of pop phenomenology where nothing appears as it seems. Each phantasm can morph or combust, resulting in either doom for the player or a reward of points or coins (with spangly bursts of enthusiasm like those Wright depicted as visual onomatopoeia in *Scott Pilgrim vs. the World*).

This demolition derby suggests a kinetic version of *A.I.*'s Flesh Fair—but without the moral or emotional consequences. It's a breathless bender that, as it goes along, hollows out Parzival's symbolic quest for an unspecified holy grail. The pell-mell action never pauses so that we can consider how this relentless excitation rattles the senses. And that, tragically, is how gaming's trash pop culture has deprived several generations of spiritual reflection. It merely reflects their alienation (which was the underlying theme of Anderson's *Death Race* but here is virtually forgotten).

The fallacy at the heart of *Ready Player One* is that Wade's win as Parzival takes on sentimental, if not philosophical, dimensions; that the puzzlingly violent, razzle-dazzle workout prepares its characters for life; and that gaming implicitly provides new cognitive patterns for its players. Spielberg immerses himself in the delusion that virtual reality equates to cinema, the photographic reflection of life. Although the film moves with Spielberg's signature flair, it is slowed down intellectually when Wade's anxiety and desperation are replaced with an unreal commitment to demigod Halliday and his ersatz principles. The "fun" becomes meaningless.

*Ready Player One*'s concept is so apologetic about pop-culture deception that it is kryptonite for a director who doesn't apply all his intelligence or discover anything new. Note how the pop music cues feign nostalgia: Spielberg's synthetic *Saturday Night Fever* (1977) homage should rightly refer to Michael Jackson's *Thriller* (a genuine civilizing phenomenon that belongs to the film's '80s gestalt); it might have elevated the film's concept of pop-culture bliss. This pop jamboree demands satire, but Spielberg doesn't go there, either for fear of losing his audience or because the movie is fundamentally empty.

A once-great filmmaker has taken on a new avatar less heroic than Parzival. It is the avatar of a pandering crowd-pleaser. Spielberg, the D. W. Griffith of the sound era—who ironically, when the politically correct putsch began in 1999, turned his back on Griffith by failing to speak up as the Directors Guild of America stripped Griffith's name and legacy from its awards—now celebrates Hollywood's most craven tendencies. The crowd-pleaser has outdone himself.

*National Review*
May 2018

# SPIELBERG MEETS THE ZEITGEIST

---

## Spielberg in the Whorehouse of Cannes

*B*LUE *I*S *THE* *Warmest Color* (2013) is distinguished by being the Palme d'Or winner at the Cannes Film Festival when Steven Spielberg was President of the Jury. It was a shocking choice only because the film is so meaningless, not due to its supposed "shocking" lesbian sex scenes. Such "explicitness" couldn't have fazed Spielberg who dared Hollywood's pioneering lesbian content in 1985's *The Color Purple*—a film that has yet to get its due from critics but has become a staple for Black academics and proved globally popular; note its frequent TV showings, even on the hipster station Sundance Channel. (The Cannes festival began with a tribute to Spielberg featuring a performance of *The Color Purple*'s theme song "Ms. Celie's Blues (Sister)," a song that transcended sexuality with a sympathetic expression of female solidarity.)

Given Spielberg's humanist sophistication, the Jury's choice of *Blue Is the Warmest Color* is puzzling; it reverses the progress of *The Color Purple* with a meandering focus on sexual license. Director Abdellatif Kechiche's story of a Parisian high school girl Adele (Adèle Exarchopoulos) who succumbs to the butch charms of a blue-haired art student Emma (Léa Seydoux), then loses all sense of herself is neither pro-humanist nor pro-gay. Kechiche, adapting a graphic novel by Julie Maroh, emphasizes the physical aspects of romance—sexual attraction, sexual coupling—that makes the stability of gay romance questionable. In *The Color Purple*, Spielberg's adaptation of Alice Walker's novel featured a mature understanding of the need for love between women as well as between opposite genders.

*The Color Purple*'s Hollywood discretion (and pop universality) may not have pleased 1985 status-keepers who preferred *Out of Africa* but Spielberg and screenwriter Menno Mayjes wonderfully recognized the humane essence of Celie (Whoopi Goldberg) discovering herself through an attraction to blues singer Shug Avery (Margaret Avery). Their relationship, based in Black blues folk culture, was less about sex than the larger issue of emotional fulfillment—personal wholeness and spiritual salvation. Kechiche, a politically-correct operator whose monotonous *The Secret of the Grain* (2007) exploited Muslim immigrancy, uses gayness to support dubious ideas about romance and identity. His long, obvious concentration on female sexuality doesn't celebrate womanhood but exploits it in that grayish-blue area of gynophilia (heterosexual men's excitement at watching women copulate—and teenage Adele's shaved pudenda).

Really, what is there to learn from watching Adele and Emma bumping-and-grinding? Or repetitive close-ups of Exarchopoulos' wet, open mouth (obvious vaginal symbolism)? She gives up her intellectual interest in literature to implausibly become a hausfrau to please her social-climbing woman. (Seydoux's tomboy manner as a woman who puts her career before her personal life recalls Rainer Werner Fassbinder's trollish look.)

In Robert Towne's 1982 *Personal Best*, female sex scenes were emotionally intimate yet without all the huffing, puffing and bumping uglies. Director John Huston once suggested certain private acts should never be shown which Kechiche confirms with the silly pointlessness of Adele and Emma's extended exertions. As with the belly dancing in *The Secret of the Grain*, Kechiche doesn't know when enough is enough.

All this is as unprofound as Woody Allen's self-justifying, "The heart wants what it wants"—a way to avoid examining the depths of human interaction. Kechiche gets no credit for a gay sex breakthrough; anyone who has followed the cultural progress of gay filmmakers are already ahead of this film through the dazzling experiences of Andre Techine's *Wild Reeds* (1995), Gael Morel's *Full Speed* (1996), Ducastel-Martineau's *My Life on Ice* (2003) and Lionel Baier's *Garçon stupide* (2005)—for starters. Otherwise we're back to the ignorance of thinking *Brokeback Mountain* was an innovation.

Kechiche emulates the realism of Maurice Pialat and Mike Leigh then ruins it with dubious insights ("Tragedy is inevitable, that's the essence of human life") that are fashionable humbug. Spielberg should be embarrassed.

*CityArts*
November 2013

# Better-Than
*[Excerpts from the Annual Better-Than Lists]*

## 2008

### *Indiana Jones and the Kingdom of the Crystal Skull* > *Iron Man*
Steven Spielberg's par excellence genre expertise wrung fresh amazement out of the Indy Jones franchise; it exposed *Iron Man's* dung-like banality.

## 2011

### *The Adventures of Tintin* > *The Artist*
Spielberg restores the essence of cinema (from the Greek "kinesis," meaning movement), defying Michel Hazanavicius' too-cute silent movie hoax. Joy vs. Inanity.

### *War Horse* > *Hugo*
Spielberg revives genre aesthetics as spiritual expression, defying Martin Scorsese's fatuous history lecture. Feeling vs. Sentimentality.

## 2012

### *The Lady* > *Lincoln*
Luc Besson's bio-pic examined Aung San Suu Kyi's marital and political commitment, while Spielberg's unholy marriage to Tony Kushner pushed the cult of personality. Aphorisms vs. Propaganda.

## 2015

### *Sicario* > *Bridge of Spies*
Denis Villeneuve explores the moral parameters of the U.S. drug wars while Spielberg plays moral-equivalency games with Cold War history. Visionary boldness vs. visionary smugness.

## 2016

### *The Mermaid* > *The BFG*
Stephen Chow's action-fantasy just happens to make ecological points while defending the ethics of the forgotten working class. Spielberg's political parable is a transparent valedictory salute to Obama's ruling-class elitism, normalized as childhood fantasy. The most popular film in China's history vs. an American election-year flop.

## 2017

### *The Square* > *The Post*
Ruben Östlund satirizes art (the media) in the age of political correctness while Spielberg idealizes the media (journalism) for its seditious self-justification. High-culture chagrin vs. the normalizing of what used to be called yellow journalism.

## 2018

### *Mom and Dad* > *Ready Player One* / *Isle of Dogs* / *The Ballad of Buster Scruggs*
Brian Taylor's uncanny update of *Les Parents terribles* (1948) is an audacious domestic comedy that advances from its source

in cult-movie idiosyncrasy to outpace the tired mainstream exertions of Spielberg. Wes Anderson and the Coen Brothers, formerly great artists, now at their most confused, manic, and depressed (respectively). Fun vs. exhaustion. Insight vs. capitulation. Exhilaration vs. sullen nihilism.

# Spielberg Recovers His Political Courage

**H**YSTERIA OVER STEVEN Spielberg's intention to address how the Academy of Motion Picture Arts and Sciences gives its Oscar awards to live streaming content rather than movies, has ignited new millennial panic. The Internet is crazily enraged that Hollywood's youngest titan hasn't bowed down to the latest shift in content delivery like everybody else.

Few people can think for themselves these days and pop culture consumption is one of the most pathetic examples of the public rendered susceptible to media suasion. This is the same non-analytical, TV-loving mania as left media blaming itself for promoting President Trump's election; they're unrational about media and its impact. The anti-Spielberg protests are ridiculous first of all because Spielberg hasn't even made his statement yet. Why have the Inter-Webs jumped the shark?

Spielberg's recent box-office flops lost him cultural clout, especially for those who easily fall for the latest trends—it's bias confirmation of their non-discriminating taste and shoppers' idiocy along with shoppers' remorse. Spielberg's earlier pronouncement on what's artistically distinctive about theatrical cinema dares to oppose the speciously labeled "Golden Age of Television." He has riled the lemmings who give in to binge-watching and devoted themselves to cable presentations (what academics call "corporate autism"). They don't appreciate the heightened visual and sensual awareness that makes Spielberg's particular art form—the cinema—special.

I have not been a fan of Spielberg's recent politically-influenced films (*Lincoln*, *Bridge of Spies*, *The BFG*, *Ready Player*

*One*) so it is surprising that he appears to be going against the progressive mob. But Spielberg's plan to address the Academy's Board of Governors (of which he is its most prestigious member), proposing to change awards criteria, indicates that he has beliefs that go deeper than populist politics. The anticipated articulation of these beliefs (that cinema, unlike television, is an irreducible, visually kinetic art form and is inseparable from the mass human experience) reminds true Spielberg fans that some spark of artistic valor still remains.

Maybe Spielberg can no longer woo ticket buyers in the vast numbers he once did, but he seems to have grown testicular fortitude.

Could this be Spielberg's proudest moment? It nearly makes up for him succumbing to stupid political correctness in 1999, going along with the Directors Guild of America removing D.W. Griffith's name from its awards, thus betraying the movie pioneer Spielberg recalls at his best and to whom he, and all of us, are most indebted.

Spielberg may be "on the wrong side of history," but that was always a specious axiom, favored by the dictator mentality of the previous administration that Spielberg like many others fell for from 2008 to 2016.

When Spielberg actually makes his Board of Governors appeal, his opponents may find that he fights for more than the organization's prestige. He cannot ignore that television and electronic media have beaten the movies in the popularity contest. But neither can the fact of cinema's kinetic, spatial essence be ignored. Those qualities have also lost popularity (degraded by aesthetically inert films like *The Lord of the Rings* series and any Marvel Comics film you can name) and I think that's implicit in Spielberg's complaint.

The Academy's erratic protocol is obviously full of mishaps and contradictions. (It has fallen for new media trends and p.c. activism and ruined its former standards—such as the embarrassing case of ESPN's *O.J.: Made in America* (2016) TV series winning the Best Documentary Feature prize in 2016.) But when the aesthetics of film presentation are forgotten, so is the phenomenon of filmgoing that once upon a time was literally, socially unifying. In the upcoming political revolution epic *Peterloo* (2019), director Mike Leigh yearns for unity through intense, fascinated concentration on faces and emotional sweep that would be imperceptible on television or computer screens. (*Peterloo* is being released by Amazon Studios, a misnomer that pretends to Hollywood tradition while, actually, opposing it. At least *Peterloo* is experientially superior to anything so far released by Netflix.)

Movie review shills never educate audiences about aesthetics, they simply provide hype, going along with the cultural collapse: Film = TV. If an egghead critic argues against this, the point gets dismissed. When Spielberg makes the point, even dummkopfs must pay attention.

Consumers who are suckers for the independent movie trend are complaining that Spielberg is against them; they don't realize how few indie films keep the promise of Griffith, Eisenstein, Sternberg, Welles, Cocteau, Visconti and Godard. They don't understand that Spielberg, for the first time in recent years, is thinking independently. They don't see that independent thinking is the rarest, most necessary attribute in this political era. Spielberg may be fighting a losing battle, but it's honorable.

*National Review*
December 2019

# Spielberg Meets the Zeitgeist

*Scholar Daniel McNeil responded to an Internet discussion on Spielberg's relevance in the Millennium and asks: "But does this show that Spielberg has lost the 'feel for the zeitgeist?' Or that he can only convey the zeitgeist as thought and felt by the 1%?"*

LIKE MOST MIDDLE-CLASS filmmakers, Spielberg's cultural-economic background influences his approach to the world and to filmmaking. His feel for the zeitgeist, apparent in his early hits that were in-sync with popular attitudes and tastes, derives from the cultural familiarity and knowledge that is gained from one's participation in middle-class society and its conventions and rituals.

It's not commonly recognized that filmmakers (like all authors of art products) express the cultures that created them, that they belong to—that's basic Structuralism, the system of understanding and examining social relations and connections that American universities began to teach in the late-20th century. But that insight into how ideology functions, how it is casually concealed even in films, books, music, theater that appear non-political (such as Pixar and Marvel for you uninitiated) is now conveniently forgotten by the educated classes when it becomes unfavorable.

Instead of taking-in the political ideas clearly apparent in Spielberg's Obama-era films (*Lincoln*, *Bridge of Spies*, *The BFG*, *The Post*), some prefer the approach of regarding the films disingenuously—as entertainments or innocuous patriotic histories. This delusion grows from the peculiar cultural and ideological satisfaction that liberals enjoyed during the Obama administration (the period when those films were made) which fostered the belief that their sense of social justice was historically, politically, morally correct and thus inarguable—a point that Spielberg's films reinforced. (Having finally wrested the government from George W. Bush and achieved ideological and cultural dominance, liberals put into effect the implication that ideology was not a means of thinking to be analyzed or explicated but, now under Obama, was simply, good and true.)

This anti-ideology phase had a short-lived label: "Post-Racial." That opportunistic title (a hasty progressive boast) was too erroneous to stick. We laugh about it now but for various, obscure reasons it never stuck to Spielberg who was in the process of subsuming all his racial ideas into the strange displacement of the proto-Communist iconography of Tony Kushner's *Lincoln* which was "post-racial" in its transmutation of Obama's biracial identity into a Republican figure whom contemporary Democrats now hijack for racialist rhetoric. "Post-racial" certainly could not stick the way left critics during the 1980s condescendingly demeaned Spielberg by accusing him of being a representative of Reagan Era populism.

That notion was asserted as calumny, intended to scrutinize, undercut and diminish Spielberg's ("unhip") popularity. But no such scrutiny took place in the Obama Era when the ideology evoked by Spielberg's films remained unexamined. The films, despite positive acclaim, were relatively unpopular; their failure was overlooked as if to erase any traces of non-triumphant Obamaism (the perfect term for Daniel Day-Lewis and Mark Rylance's less-than-exhilarating Oscar wins) or, more to the point, to ignore an ideology that was superficial and, shamefully, not taken to heart.

To hide or ignore Spielberg's ideology at this point is to practice the political obfuscation which contradicts leftist critical theory for fear that it would expose the manipulations of leftist cultural practice.

The reality of Spielberg having lost popular favor (or losing the feel for the zeitgeist that he at one time seemed to possess intuitively) forces one to rethink whether or not Spielberg ever addressed the zeitgeist as a cultural response or a cultural power. Did he truly effect popular thought (as his early hits *Jaws*, *Close Encounters*, *Raiders of the Lost Ark*, *E.T. the Extra-Terrestrial* and *The Color Purple* seemed to indicate) or did he simply reflect it (as his later films *A.I. Artificial Intelligence*, *Minority Report*, *War of the Worlds*, *Munich* suggest)?

The incongruousness of Spielberg's *The Post*, a reenactment of a moment in political history that is guilefully-conceived as a reaction to recent politics, makes it a break away from the unsettled spirit of the times. Not a misreading of the zeitgeist but a deliberate attempt to alter (or in post-election left parlance, to "resist") the popular spirit of the times and replace it with an anti-harmonious, disunited ideology of deceit and treachery and sedition. The film does not reflect disharmony—it clearly is not caught in the middle of the mainstream media's fantasies about itself as "the free press" and the distress of millions of Americans who can no longer trust the media's naked agenda. But, rather, it is a disingenuous film that pretends most Americans consent to the actions of the privileged characters on screen—that there is harmony in agreed-upon dissent. It is an effort toward honoring, affecting and achieving the treachery and faithlessness—a betrayal of populism and the popular instinct—that Paul Joseph Watson summarized in his exquisite reproof, "You cannot be the counterculture and the dominant culture." It's impossible, yet Spielberg, the formerly great and formerly *popular* popular artist now lives the lie.

# INDEX

**#**

*1776* play. 205, 326

*1941* (1979) film. 49-53, 63, 126, 144, 145, 146, 149, 152, 160, 230, 262, 280, 311

*2001: A Space Odyssey* (1968) film. 250

*227* tv series. 97

*25th Hour* (2002) film. 261

*4 Little Girls* (1997) film. 179, 219

*400 Blows, The* (1959) film. 46

**A**

*À nous la liberté* (1931) film. 47

*A.I. Artificial Intelligence* (2001) film. xiii, 69, 71, 127, 241-247, 248-253, 296, 343, 354, 368

*About Schmidt* (2002) film. 261

Adams, Ken. 51

*Adventures of Tintin, The* (2011) film. xiv, 307-315, 342, 354, 360

*Ain't Misbehavin'* play. 89

*Air Force One* (1997) film. 178

*Alien* (1979) film. 70

*Alien Nation* (1988) film. 199

*All the President's Men* (1976) film. 346

Allen, Debbie. 179, 221

Allen, Karen. 122, 293

Allen, Nancy. 52

Allen, Woody. 99, 158, 184, 359

*Allonsanfàn* (1974) film. 197

Almagor, Gila. 287

Alonzo, John A. 43

*Alphaville* (1965) film. *256*

Althusser, Louis. 201

Altman, Robert. xii, 49, 197, 224, 235, 263, 311

*Always* (1989) film. xiii, 123-128

Amalric, Mathieu. 287

*Amazing Grace* (2007) film. 325-326

"Amazing Grace" song. 202

*Amazing Stories* tv series. 124

*American Beauty* (1999) film. 306

*American Cinema: Directors and Directions 1929-1968, The* book. 147

*American Hot Wax* (1978) film. 53

*American Playhouse* tv series. 99

*American Ruling Class, The* (2005) film. 320

*American Werewolf in London, An* (1981) film. 73

*Amistad* (1997) film. xiii, 68, 126, 173-178, 179-185, 186-194, 195-215, 216-222, 224, 225, 226, 227, 228, 229, 230, 232, 233, 234, 235, 244, 274, 284, 304, 312, 320, 323, 324, 325, 326, 327, 335

*Anaconda* (1997) film. 170

Andersen, Hans Christian. 83

Anderson, Paul W.S. 71, 311, 321, 352, 354, 361-362

Anderson, Wes. 125

*Angel Eyes* (2001) film. *245*

*Angels in America: A Gay Fantasia on National Themes* play. 326

*Animal House* (1978) film. 51, 52

Ann-Margret. 52

*Another 48 Hrs.* (1990) film. 130

Antonioni, Michelangelo. 125, 257

*Antwone Fisher* (2002) film. 261

*Apocalypse Now* (1979) film. 49, 169, 278

*Apocalypse Now Redux* (2001) film. 287

Apted, Michael. 325

*Arabian Nights* book. 192

Arestrup, Niels. 312

Aronofsky, Darren. 251

*Artist, The* (2011) film. 360

Astaire, Fred. 125

Atherton, William. 28, 30, 32

Attenborough, Richard. 139, 168, 236, 323

Auto Focus (2002) film. 261

Avery, Margaret. 90, 94, 97, 104, 358

Axton, Hoyt. 79

Aykroyd, Dan. 73


**B**

*Back to the Future* (1985) film. 294

*Bad Santa* (2003) film. 279

Badham, John. 69

*Badlands* (1973) film. 31

Baier, Lionel. 359

Baker, Anita. 98

Baldwin, James. 209

Bale, Christian. 109

*Ballad of Buster Scruggs, The* (2018) film. 361-362

Ballard, J.G. 111

Bana, Eric. 281, 284

Barnhill, Ruby. 340

Barrie, James M. 129, 130, 133, 134, 340

Barthelmess, Richard. 124

Baskett, James. 96

Bates, Kathy. 177

Bay, Michael. 249, 258, 262, 310

Baye, Nathalie. 261

Bazin, Andre. 309

Beatty, Ned. 52

*Beauty and the Beast* (1991) film. 132

Bellocchio, Marco. 285

Bellow, Saul. 281

*Beloved* (1998) film. *327*

Belson, Jerry. 124

Belushi, John. 51

Benchley, Peter. 33, 34

Benson, Lucille. 52

Berry, John. 220

Bertolucci, Bernardo. 80

Besson, Luc. 58, 353, 360

Bettelheim, Bruno. 245

*BFG, The* (2016) film. 339-344, 361, 363, 366

Biberman, Herbert. 220

*Bicentennial Man* (1999) film. *244*

*Birds, The* (1963) film. *277*

*Birth of a Nation, The* (1915) film. 89, 95, 102, 184, 186, 189, 190, 206, 324

*Birth of a Nation'hood: Gaze, Script, and Spectacle in the O. J. Simpson Case* book. 206

*Black Christmas* (1975) film. 37-39

*Black Like Me* (1964) film. 99

Black, Carol. 99

Blackmun, Harry. 214, 218

Blanchett, Cate. 104, 291, 294

Blondell, Joan. 38

*Blow* (2001) film. 265

*Blow Out* (1981) film. 257, 258

*Blow-Up* (1966) film. 257, 258

*Blue Is the Warmest Color* (2013) film. 357-359

*Blue Jean* music video. 244

*Blues Brothers, The* (1980) film. 64

Boam, Jeffrey. 115, 120

Bong Joon-ho. 353

*Bonnie and Clyde* (1967) film. 29, 31, 77

Boorman, John. 110

Borgnine, Ernest. 234

*Born on the Fourth of July* (1989) film. 278

Borzage, Frank. 125, 244

*Bourne Identity, The* (2002) film. 260

Bowie, David. 244

*Boxer, The* (1997) film. 176

Brando, Marlon. 104, 294

Brantley, Ben. 102

Bray, Stephen. 104

*Breathless* (1960) film. 250

Brecht, Bertolt. 171, 332

Bresson, Robert 244, 337

*Bridge at San Luis Rey, The* novel. 127

*Bridge of Spies* (2015) film. 335-338, 340, 361, 363, 366

*Bridges of Madison County, The* book. 177

*Bringing Up Baby* (1938) film. 141

*Brokeback Mountain* (2005) film. 103, 104, 359

Brooks, Albert. 73

*Brother from Another Planet, The* (1984) film. 87

Brothers Grimm. 246

Brown, Georgia. 121

Bruckheimer, Jerry. 231, 249

Buckens, Celine. 312

*Bulworth* (1998) film. 231, 235

Buñuel, Luis. 244, 257, 258

*Burn!* (1970) film. 220

Burnett, Charles. 203

Bush, George W. 275, 330, 332, 367

Busia, Akosua. 89, 150

*Butcher Boy, The* (1998) film. 231

*Bye Bye Birdie* (1963) film. 52


# C

*Cabinet of Dr. Caligari, The* (1920) film. 74

*Caesar Must Die* (2012) film. 321

Caesar, Adolph. 91

Cameron, James. 173-178, 258, 311

*Camp de Thiaroye* (1988) film. 204

Campbell, Joseph. 119

Campion, Jane. 210

"Can't Truss It" song. 161, 185, 195, 212

*Cape Fear* (1991) film. 250

*Capote* (2005) film. *282*

Capra, Frank. 211, 326

Capshaw, Kate. 122, 252

*Captain EO* (1986) film. 133

*Carol* (2015) film. 103, 104

*Carousel* play. 125, 127

*Carrie* (1976) film. *77*

Carter, Thomas. 156

*Casablanca* (1942). 114, 299

*Casualties of War* (1989) film. 214

*Catch Me If You Can* (2002) film. xiii, 261-266, 310

*Cats* play. 133

*Cave of Forgotten Dreams* (2010) film. 311

*Chameleon Street* (1991) film. 264, 265

Chaplin, Charles. xi, 141, 250, 303

Charman, Matt. 336

Chatwin, Justin. 275

Chester, Vanessa Lee. 168, 170, 171

Chic. 55

*Chinatown* (1974) film. 77

*Chinese Ghost Story, A* (1987) film. 117

*Chitty Chitty Bang Bang* (1968) film. 133

Chow, Stephen. 361

Christie, Agatha. 257

Chuck D. 212

*Citizen Kane* (1941) film. xvi, 299, 352

Clark, Bob. 37-39

Clayburgh, Jill. 88

Clinton, Bill. 301, 332

Clinton, Hillary. 328, 332, 350

*Clockwork Orange, A* book. 340

*Close Encounters of the Third Kind* (1977) film. xi, xii, xvi, 31, 41-47, 49, 51, 53, 59, 62, 65, 77, 78, 87, 93, 96, 111, 125, 127, 140, 143, 149, 152, 160, 214, 218, 225, 246, 274, 302, 340, 342, 368

Cocteau, Jean. 249, 365

Coen, Joel and Ethan. 336, 361-362

Cohen, Larry. 349

Cohen, Lynn. 284

*Color Purple, The* (1985) film. xi, xii, xvi, 31, 63, 67, 70, 85-91, 92-94, 95-99, 100-101, 102-105, 109, 111, 113, 116, 117, 129, 132, 143, 144, 148, 149, 150, 151, 152, 153, 158, 159, 160, 162, 163, 180, 181, 198, 205, 208, 213, 218, 221, 225, 244, 252, 262, 274, 291, 312, 357, 358, 368

*Color Purple, The* book. 85, 90, 92, 96, 101, 102, 103, 151, 358

*Color Purple, The* play. 102-105

"Come Fly with Me" song. 263

*Company of Wolves, The* (1984) film. 245

*Company, The* (2003) film. 311

*Con Air* (1997) film. 178

*Confessions of a Dangerous Mind* (2002) film. 261

Connery, Sean. 114, 121, 298

*Conrack* (1974) film. *221*

*Conversation, The* (1974) film. 35, 257, 286

Cooke, Olivia. 353

Coppola, Francis Ford. xii, 49, 78, 133, 208, 257, 258, 287, 313

Cornish, Joe. 309

*Cosby Show, The* tv series. 89, 97, 98

Cosby, Bill. 89, 95, 97

Craig, Daniel. 283

*Crash* (1996) film. 245

Crawford, Joan. 104

*Creature From the Black Lagoon, The* (1954) film. *35*

Crichton, Michael. 138, 140

*Crimson Pirate, The* (1952) film. 58

*Crisis of the Negro Intellectual: A Historical Analysis of the Failure of Black Leadership, The* book. *218*

Cronenberg, David. 80, 245, 294

Crosby, Bing. 56

Crothers, Scatman. 73, 74

Cruise, Tom. 64, 255, 259, 272, 275, 280, 348

Cruse, Harold. 218

*Crusoe* (1988) film. 120

*Cry Freedom* (1987) film. 182, 199, 221

Cundey, Dean. 133


**D**

da Vinci, Leonardo. 45, 255, 257, 260

Dahl, Roald. 340

*Daily Show, The* tv series. 333

Daldry, Stephen. 69

Damon, Matt. 224

*Dances with Wolves* (1990) film. 190

Dante, Joe. 73-75, 77-83, 232

Daviau, Allen. 86, 144

Davies, Jeremy. 235

Davies, Terence. 241

De Sica, Vittorio

*Day After Tomorrow, The* (2004) film. 276

Day-Lewis, Daniel. 176, 323, 324, 330, 331, 332, 367

Dayan, Moshe. 143

De Niro, Robert. 186, *336*

De Palma, Brian. 62, 78, 79, 80, 82, 111, 170, 185, 214, 226, 257, 258, 320

*Death Race* (2008) film. 352, 354

*Deconstructing Harry* (1997) film. *184*

Deezen, Eddie. 52

*Defiant Ones, The* (1958) film. 199

Defoe, Daniel. 120

Delrogh, Dennis. 312

*Delta Force, The* (1986). *286*

DeMent, Iris. 227, 321

Demetry, John. 267, 268

DeMille, Cecil B. 59, 65

Demme, Jonathan. 262, 286, 327

Demy, Jacques. 224, 244, 249

Denby, David. 143, 156, 181, 191

Dennis, Sandy. 62

*Descendants, The* (2011) film. 315

Deschanel, Caleb. 120

Devlin, Dean. 231

*Diary of Anne Frank, The* (1959) film. *163*

DiCaprio, Leonardo. 174, 176, 261, 263, 264

Di Cicco, Bobby. 52

*Dick Van Dyke Show, The* tv series. 124

Dick, Philip K. 256, 259

Dickens, Charles. 85, 90, 93

Dillon, Melinda. 42

*Dirty Dozen, The* (1967) film. 286

Disney, Walt. xi, 67, 96, 139, 352

*Disturbing Behavior* (1998) film. 231-236

*Do the Right Thing* (1989) film. 161, 181, 185

Doctorow, E.L. 121

Donner, Richard. 231

Doody, Alison. 114, 122

Doyle, Arthur Conan. 257

Doyle, John. 102-105

*Dreamgirls* (2006) film. 305

*Dreamgirls* play. 89

*Dreams From My Father: A Story of Race and Inheritance* book. 327

Dreyer, Carl Theodor. 71, 244

Dreyfuss, Richard. 34, 39, 40, 42, 123, 171

*Driving Miss Daisy* play. 88
*Drums Along the Mohawk* (1939). 117
Ducastel, Olivier. 359
*Duel* (1971) tv movie. *31-32*
Dullea, Keir. 38
Dunne, Irene. 123

**E**

*E. T. the Extra-Terrestrial* (1982) film. xi, xii, xvi, 64, 67-72, 74, 77,
    87, 89, 93, 96, 117, 129, 131, 132, 137, 140, 143, 149, 152,
    153, 157, 159, 194, 203, 214, 217, 246, 273, 343, 368
Ebert, Roger. 197, 208, 331
Edison, Thomas. 45
Eisenstein, Sergei. 35, 198, 230, 362, 365
Eisner, Brett. 292
Ejiofor, Chiwetel. 201
Emmerich, Roland. 231, 276
*Empire of the Sun* (1987) film. 109-112, 116, 118, 124, 129, 132,
    144, 152, 160, 205, 218, 230, 245, 252, 262, 270
*Empire Strikes Back, The* (1980) film. 116, 130, 298
*Enemy Mine* (1985) film. 87
*English Patient, The* (1996) film. 167
Evans, Walker. 152
Exarchopoulos, Adèle. 357, 358
*Exorcist, The* (1973) film. 34, 62, 63, 64
*Eyes on the Prize* tv series. 162

**F**

*Fahrenheit 9/11* (2004). 267, 268
Fairbanks, Douglas. 303
Fallaci, Oriana. xv, xvii

*Family Ties* tv series. 99

Fanning, Dakota. 272

*Far from Heaven* (2002) film. 261

*Farm: Angola USA* , The (1998) film. 231

Farrell, Colin. 259

Fassbinder, Rainer Werner. 358

*Fast and the Furious, The* (2001) film. 248

*Fast, Cheap & Out of Control* (1997) film. 179

*Faust* (1926) film. 252

Fellini, Federico. 250

Ferber, Edna. 90

Ferrara, Abel. 264

Fiedler, Leslie. 331

Fields, Sally. 324

Fiennes, Ralph. 153, 164

*Fight Club* (1999) film. 260

*Film Socialisme* (2010). 307

Fincher, David. 251, 258

Finney, Albert. 326

Fisher, Frances. 176

"Flashback" song. 55

Fleming, Victor. 123, 124, 126, 127

*For Colored Girls Who Have Considered Suicide / When the Rainbow Is Enuf* play. 90

Ford, Harrison. 56, 113, 119, 171, 291, 293, 295, 297

Ford, John. 85, 101, 114, 115, 116, 118, 120, 150, 210, 223, 278, 298, 313, 324, 325, 347

Fosse, Bob. 35

*Four Feathers, The* (1939). 117

Fraker, William A. 43, 53, 144

Franklin, Aretha. 98

Franzone, David. 188

Freeman, Morgan. 193, 200, 2014, 209

*French Connection, The* (1971) film. 34

*French Provincial* (1975) film. 313

Friedkin, William. 34, 62, 63, 64

*Full Metal Jacket* (1987) film. 278

*Full Speed* (1998) film. 231, 359

Fuller, Sam. 69, 223

*Funeral, The* (1996) film. 264

*Funhouse, The* (1981) film. 64

Furthman, Jules. 124

*Fury, The* (1978) film. 62, 78, 79, 82, 246


**G**

Gale, Bob. 50, 52, 333

Galligan, Zach. 79

Gamble, Kenny. 183

*Gandhi* (1982) film. 68, 147, 323

*Gangs of New York* (2002) film. 261, 331

*Garçon stupide* (2005) film. 359

*Garden of the Finzi-Continis, The* (1971) fiim. 155

Gardner, Keith. 234

Garner, Jennifer. 265

Gary, Lorraine. 52

Gates Jr., Henry Louis. 221

Geffen, David. 301-306

*General, The* (1926) film. 298

Gerima, Haile. 186, 195, 220

*Geronimo: An American Legend* (1993) film. 155

Gershwin, George. 95

*Getaway, The* (1972) film. 30

*Ghost* (1990) film. 132

Gibson, Mel. 348

*Gimme a Break!* tv series. 97

*Gingerbread Man, The* (1998) film. 231

*Girl 6* (1996) film. 180

"Girl from Ipanema, The" song. 263

Gish, Dorothy. 89

Gish, Lillian. 89, 197

*Gladiator* (2000) film. 304

*Glory* (1989) film. 179, 226

Glover, Danny. 89, 91, 94

"God Bless the Child" song. 164

Godard, Jean-Luc. xii, 100, 131, 191, 250, 256, 296, 307, 365

*Godfather, The* (1972) film. xii, 68, 208, 287

*Godfather Part II, The* (1974) film. 78, 130, 178

*Godfather Part III, The* (1990). 130

*Godzilla* (1998) film. 292

*Gold Rush, The* (1925) film. 141

Goldberg, Whoopi. 90, 92, 93, 95, 96, 98, 104, 150, 358

Goldblum, Jeff. 138, 168, 170, 171

*Goldfinger* (1964) film. 51, 263

*Gone With the Wind* (1939) film. 111, 313

*Good Shepherd, The* (2006) film. 336

*Good Times* tv series. 97

Goodman, Hazelle. 184

Goodwin, Doris Kearns. 324

*Goonies, The* (1985) film. 88

Gordon, Dexter. 99

Grant, Cary. 124

*Great Gatsby, The* (1974) film. 30

*Great Race, The* (1965) film. 51

*Greatest Showman, The* (2017) film. 352

*Green Pastures, The* (1936) film. 89

Greene, Eric. 267, 268, 270

Greenwood, Bruce. 349

*Gremlins* (1984) film. 77-83, 88

*Gremlins 2: The New Batch* (1990) film. 130, 232

Grier, Pam. 185

Griffith, D.W. xii, xiv, xv, 68, 69, 85, 89, 90, 93, 95, 100, 101, 120, 129, 130, 153, 160, 184, 186, 189, 190, 191, 192, 197, 201, 208, 211, 212, 214, 223, 235, 245, 252, 289, 294, 303, 312, 324, 355, 364, 365

*Grind* play. 89

*Grindhouse* (2007) film. 295

Grisham, John. 203

Gross, Larry. 155

*Guess Who's Coming to Dinner?* (1967) film. 96

Guffey, Cary. 42, 51

Gugino, Carla. 353

*Gunga Din* (1939) film. 117

*Guy Named Joe, A* (1943) film. 123, 126, 127


**H**

*Hacksaw Ridge* (2016) film. 348

*Hallelujah!* (1929) film. 89

Hamilton, Murray. 52

Hammerstein, Oscar. 125

Hammett, Dashiell. 257

*Hands Over the City* (1963) film. 323

Handy, Bruce. 341

Hanks, Tom. 224, 228, 238, 262, 265, 268, 273, 335, 336, 337, 345, 348

"Hansel and Gretel" fairy tale. 245

Harbach, Otto. 125

*Hard Copy* tv series. 144

Hardy, Thomas. 100

Harris, Wendell B. 264

Haskell, Molly. 341

Haskin, Byron. 87, 274

*Hatari* (1962) film. 168

Havers, Nigel. 110

Hawks, Howard. 116, 124

Hawn, Goldie. 28, 29, 32

Hawthorne, Nathaniel. 246

Hawthorne, Nigel. 199

Haynes, Todd. 294

Hazanavicius, Michel. 360

*Heaven's Gate* (1980) film. 176

*Hellboy* (2004) film. 288

*Hellzapoppin'* (1941) film. 63

Hepburn, Audrey. 126, 127, 128

*Here Comes Mr. Jordan* (1941) film. 126

Hergé. 307, 309, 311

Herzog, Werner. 311

Hier, Marvin. 219

Hill, Jack. 183

Hill, Walter. 78, 80, 155

Hinds, Ciarán. 283

*Histoire(s) du cinema (1988-1998)* film. 296

Hitchcock, Alfred. xi, 35, 64, 69, 249, 251, 258, 277, 309

Hoffman, Dustin. 132, 133, 134, 186, 346

Hoffmann, E.T.A. 45

Holden, William. 234

Holiday, Billie. 164

Holland, Agnieszka. 154, 163

*Hollywood Shuffle* (1987) film. 99

*Holocaust* (1978) tv mini-series. 163

Holt, Tim. 246

*Hook* (1991) film. 129-135, 138, 139, 149, 160, 171, 244, 340

Hooper, Tobe. 61-65

*Hope and Glory* (1987) film. 110

Hope, Bob. 56

Hopkins, Anthony. 199, 210, 323

Hora, John. 74

"Hound Dog" song. 293

Hounsou, Djimon. 182, 187, 195, 208, 209, 219, 323

*Hours, The* (2002) film. 261

Houston, Whitney. 95, 98

Howard, Arliss. 168, 200

Howard, Ron. 69

*Howling, The* (1981) film. 82

Huff, Leon. 183

Hughes, Robert. 168

*Hugo* (2011) film. 309, 311, 315, 343, 360

Hunter, Holly 123

Hurst, Fannie. 90, 101

Hurston, Zora Neale. 101

Hurt, John. 291

Hurt, William. 241

Hussey, Olivia. 38, 39

Huston, John. 121, 223, 359


**I**

*I Wanna Hold Your Hand* (1978) film. 52

*Ice Storm, The* (1997) film. 182

*Imitation of Life* book. 90, 91

*In the Bedroom* (2001) film. 259

*In the Heat of the Night* (1967) film. 214

*Incendies* (2011) film. 308

*Independence Day* (1996) film. 167, 168, 170, 276

*Indiana Jones and the Kingdom of the Crystal Skull* (2008) film. 289-296, 297-300, 337, *360*

*Indiana Jones and the Last Crusade* (1989) film. xiii, 113-115, 116-122, 132, 145, 146, 147, 151, 152, 160, 190, 205, 228, 230, 251, 262, 289, 290291, 292, 294, 297-300, 309, 310

*Indiana Jones and the Temple of Doom* (1984) film. 77-83, 88, 113, 117, 118, 120, 122, 290, 297-300, 311

Indiana Jones film series. 56, 67, 117, 118, 122, 124, 130, 145, 151, 195, 262, 269, 289, 290, 297-300, 315, 320, 340

*Indiana Jones: The Complete Adventures* blu-ray. 297-300

*Inglourious Basterds* (2009) film. 313

Ingram, Rex. 192, 193, 211

*Intolerance* (1916) film. 189, 191, 197, 208, 212, 252

*Invasion of the Body Snatchers* (1978) film. 77

*Iron Horse, The* (1924) film. 120, 298

*Iron Man* (2008) film. 292, *360*

*Iron Man* film series. 315

Irvine, Jeremy. 312

*Isle of Dogs* (2018) film. 361-362

*It's a Mad, Mad, Mad, Mad World* (1963) film. 50

Ivey, Dana. 88

## J

*Jackie Brown* (1997) film. 179, 180, 183, 184

Jackson, Desreta. 89, 94,

Jackson, Janet. 95, 98

Jackson, Michael. 133, 355

Jackson, Peter. 291, 292, 309

Jackson, Samuel L. 180, 183, 184, 185, 209

James Bond film series. 51, 56, 291, 298

Jancsó, Miklós. 229

*Jarhead* (2005) film. 277, 278

*Jaws* (1975) film. xi, xii, xvi, 33-36, 37-39, 40, 41, 42, 49, 51, 53, 61, 67, 71, 77, 81, 92, 114, 116, 126, 140, 146, 171, 186, 195, 225, 256, 302, 340, 368

*Jeffersons, The* tv series. 97

*Jewel in the Crown, The* (1984) tv mini-series. 120

*Jo Jo Dancer, Your Life is Calling* (1986) film. 98

Johnson, Ben. 29, 32

Johnson, Brad. 124

Jones, Quincy. 91, 93

Jones, Tommy Lee. 324

Jordan, Neil. 245

*Journey to the Center of the Earth* (1959) film. 311

Jovovich, Milla. 71

*Jules and Jim* (1962) film. 253

*Jumpin' Jack Flash* (1986) film. 98

*Jungle Fever* (1991) film. 180, 183

*Jurassic Park* (1993) film. xiii, 67, 137-141, 165, 167, 168, 169, 171, 232, 302, 354

*Jurassic Park* film series. 175, 195


**K**

Kael, Pauline. 68, 126, 153, 163, 306

Kahn, Joseph. 298

Kahn, Michael. 51, 292

Kamiński, Janusz. 144, 171, 213, 246, 263, 294, 297, 312, 313, 324

Karina, Anna. 100

Karyo, Tchéky. 253

Kasdan, Lawrence. 55, 290

Kassovitz, Mathieu. 283

Katzenberg, Jeffrey. 301-306

Kaufman, Philip. 290

Kay, Dianne. 52

Keaton, Buster. 298

Kechiche, Abdellatif. 357-359

Kelly, Gene. 53

Kelly, Richard. 295

Keneally, Thomas. 152

Kern, Jerome. 125

Kershner, Irvin. 116

Kidder, Margot. 38, 39

*Killer Elite, The* (1975) film. 286

*King Kong* (1933) film. 168, 192, 354

*King Kong* (2005) film. 291

Kingsley, Ben. 153

Kipling, Rudyard. 115, 121

Koepp, David. 171, 292, 293, 294

Konchalovsky, Andrei. 250

Korda, Alexander. 57

Korine, Harmony. 251

Kovács, László. 43

Kramer, Stanley. 50, 52, 93

*Kriemhild's Revenge* (1924) film. 252

Kubrick, Stanley. 31, 74, 175, 244, 245, 249, 250

*Kundun* (1997) film. 212

Kureishi, Hanif. 120

Kurosawa, Akira. 156, 223, 249, 250, 313
Kushner, Tony. xiv, 284, 287, 324, 325, 326, 327, 330, 331, 333, 336, 339, 342, 360, 367

**L**

*L.A. Confidential* (1997) film. 190, 212
*L'Avventura* (1961) film. 295
*La Marseillaise* (1938) film. 197
*La vie de Jésus* (1998) film. 231
LaBeouf, Shia. 293
*Lady, The* (2012) film. 360
Landis, John. 64, 73-75
Lang, Fritz. 252
LaPorte, Nicole. 301-306
*Lara Croft: Tomb Raider* (2001) film. *248*
*Last Days of Disco, The* (1998) film. 231
*Last of the Mohicans, The* (1992) film. *331*
Law, Jude. 242
*Lawrence of Arabia* (1962) film. 211, 310
*Le mani sulla città* (1963) film. 204
*Le prise de pouvoir de Louis XIV* (1966) film. 197
Lean, David. 111, 249, 310, 313, 342
Lear, Norman. 97
Leary, Denis. 232
*Leaving Las Vegas* (1995) film. 167
Lee, Christopher. 52
Lee, Spike. 95, 98, 156, 157, 158, 159, 161, 162, 179-185, 211, 212, 219, 220, 252
*Left-Handed Gun, The* (1958) film. 165
*Legend of the Guardians: The Owls of Ga'hoole* (2010) film. 311
*Lego Movie, The* (2014) film. 353

Leigh, Mike. 171, 359, 365

*Les Parents terribles* (1948) film. 361

*Lethal Weapon* (1987) film. 199

Li, Jet. 253

*Lili* (1953) film. 133

*Lilies of the Field* (1963) film. 96

*Liliom* (1930) film. 125, 127

*Lincoln* (2012) film. 126, 319-321, 322-327, 328, 329, 330, 331, 333, 335, 336, 338, 339, 340, 342, 346, 352, 360, 363, 366, 367

*Lions for Lambs* (2007) film. 348

Lithgow, John. 75

*Little Nikita* (1988) film. 96

*Live Flesh* (1998) film. 231

*Lives of a Bengal Lancer* (1935) film. 117

*Lola* (1962) film. 224

*Long Day Closes, The* (1993) film. 241

*Long Riders, The* (1980) film. 78

*Long Way Home, The* (1997) film. 219

Lonsdale, Michael. 287

"Look of Love, The" song. 263

*Lord of the Rings, The* film series. 291, 309, 364

*Lost World: Jurassic Park, The* (1997) film. xiii, 167-172, 230,

*Love and Death in the American Novel* book. *331*

*Love Story* (1970) film. 33

Lubitsch, Ernst. 122

Lucas, George. 55, 56, 57, 82, 114, 116, 117, 119, 279, 290, 292

Luhrmann, Baz. 176

Lumet, Sidney. 93

Luna, Diego. 269

# M

*M\*A\*S\*H* (1970) film. xii, 30, 77, 224

MacNaughton, Robert. 69

*Mad Max* film series. 75

Maddin, Guy. 32

*Magic Flute, The* opera. 126

*Magnificent Ambersons, The* (1942) film. 100, 246

Mailer, Norman. 306

*Make Room for Daddy* tv series. 89

*Malcolm X* (1992) film. 156, 157, 162, 179, 181, 182

Malkovich, John. 110

*Man Who Would Be King, The* (1975) film. 121

*Man With Two Brains, The* (1983) film. 343

*Manchurian Candidate, The* (2004) film. 286

Mara, Rooney. 104

Maroh, Julie. 358

Martin, Steve. 343

Martineau, Jacques. 359

*Mary Poppins* (1964) film. 133

*Master, The* (2012) film. 320

Matheson, Tim. 52

*Matrix, The* (1999) film. 70, 260

Matthau, Walter. 310

Maupassant, Guy du. 100

McBride, Chi. 269

*McCabe & Mrs. Miller* (1971) film. 29, 78

McConaughey, Matthew. 200, 203

McCrea, Joel. 338

McGavin, Darren. 62

McNeil, Daniel. 366

Medavoy, Mike. 320

*Memento* (2000) film. 248, 260

*Men in Black* (1997) film. 178

*Men Who Would Be King: An Almost Epic Tale of Moguls, Movies, and a Company Called DreamWorks, The* book. 301-306

Mendelsohn, Ben. 363

Mendes, Sam. 277, 278

*Mermaid, The* (2016) film. 361

*Metropolis* (1927) film. 47, 252, 257

Meyjes, Menno. 86, 87, 92, 115, 120

*Midnight in Paris* (2011) film. 315

*Midsummer Night's Dream, A* play. 340

Mifune, Toshiro. 52

Milius, John. 50, 155, 226, 279

Miller, George. 73-75

Milloy, Courtland. 221

*Minority Report* (2002) film. xiii, 63, 255-260, 322, 368

*Miracle, The* (1947) film. 250

*Mississippi Burning* (1988) film. 120, 182, 188, 221

*Mo' Better Blues* (1990) film. 184

*Modern Times* (1936) film. 47

Moffat, Steven. 309

"Molasses to Rum to Slaves" song. 205, 325-326

*Mom and Dad* (2018) film. 361

*Monsieur Verdoux* (1947) film. 250

*Monster House* (2006) film. 310

Moore, Julianne. 168, 170

Moore, Michael. 267, 268

Morel, Gael. 359

*Morning Joe* tv series. 333

Morrison, Toni. 206

Morrissey. 345, 349, 350

Morrow, Vic. 73

Morton, Samantha. 257

*Moulin Rouge!* (2001) film. 245

*Mr. Smith Goes to Washington* (1939) film. 325

Mr. T. 89

"Ms. Celie's Blues (Sister)" song. 104, 357

*Mummy, The* (1999) film. 292

*Munich* (2005) film. xiv, 268, 281-296, 305, 326, 339, 368

Murnau, F.W. 252

Murphy, Eddie. 97

*My Life on Ice* (2003) film. 359

*My Night at Maud's* (1969) film. 123

*My Summer of Love* (2004) film. 288


**N**

Nabokov, Vladimir. 249

*Naked Lunch* (1991) film. 131

Napier, John. 133

*Nashville* (1975) film. 77

*Nasty* music video. 98

Nathanson, Jeff. 264

*National Treasure* (2004) film. 292

*Native Son* book. 99

"Nature Boy" song

Neeson, Liam. 245

Nelson, Craig T. 63

*NeverEnding Story, The* (1984) film. 82

Nichols, Mike. 278

*Night America Panicked, The* (1975) tv movie. 50

*Night Gallery* (1969) tv movie. 260

*Night of the Hunter, The* (1955) film. 245

*Nightjohn* (1996) film. 203

*Nightline* tv series. 174

Noble, Gil. 180

Northam, Jeremy. 207


## O

*O.J.: Made in America* (2016) tv mini-series. 365

O'Connor, Frances. 241

Oates, Warren. 52

Obama, Barack. xiv, 328, 329-333, 337, 342, 343, 346, 349, 361, 366

Oberon, Merle. 38

*Odd Couple, The* tv series. 124

*Oh! What a Lovely War* (1969) film. 236

*Okja* (2017) film. 353

*Oliver Twist* novel. 93

*Oliver!* (1968) film. 133

*On the Waterfront* (1954) film. 104

"Once Upon a Dream" song. 246

*One Night Stand* (1997) film. 199

*Only Angels Have Wings* (1939) film. 124

*Ordet* (1955) film. 71

*Orphans of the Storm* (1921) film. 89, 93, 153, 189, 235

Osment, Haley Joel. 241, 246

Östlund, Ruben. 361

*Our Town* play. 127

*Out of Africa* (1985) film. 120, 358

*Out of Sight* (1998) film. 231

*Outsiders, The* (1983) film. 313

"Oval Portrait, The" short story. 100

Ozu, Yasujirō. 244

# P

Pallana, Kumar. 269

Paquin, Anna. 198

*Paradise Now* (2005) film. 285

*Parallax View, The* (1974) film. 35

*Passage to India, A* (1984) film. 120

*Passion* (2012) film. 320

*Patton* (1970) film. 208

"Paul's Mistress" short story. 100

Paulson, Sarah. 349

*Pay It Forward* (2000) film. 246

*Pearl Harbor* (2001) film. 249

Peck, Gregory. 338

Peckinpah, Sam. 30, 116, 223, 228, 234, 286

Peebles, Melvin Van. 180

Pendergrass, Teddy. 209

Penn, Arthur. 165

*Perfect Couple, A* (1979) film. 49

*Persona* (1966) film. 246

*Personal Best* (1982) film. 359

*Peter Pan, or The Boy Who Wouldn't Grow Up* play. 74, 129, 130, 133, 340

*Peterloo* (2019) film. 365

Petersen, Wolfgang. 82

Phoenix, River. 119, 298, 309

Pialat, Maurice. 359

*Piano, The* (1993) film. 210

Picasso, Pablo. 85

Pickens, Slim. 52

Pickford, Mary. 303

*Pickpocket* (1959) film. 337

*Pina* (2011) film. *311*

*Pink Panther, The* (1963) film. 263

*Pinocchio* (1940) film. 249, 252

"Pinocchio" fairy tale. 245

Pirandello, Luigi. 274

*Pirates* (1986) film. 310

*Pirates of the Caribbean* film series. 291, 310

*Place in the Sun, A* (1951) film. 56

*Platoon* (1986) film. 98, 227, 278

Platters, The. 125

*Playtime* (1967) film. 47

*Pledge, The* (2001) film. 259

Poe, Edgar Allan. 100

*Point Blank* (1967) film. 77

Poitier, Sidney. 91, 95

Polanski, Roman. 310

*Polar Express, The* (2004) film. 310

Pollack, Sydney. 68

*Poltergeist* (1982) film. 61-65, 74

Pontecorvo, Gillo. 154, 220

*Pootie Tang* (2001) film. 250

*Porgy and Bess* (1959) film. 95

*Porgy and Bess* play. 95

*Poseidon Adventure, The* (1972) film. 175

*Post, The* (2017) film. 345-350, 353, 366, *368*

Postlethwaite, Pete. 170, 205, 345-350, 353, Spielberg Meets the Zeitgeist

*Power of One, The* (1992) film. 209

*Precious* (2009) film. 102

Presley, Elvis. 293

*Price Above Rubies, A* (1998). 231

Prince. 97

*Prince of Egypt, The* (1998) film. 302

*Prospero's Books* (1991) film. 131

Pryor, Richard. 97, 98

Public Enemy. 161, 185, 195

Pugh, Willard E. 91

*Pulp Fiction* (1994) film. 70, 167

"Push the Button" song. 104


## Q

*Quiz Show* (1994) film. 190


## R

*Rachel Maddow Show* tv series. 333

*Ragtime* book. 121

*Raiders of the Lost Ark* (1981) film. xi, xii, xvi, 31, 55-65, 77, 114, 118, 122, 251, 290, 292, 293, 294, 295, 297-300, 302, 368

Rainer, Peter. 104

*Rambo: First Blood Part II* (1985) film. 114

Ray, Nicholas. 69

*Ready Player One* (2018) film. 351-355, 361-362, 363-364

Reagan, Ronald. 55, 57, 70, 114, 177, 290, Spielberg Meets the Zeitgeist

*Real Time with Bill Maher* tv series. 333

*Rear Window* (1954) film. 257

*Red Badge of Courage, The* (1951) film. 226

*Red Desert* (1964) film. 125

Redford, Robert. 346

*Reincarnation of Peter Proud, The* (1975) film. 38

*Relic, The* (1997) film. 171

Renoir, Jean. 44, 46, 81, 197, 223, 248, 287, 342

*Resident Evil* (2002) film. 67-72

*Resident Evil: Afterlife* (2010) film. 311

Reynolds, Burt. 51

*Rhapsody in August* (1991) film. 156

Rhys, Matthew. 347

Rich, Frank. 154

Richardson, Miranda. 110

Ritchie, Michael. 124

Richter, Gerhard. 314

Riefenstahl, Leni. 209

Ritt, Martin. 221, 222

*Road Warrior, The* (1982) film. 75

Robards, Sam. 241

Robbins, Tim. 279

Roberts, Julia. 279

*RoboCop 2* (1990) film. 130

Rockwell, Norman. 225

Rodgers, Richard. 125

Rogers, Ginger. 125

Rohmer, Eric. 123

*Romeo + Juliet* (1996) film. 176

*Roots* (1977) tv miniseries. 96, 153, 162, 220

*Rosewood* (1997) film. 194, 204

Rosi, Francesco. 204, 205, 206, 229, 323

Ross, Steve. 147

Rossellini, Roberto. 197, 250

Roth, Eric. 284

*Rough Riders* (1997) tv mini-series. 226

*Round Midnight* (1986) film. 99

Rubinstein, Zelda. 64

*Runaway Train* (1985) film. 250

*Rush Hour 2* (2001) film. 264
Russell, Brenda. 104
Russell, David O. 278
Rylance, Mark. 337, 340, 352, 367

**S**
*S\*P\*Y\*S* (1974) film. 35
Sabu. 57
Sacks, Michael. 28, 30
*Sahara* (2005) film. 292, 293, 294
Said, Edward. 57, 190
Saldana, Zoe. 269
Salomon, Mikael. 125, 127
*Salvatore Giuliano* (1962) film. 323
*Samson and Delilah* (1949) film. 65
*Sankofa* (1994) film. 186, 195, 220
Sarris, Andrew. 123, 147
*Saturday Night Fever* (1977) film. 355
*Saturday Night Live* tv series. 332
*Saving Private Ryan* (film) 1998. xiii, 67, 124, 223-230, 231-236,
    252, 274, 280, 313, 341
Sawyer, Forrest. 182
Saxon, John. 39
*Scarface* (1983) film. 185
Schama, Simon. 212
Scheider, Roy. 34, 39, 40
*Schindler's List* (1993) film. xiii, 31, 67, 143-157, 158-166, 167,
    181, 190, 193, 196, 205, 208, 213, 214, 216, 217, 218, 219,
    220, 225, 228, 274, 283, 299, 302, 305, 341
Schrader, Paul. 279
Schumacher, Joel. 203

Schwarzenegger, Arnold. 137, 177

Scorsese, Martin. 78, 250, 279, 309, 310, 311, 331, 343, 360

*Scott Pilgrim vs. the World* (2010) film. 352, 354

Scott, Ridley. 252, 258

Scott, Tony. 258

*Searchers, The* (1956) film. 150, 151, 278, 279, 280

*Secret of the Grain, The* (2007) film. 358, 359

*Secrets & Lies* (1996) film. 171

Sembene, Ousmane. 204, 205, 206

Serling, Rod. 73, 74, 75

*Seven* (1995) film. 71

Seydoux, Léa. 357, 358

Shange, Ntozake. 85

Shaw, Robert. 34, 39, 40

*She's Gotta Have It* (1986) film. 98

Sheridan, Tye. 351, 353

*Shining, The* (1980) film. 74

*Short Cuts* (1993) film. 235

*Show Boat* book. 90, 91

*Shrek* (2001) film. 305

Shyamalan, M. Night. 245

*Sicario* (2015) film. 361

*Sick: The Life and Death of Bob Flanagan* (1997) film. 179

*Sid and Nancy* (1986) film. 99

*Siegfried* (1924) film. 252

*Silence of the Lambs, The* (1991) film. 71

*Silent Night, Evil Night* (1974) film. 37

Sinatra, Frank. 263

Singleton, John. 194, 204

Siodmak, Robert. 58

Sirk, Douglas. 101

Siskel, Gene. 197

*Sixth Sense, The* (1999) film. 246

Skarsgård, Stellan. 200, 207

*Slaughterhouse-Five* (1972) film. 30

*Slaves* (1969) film. 220

Slocombe, Douglas. 43, 295, 297

*Small Change* (1976) film. 245

*Small Soldiers* (1998) film. 232

*Smile* (1975) film. 124

Smith, Bessie. 90, 104,

Smith, Lois. 259

Smith, Maggie. 130

"Smoke Gets in Your Eyes" song. 125

"Snow Queen, The" fairy tale. 245

Snyder, Zack. 311

Solman, Gregory. 174, 232, 267, 268

*Something Evil* (1972) tv movie. *62, 63, 64*

*Something Wild* (1986) film. 99, 262

*Song of the South* (1946) film. 87, 96

*Sophie's Choice* (1982) film. 153, 163

*Sophisticated Ladies* play. 89

*Soul Man* (1986) film. 99

*Sounder* (1972) film. 221

Spader, James. 324

*Speed* (1994) film. 168, 170, 178, 212, 249

*Speed Racer* (2008) film. 295

Sperber, Wendie Jo. 52

*Splash* (1984) film. 83

*Square, The* (2017) film. 361

*Squid and the Whale, The* (2005) film. 288

Stack, Robert. 52

*Stage Door* (1937) film. 38

Stallone, Sylvester. 137

Stanley, Frank. 43

*Star Wars* (1977) film. 43, 56, 250, 290, 292, 298

*Star Wars* film series. 119, 292

*Star Wars: Episode III – Revenge of the Sith* (2005) film. 275

*Star Wars: The Last Jedi* (2017) film. 353

*Stars in My Crown* (1950) film. 338

*Steel Helmet, The* (1951) film. 226

Steiger, Rod. 104

Sternberg, Josef von. 124, 362, 365

*Steven Spielberg: A Life in Films* book. 341

*Steven Spielberg's Obama* (2013) short film. 329-333

Stevens, George. 56

*Sting, The* (1973). 262

Stone, Oliver. 174, 185, 190, 227, 278

Stoppard, Tom. 111

Storr, Robert. 314

Stowell, Austin. 338

Streep, Meryl. 345, 348, 350

Streisand, Barbra. 321

Stuart, Gloria. 177

Sturges, Preston. 52

*Sugarland Express, The* (1974) film. xii, 27-30, 31-32, 34, 35, 37, 41, 49, 53, 87, 111, 127, 149, 244

*Sum of All Fears, The* (2002) film. 260

*Sun Shines Bright, The* (1953) film. 210

*Sweet Hereafter*, The (1997) film. 182, 212

*Swing Kids* (1993) film. 156

*Syriana* (2005) film. 287

# T

*Take It Off* (1981) album. 55

*Take the Money and Run* (1969) film. 99

*Tamango* (1958) film. 220

Tarantino, Quentin. 179, 180, 183, 184, 185, 251, 290, 295, 313

Tarkington, Booth. 100

Tarkovsky, Andrei. 244

Tarr, Bela. 70

Tashlin, Frank. 87

Taviani brothers. 197, 321

Taylor, Brian. 361-362

*Taxi Driver* (1976) film. 77, 78

Techine, Andre. 80, 313, 359

*Ten Commandments, The* (1956) film. 59, 65

*Tequila Sunrise* (1988) film. 121

*Terminal, The* (2004) film. xiv, 267-270, 273, 274, 305

*Terminator, The* (1984) film. 175

*Terminator 2: Judgement Day* (1991) film. 178

*Tess of the d'Urbervilles* book. 100

*Texas Chainsaw Massacre, The* (1974) film. 61, 64

"There's a Wall in Washington" (song). 227

*Thief of Baghdad, The* (1940) film. 57, 192, 193, 211

*Thieves Like Us* (1974) film. 31

Thomas, Henry. 68, 89

Thomas, Jake. 243

*Three Kings* (1999) film. 278

*Three Musketeers, The* (2011) film. 311

*Thriller* music video. 355

*Time to Kill, A* (1996) film. 203

*Titanic* (1997) film. 68, 173-178, 189, 200, 212, 229

*Titanic* play. 174, 178

*To Be or Not to Be* (1942) film. 122

*To Kill a Mockingbird* (1962) film. 202, 338

*To Tell the Truth* tv series. 263

*Tom Thumb* (1958) film. 133

*Tommy* (1975) film. 52

*Tootsie* (1982) film. 68, 99

*Top Gun* (1986) film. 56

*Torque* (2004) film. 298

*Towering Inferno, The* (1974) film. 35, 175, 178

Towne, Robert. 359

Townsend, Robert. 99

Tracy, Spencer. 123

*Training Day* (2001) film. 260

*Transformers: Dark of the Moon* (2011) film. 310

Travolta, John. 257

Trier, Lars von. 251

*Truce, The* (1997) film. 229, 231

*True Lies* (1994) film. 170, 178

Truffaut, Francois. 42, 44, 46, 71, 131, 245, 250

*Truman Show, The* (1998) film. 231

Trumbo, Dalton. 126

Trumbull, Douglas. 43

Trump, Donald. xvi, Spielberg Meets the Zeitgeist

Tucci, Stanley. 269

Turner, Lana. 85, 104

Twain, Mark. 265

*Twilight* (1998) film. 231

*Twilight Zone, The* tv series. 73, 74

*Twilight Zone: The Movie* (1983) film. 73-75, 80, 82

## U

*Un Chien Andalou* (1929) film. 257
*Unbreakable* (2000) film. 245
*Uncle Tom's Cabin* book. 202
*Usual Suspects, The* (1995) film. 286

## V

*Valerian and the City of a Thousand Planets* (2017) film. 353
Valkenburgh, Deborah Van. 353
Verbinski, Gore. 292
Vidor, King. 89
Vigo, Jean. Xii
Villeneuve, Denis. 308, 361
Visconti, Luchino. 365
*Vitruvian Man* artwork. 255
*Volcano* (1997) film. 171
von Sydow, Max. 259

## W

Wachowskis, The. 295
Walken, Christopher. 261, 264
Walker, Alice. 85, 86, 87, 90, 91, 92, 93, 96, 101, 102, 103, 104, 151, 358
*War Horse* (2011) film. xiv, 307-315, 342, *360*
*War of the Worlds* (1938) radio drama. 50, 274, 368
*War of the Worlds* (1953) film. 274
*War of the Worlds* (2005) film. xiv, 268, 271, 272-280, 296, 305, 339, Spielberg Meets the Zeitgeist
Warshow, Robert. 229
Watson, Emily. 176
Watson, Paul Joseph. 369

*Way Down East* (1920) film. 93, 100, 197, 292, 350

Wayne, John. 121, 278, 279, 291

Weaver, Dennis. 31

Weir, Peter. 231

"Welcome to the Terrordome" song. 185

Welles, Orson. xii, 50, 100, 223, 250, 274, 362, 365

Wenders, Wim. 311

*Werckmeister Harmonies* (2001) film. 70

West, Kanye. 321

*Westworld* (1973) film. 140

*What Have You Done for Me Lately? music video.* 98

"What'll I Do" song. 30

*When I Think of You* music video. 98

"When You Wish Upon a Star" (song). 352

Whitaker, Johnny. 62

Wieseltier, Leon. 154

*Wild Bunch, The* (1969) film. 77, 228, 234

*Wild Child, The* (1970) film. 71

*Wild Reeds* (1995) film. 359

Wilder, Billy. 146

Wilder, Thornton. 127

Williams, JoBeth. 63, 64

Williams, John. 40, 44, 53, 207, 246, 263

Williams, Robin. 130, 134, 244

Williams, Treat. 52

Willis, Allee. 104

Willis, Bruce. 137

Willis, Gordon. 346

*Willow* (1988) film. 68

*Wilson* (1944) film. 342

*Wind in the Willows, The* book. 119

*Windtalkers* (2002) film. 258

Winfrey, Oprah. 90, 94, 95, 97

Winslet, Kate. 174, 176, 177

*Wizard of Oz, The* (1939) film. 64, 214

Wolfe, Tom. 306

Wollen, Peter. 315

Woo, John. 258

*Working Girl* (1988) film. 113

Wright, Edgar. 309, 352, 354

Wright, Richard. 99

Wyman, Jane. 104


**Y**

Yeston, Maury. 174

*Young Mr. Lincoln* (1939) film. 325, 326

Young, Richard. 119


**Z**

Zaillian, Steven. 155, 162, 188, 199

Zane, Billy. 176

Zanuck, Darryl F. 342

Zemeckis, Robert. 50, 52, 310, 333

Zeta-Jones, Catherine. 269

Zhai, Naishe. 109

Zischler, Hanns. 284

Zsigmond, Vilmos. 32

Zurer, Ayelet. 285

Zwick, Edward. 179-180

CPSIA information can be obtained
at www.ICGtesting.com
Printed in the USA
LVHW082250130323
741476LV00021B/447

9 780984 215911